American Scrolls

landscapes, townscapes & cityscapes

Chaim Bezalel & Yonnah Ben Levy

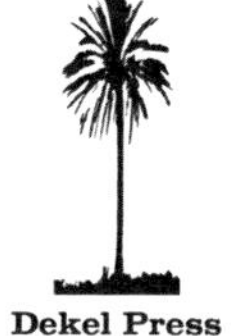

Dekel Press

ISBN: 978-0-9995958-4-8

Library of Congress: 2017964711

to our children: Judith, Chad, Maryann, Ezra, George, and Samuel

FIRST EDITION

Published by Dekel Press   www.dekelpress.com

Introduction

My father was an immigrant who, of course, loved and believed in America. He came young enough so that he did not speak with an accent, and, like many immigrants, especially those coming from hardship, never spoke of where he came from. On my mother's side, my grandparents were also immigrants, who also loved America. Had they all stayed in Europe the chances are overwhelming that they would not have survived and I would never have been born. My wife is also the descendant of immigrants, on her father's side – from Jamestown, 1600's. They were also pioneers, settling in the Pacific Northwest as far back as the late 1800's. On her mother's side there were Irish Protestants and German Jews, all moving west and further west.

My wife and I are also immigrants, and, if you will allow, pioneers. We met in Israel, both of us having taken on Israeli citizenship while maintaining our American. For various reasons, I did not return to America for nine years. Like my father, I did not look back. When I was drafted into the Israeli army reserves at age forty and spent a month each year in various postings, Yonnah would visit her friends and family in Seattle, perhaps every other year or less often. It took that long to save up for a plane ticket. In the 1980's living in Israel was still like stepping back in time, at least a couple of decades. We never expected to return to America to live. It was only after returning, to visit in 1997 and then, for family reasons, to live in 1998 that we were able to gain the perspective that comes from two different points of reference. After fifteen years in America we returned to spend half of each year in Israel.

This bi-national perspective has had a great influence on our work, both thematically and in terms of technique. It is worthwhile to compare and contrast the two nations because both are archetypes. Israel is the microcosm, the template of traditional nationhood, a unification of tribes bound together by blood and earth, language and religion. This microcosm has had and still has its effect as other nations have gained their very sense of nationhood through identifying with the story of this small nation. America, on the other hand, is the macrocosm. It is not a nation in the traditional sense, through a tribal or religious bond, but a polyglot nation of expanding borders and expanding inclusivity (at least historically though not always without a fight). Israel is deep, in fact it contains the lowest point on Earth. America is broad. Israel is the Old World, America the New. And just as Israel's influence has transcended her borders, so has America's.

The idea of "American Scrolls" came out of our own experience. At the beginning we did not know that we would be crossing the continent, and how often. We simply fell in love with the landscapes in the East and decided to try out a new style. We had been collaborating on mixed-media paintings on rice paper before, but the expanses we saw in America drew us toward a panoramic format. The technique is described on the first page of the "Autumn Scrolls" section. We made many visits to the Metropolitan Museum of Art and other museums to visit the Oriental Art exhibits to study and enjoy. The Seattle Art Museum was first established with only a collection of Oriental art. We wanted to adapt some of the styles and formats of this tradition, though we have not always been orthodox in our approach. Finally, the places depicted are places that have meaning for us. They are personal encounters and not in any sense exhaustive.

- Chaim Bezalel

Autumn Scrolls

When we returned to America, we lived for a year on a farm that was owned by Chaim's mother. The main house on the property was built in 1791 of fieldstone, like most of the oldest houses in the Hudson Valley. We lived in an apartment that had been added to one of the barns. We had not experienced a colorful autumn like this in Israel, where we had been living, and so we set out through the Catskill Mountains and the Hudson River, by car, by boat, and by kayak, intoxicated by the beauty of this unique and historic region. This was where an art movement known as the Hudson River School had given birth to the whole idea of the American landscape. In another section of the barn we set up a painting studio. For music we had a turntable and several boxes of old records which had belonged to various family members. We kept warm with a kerosene heater and were very content. For all of these paintings, Chaim transferred his panoramic photographs in sepia to sheets of Japanese rice paper, which Yonnah then painted over in acrylics.

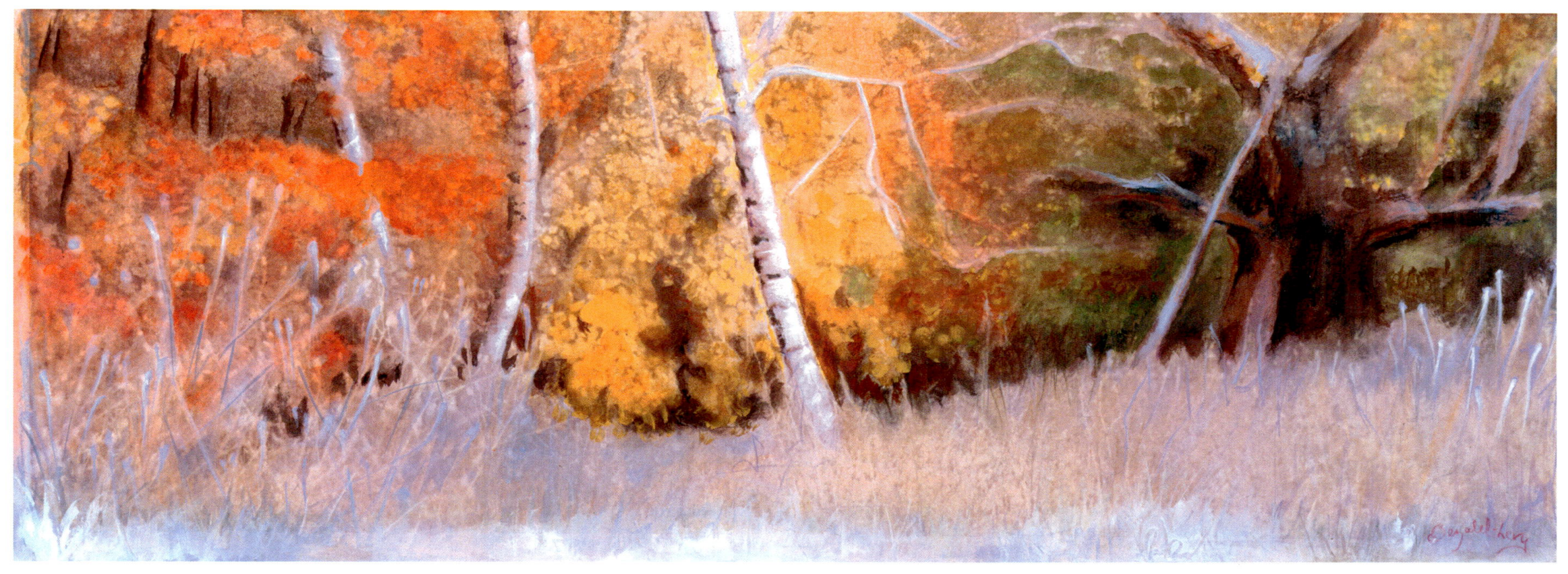

Purple Birches (1998) 18 x 48 in.

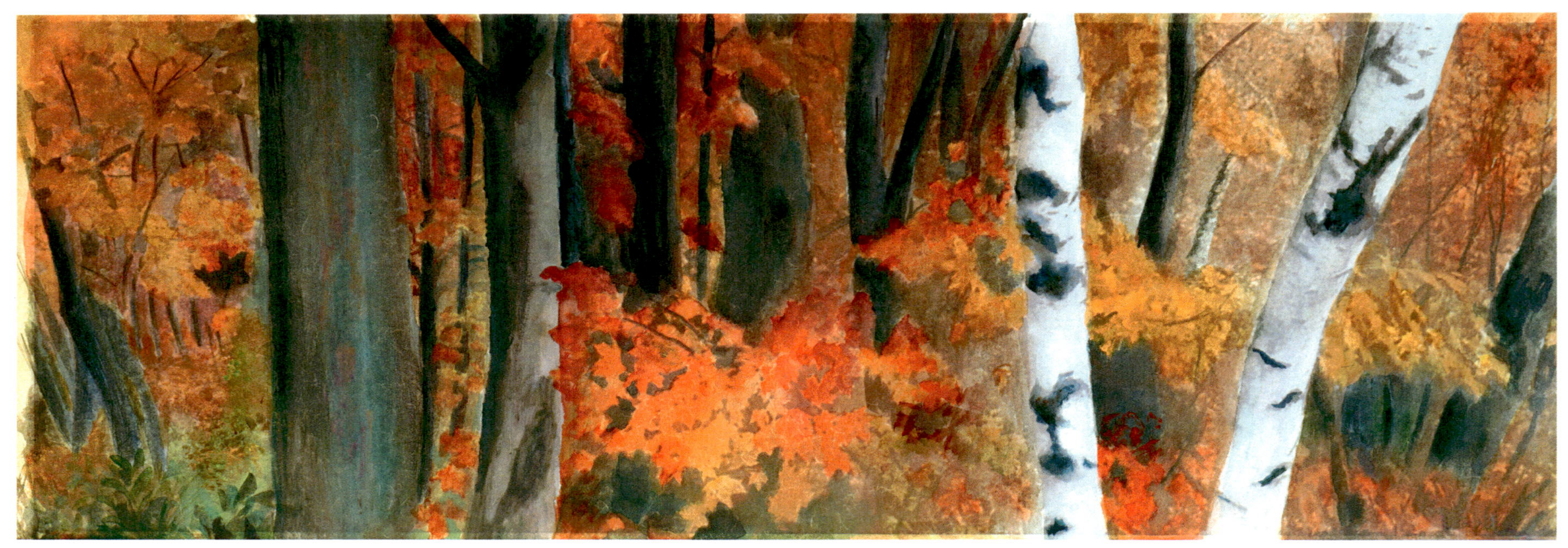

Two Birches (1998) 18 x 48 in.

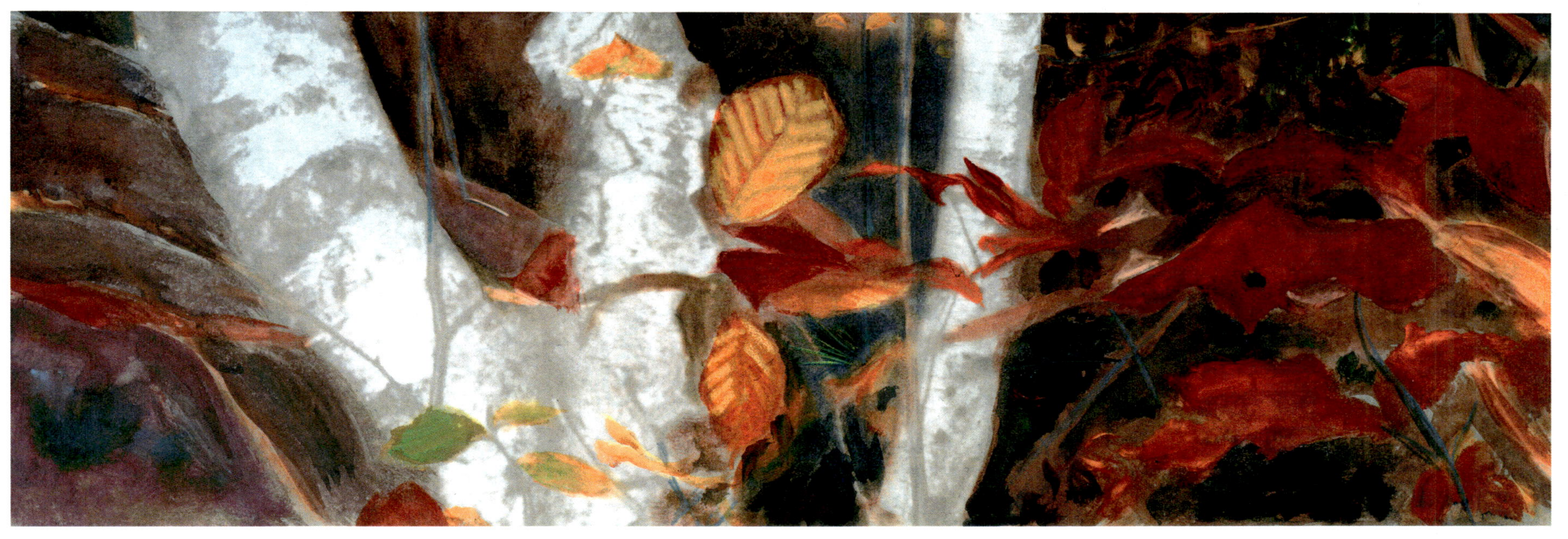

Ghost Birches (1998) 18 x 48 in.

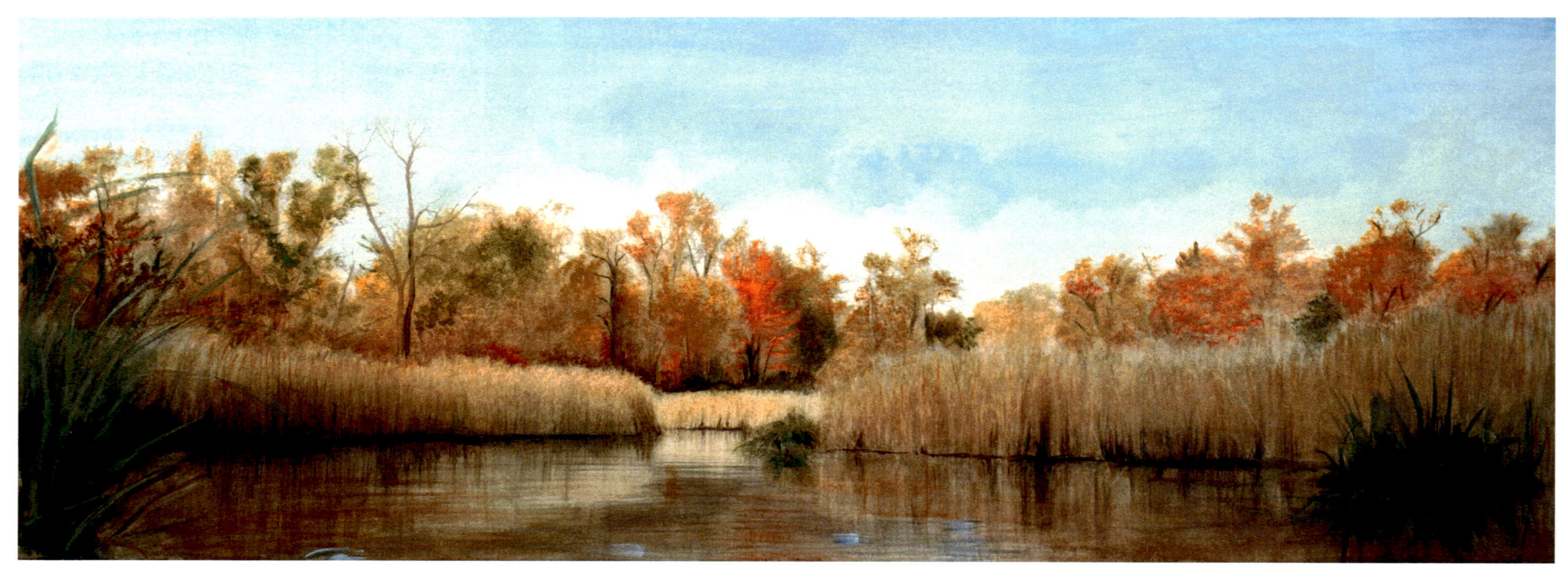

Hudson Riverbank I (1998) 18 x 48 in.

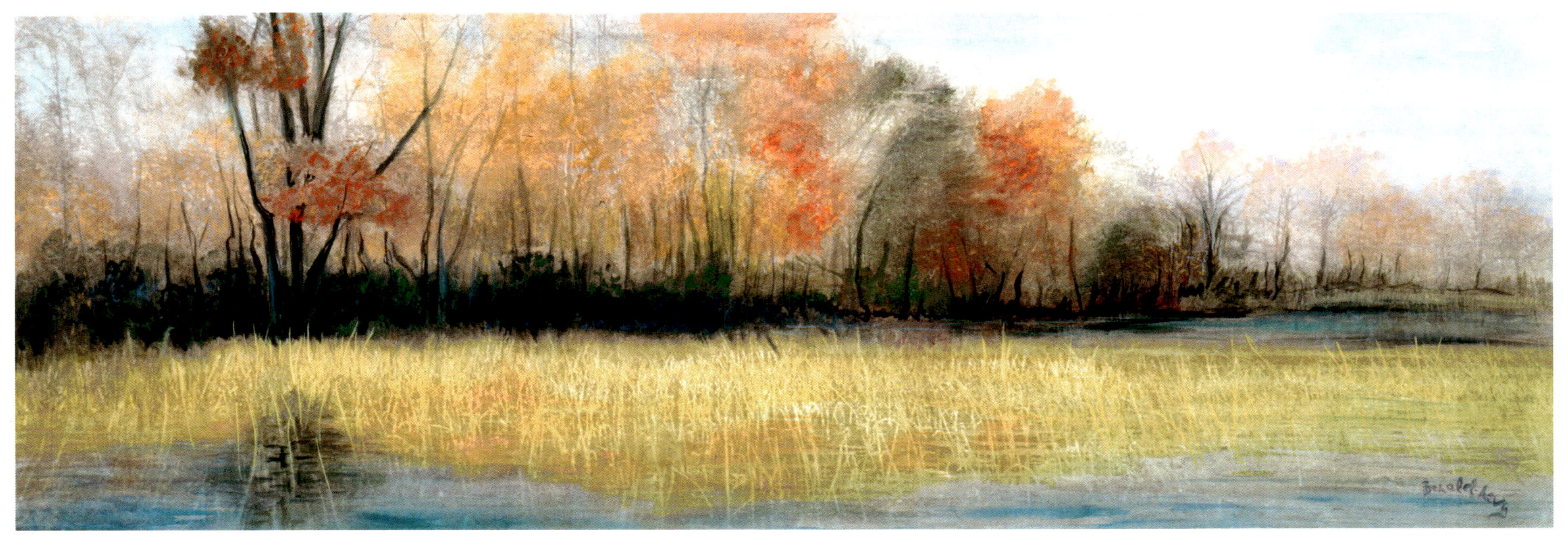

Hudson Riverbank II (1998) 18 x 48 in.

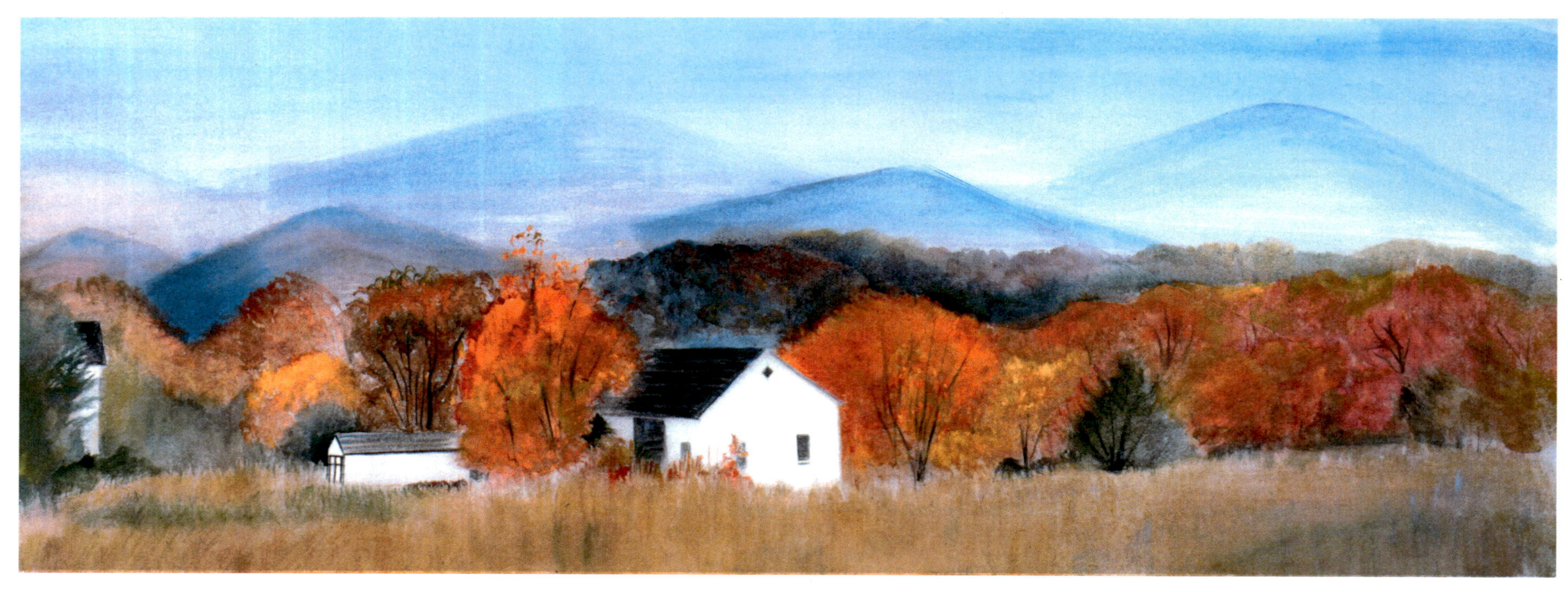

Mountain Home (1998) 18 x 48 in.

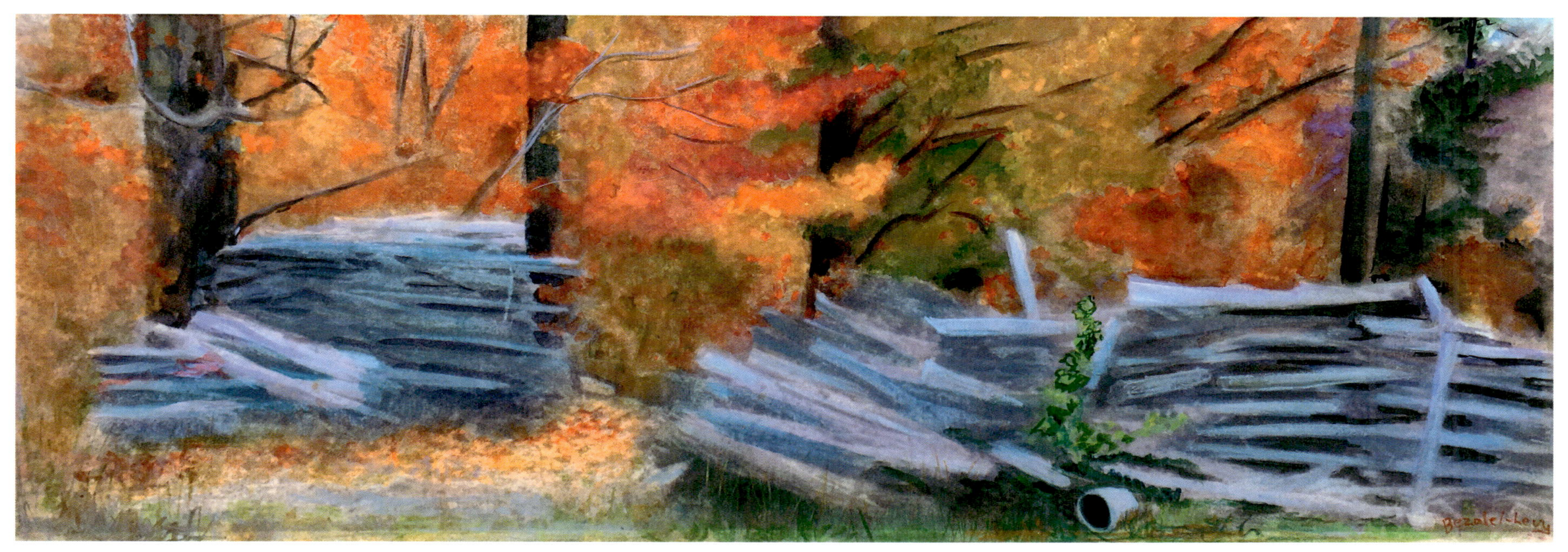

Split Rail Fence (1998) 18 x 48 in.

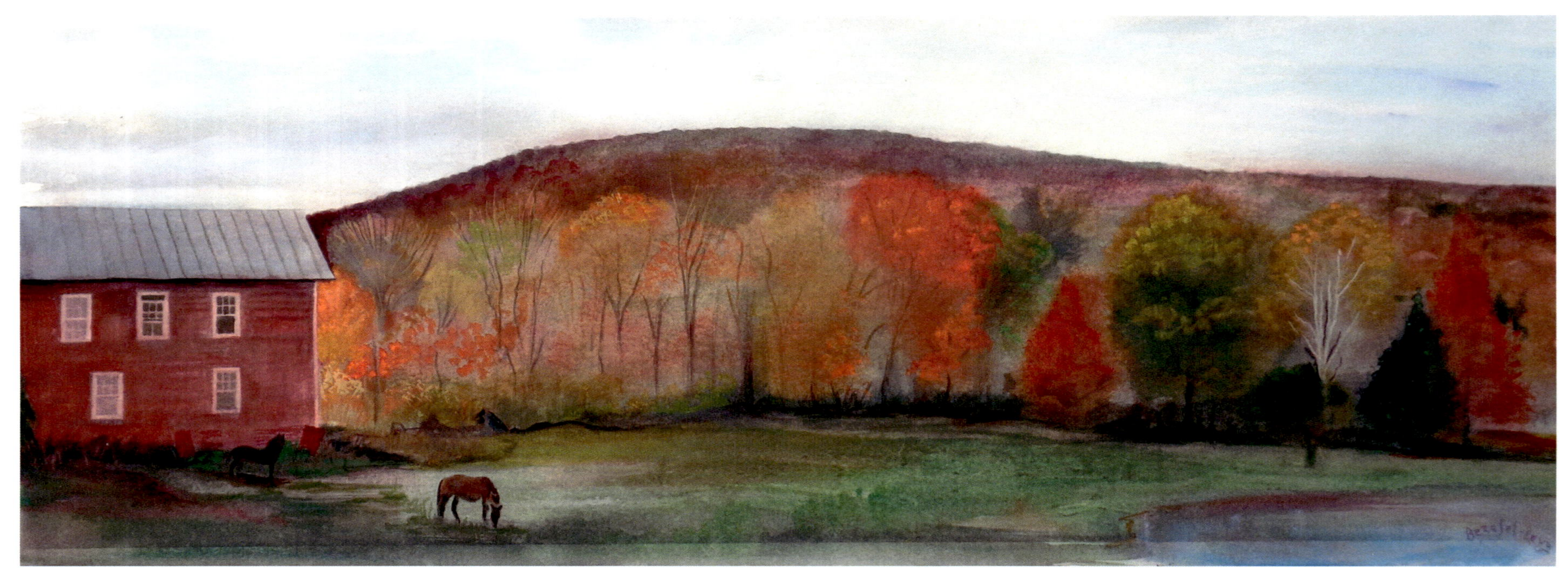

Horse and Barn (1998) 18 x 48 in.

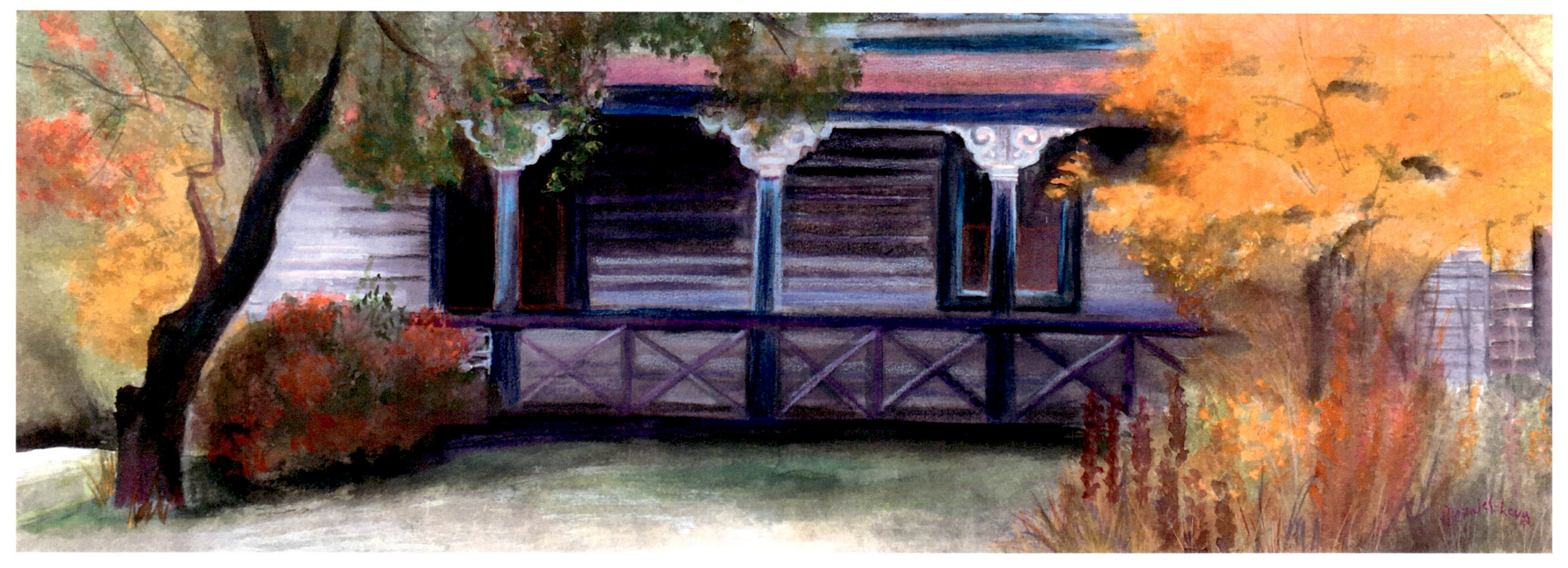

Front Porch (1998) 18 x 48 in.

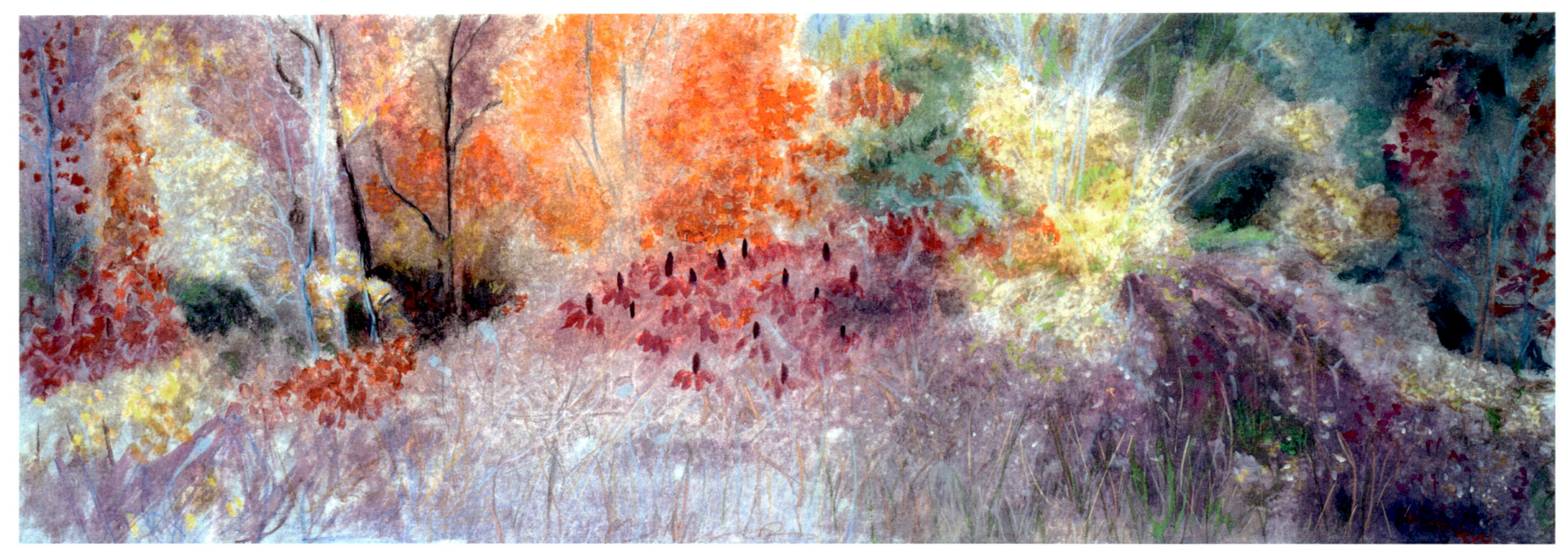

Sumac (1998) 18 x 48 in.

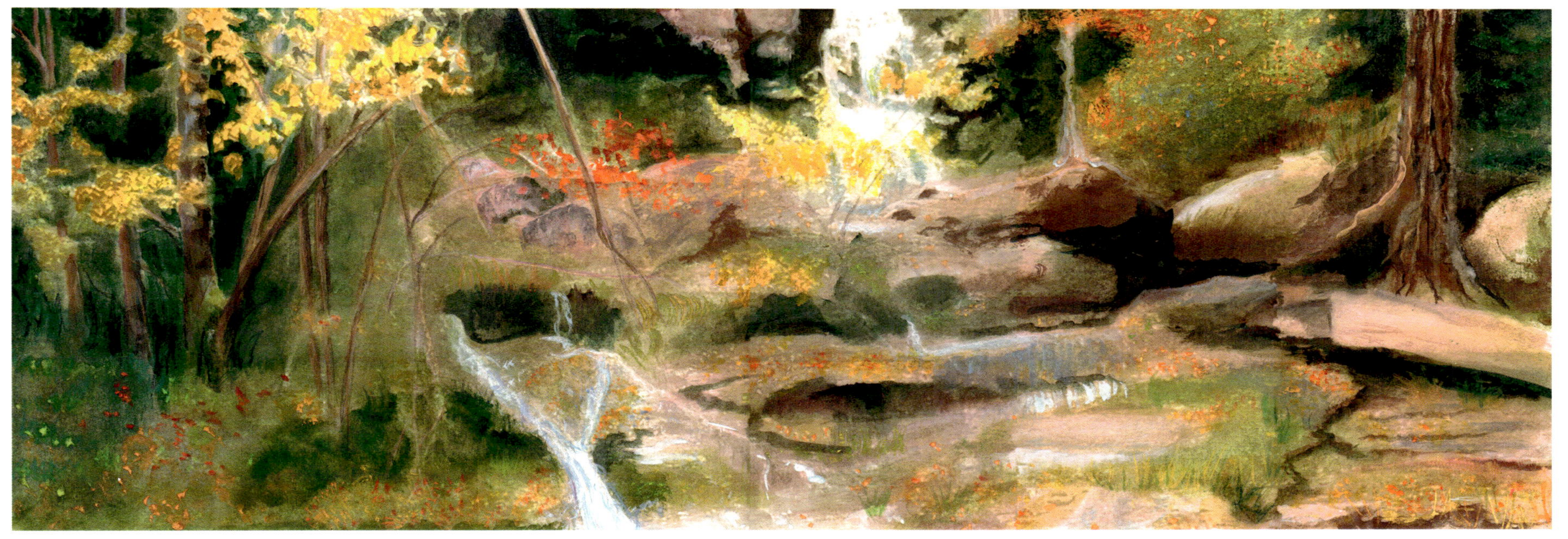

Kaaterskill Falls (1998)

Kaaterskill Falls was lauded as a place where a traveler could see a wilder image, a sort of primeval Eden. Beginning with Thomas Cole's first visit during 1825, they became a subject for painters of the Hudson River School, setting the wilderness ideal for American landscape painting. The Falls also inspired "Catterskill Falls", a poem by William Cullen Bryant:

> *"Midst greens and shades the Catterskill leaps,*
> *From cliffs where the wood-flower clings;*
> *All summer he moistens his verdant steeps,*
> *With the sweet light spray of the mountain-springs,*
> *And he shakes the woods on the mountain-side,*
> *When they drip with the rains of autumn-tide."*

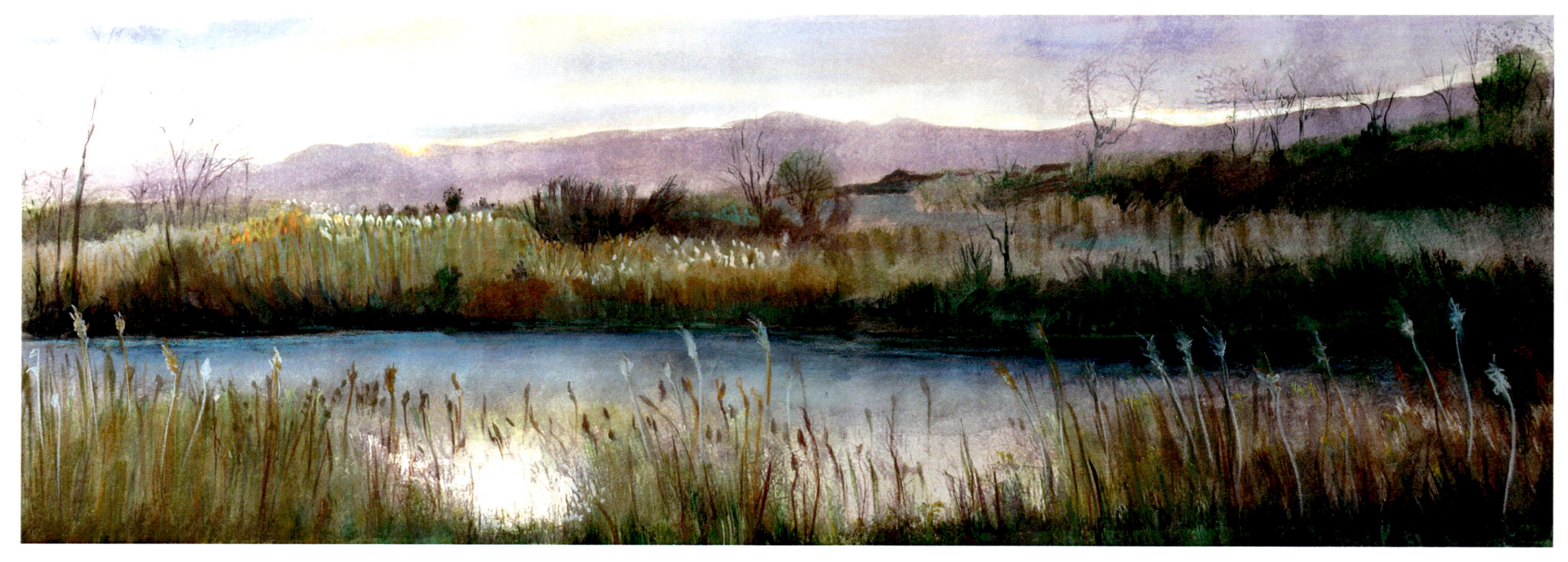

A View from Olana (1998) 18 x 48 in.

Frederic Church began as a student of Thomas Cole and became one of the most successful painters of the Hudson River School. In 1860, he purchased a 126 acre farm on the east side of the Hudson River, overlooking the river and the Catskill mountains to the west and Connecticut and the Berkshires of Massachusetts to the east. He built a mansion and named his estate Olana after an ancient treasure house in Persia.

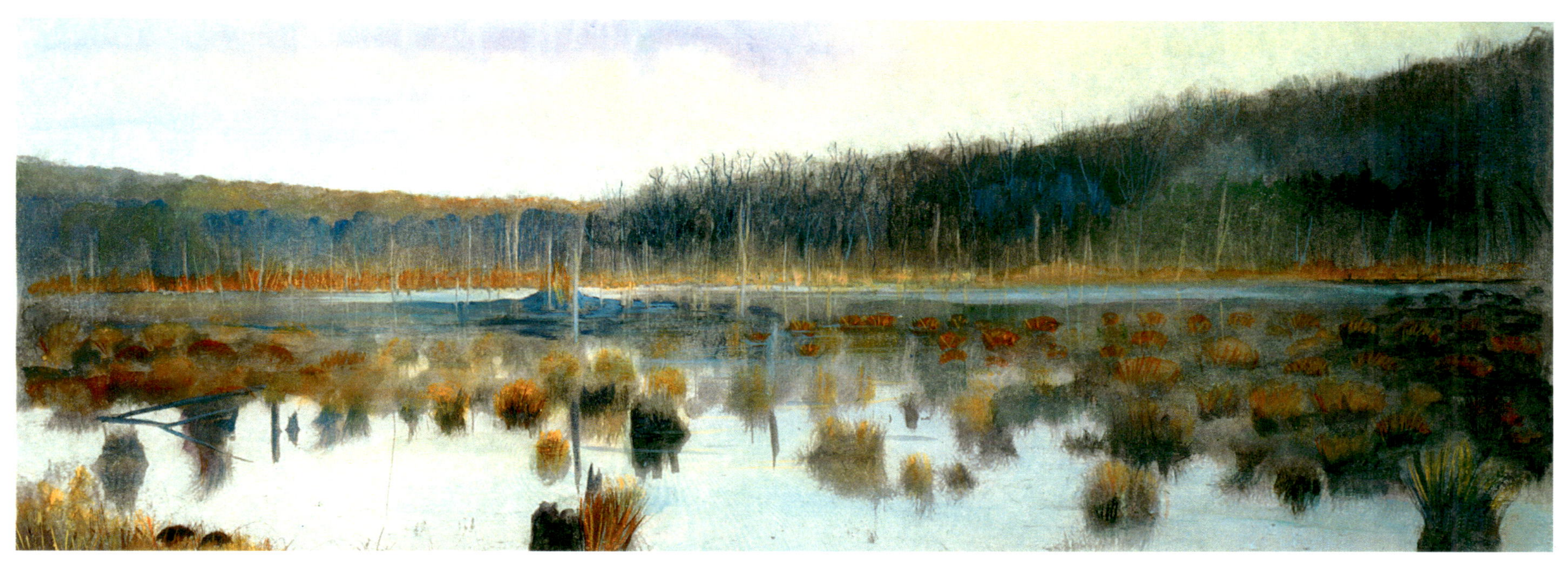

Wetlands, Kent, Connecticut (1998) 18 x 48 in.

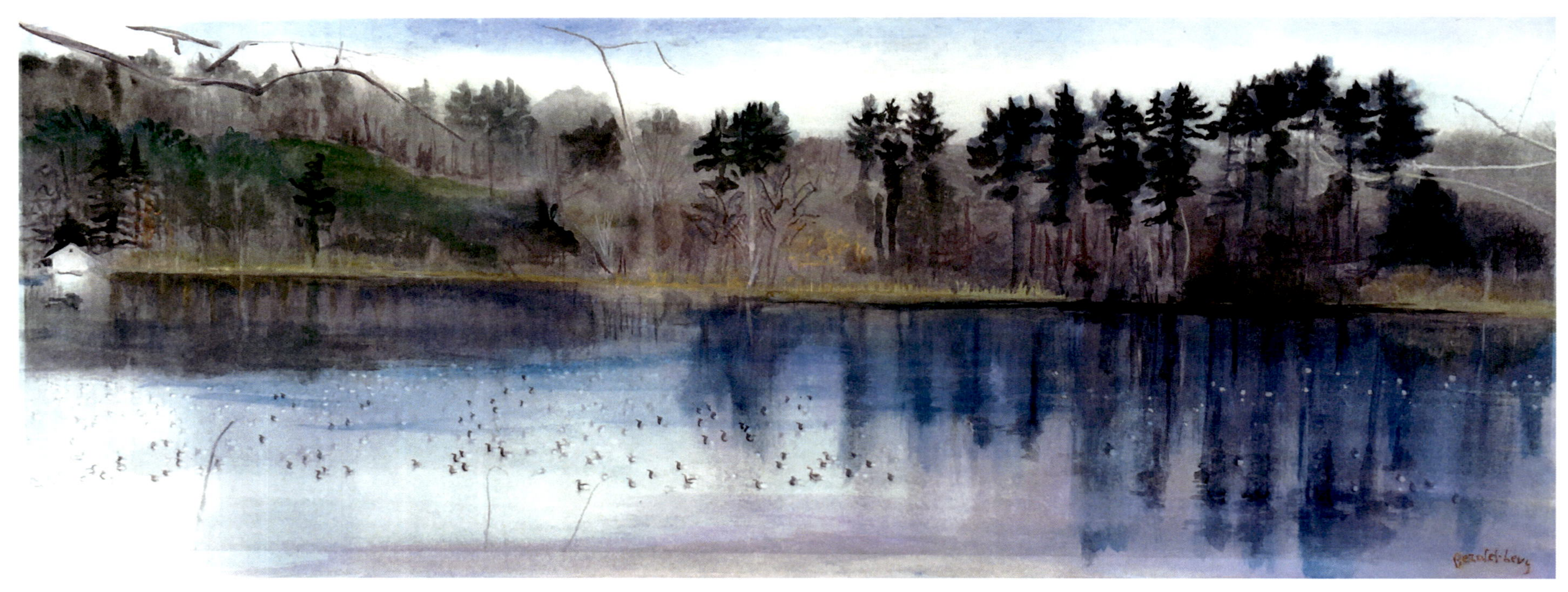

Near Hudson, NY (1998) 18 x 48 in.

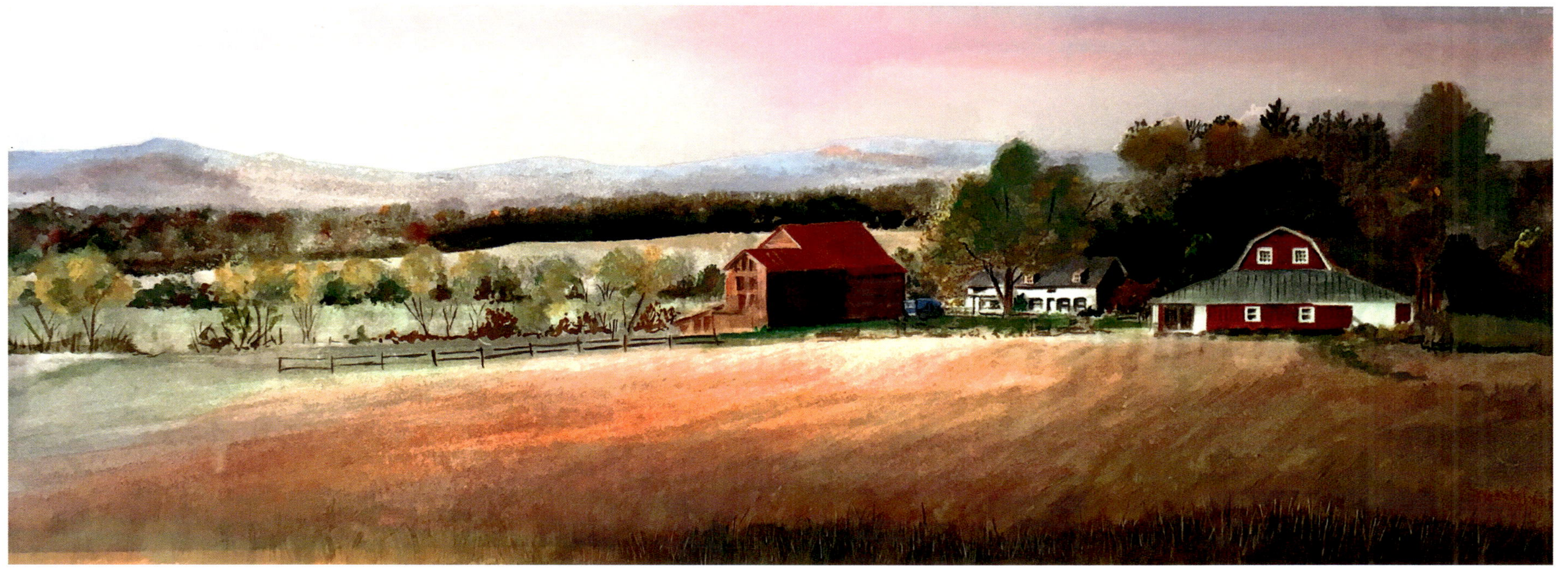

The Family Farm (1998) 18 x 48 in.

Chaim's parents bought this farm, including the stone farmhouse, built in 1791, the milking barn on the right, the original barn on the left with its massive posts and beams, and 260 acres including wetlands on the Hudson. The property had originally belonged to the Van Orden family, the ancestor of which, William Van Orden, came from Holland in the ship "Arms of Norway" about 1670. The family graves are still in a fenced area further to the left in the field. Family members still reside in the area. The property was also at an earlier time both a hunting ground and council meeting place for the Mohawk tribe. Arrowheads have been found on the property.

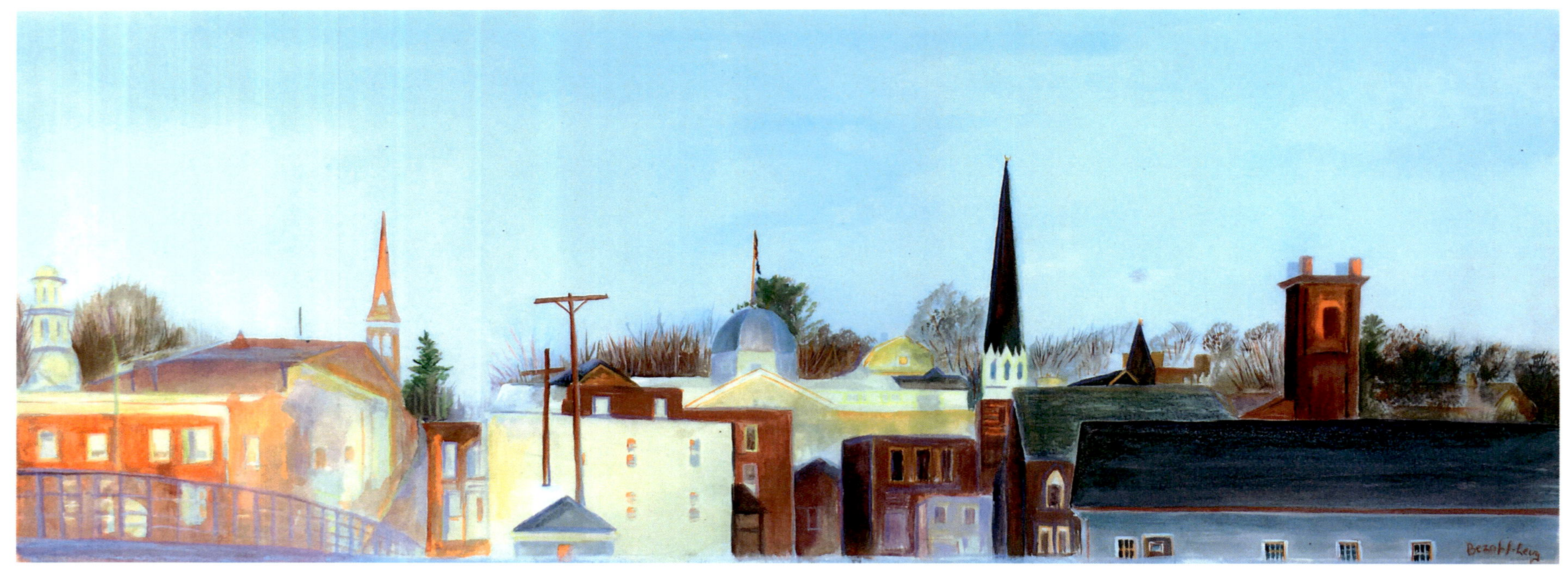

Town of Catskill (1998) 18 x 48 in.

Catskill, New York lies on the Hudson River at the Eastern edge of the Catskill Mountains 125 miles north of New York City. It is an historic town, the home of Thomas Cole (1801-1848) the founder of the Hudson River School of painting and Martin Van Buren, seventh President of the United States. In the lower left of the painting is the Uncle Sam Bridge. It is believed that the name "Uncle Sam" was derived from Samuel Wilson, a meat-packer from nearby Troy, New York who supplied rations for American soldiers during the War of 1812. There was a requirement at the time for contractors to stamp their name and where the rations came from onto the food they were sending. Wilson's packages were labeled "E.A – US." When someone asked what that stood for, a co-worker jokingly said, "Elbert Anderson (the contractor) and Uncle Sam," referring to Wilson, though the "US" actually stood for United States.

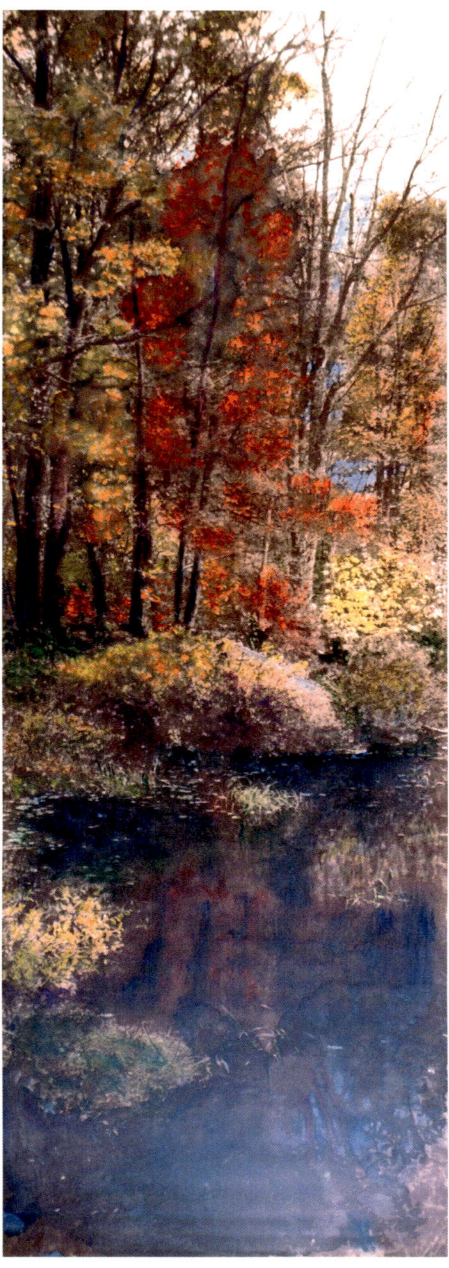

Burgett Creek (1998) 60 x 22 in.

In Between

There is a place in between
a glance around
a breath taken in
a moment
the question is out
where am I now?
where have I been?

Halfway point I would say
how fast it flew
a reassembling is needed
a looking forth
courage must displace
enthusiasm of youth

Wisdom must compensate
as the leaves drop
in the fall, turning red
in transition
so life is given the
opportunity to fulfill
its call
there is a winter of
watching and waiting
before spring and
new life bursts into green!

-Yonnah Ben Levy

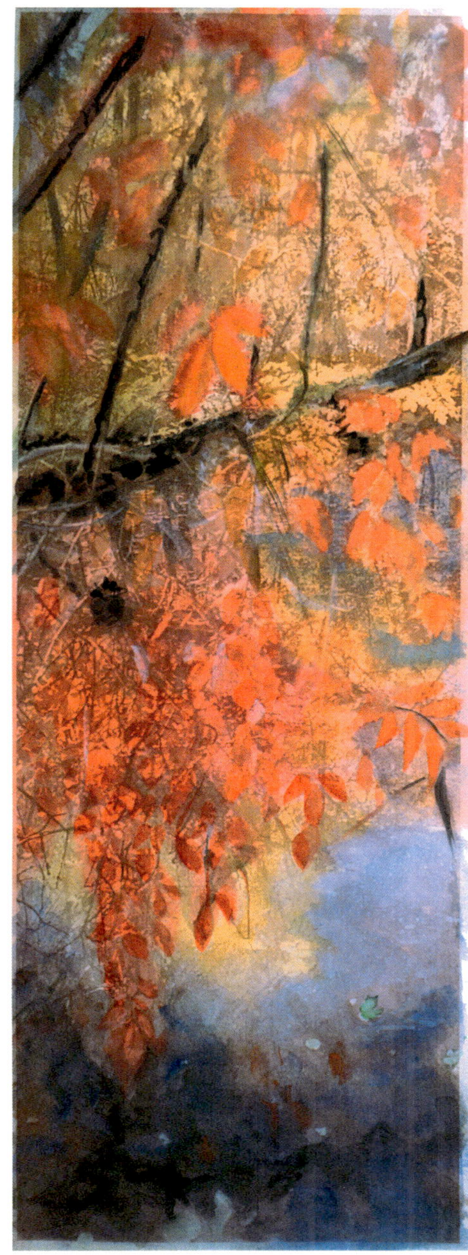

Falling Leaves (1998) 48 x 18 in.

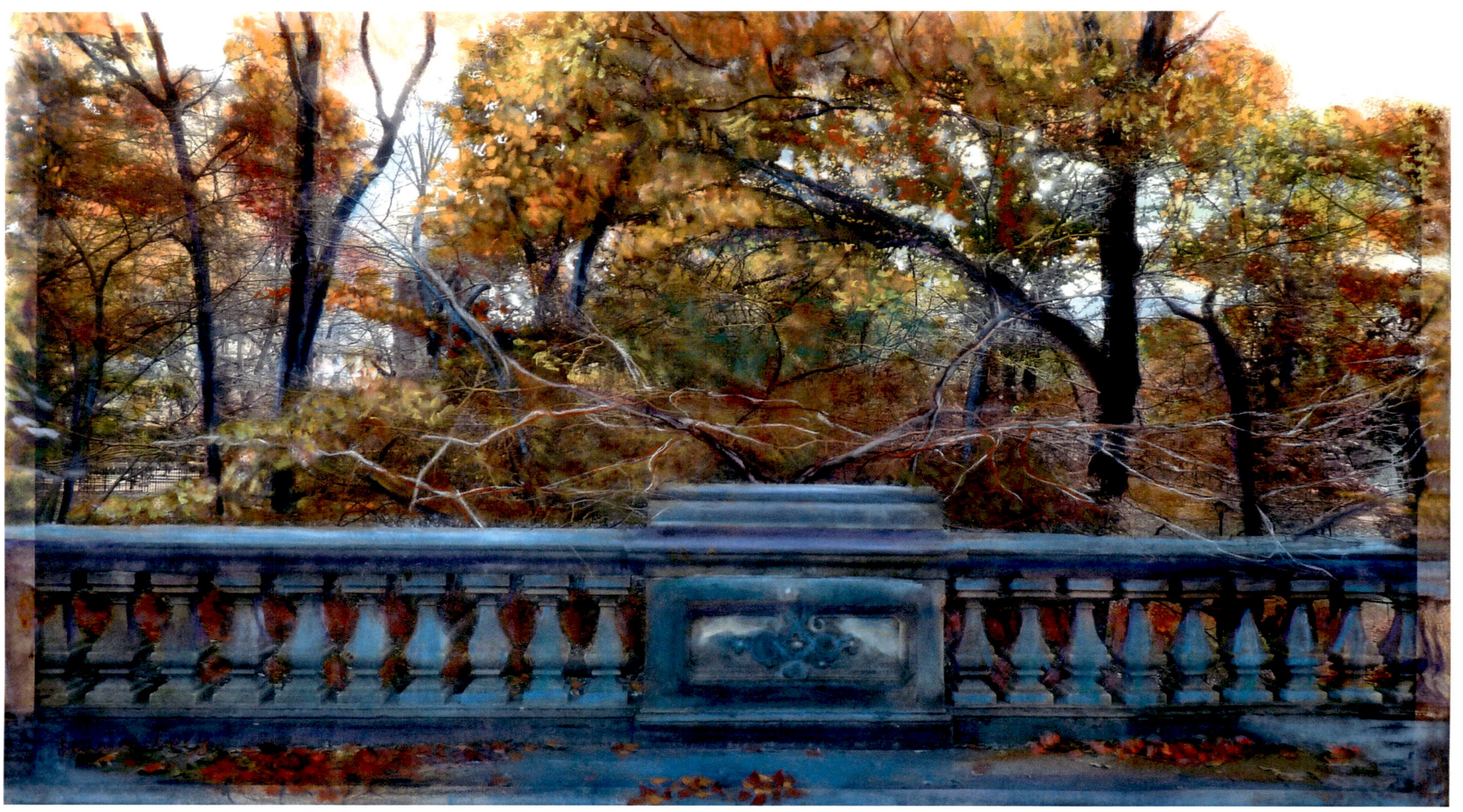

Looking in from 5ᵗʰ Avenue (2010) 22 x 39 in. mixed media with photography and acrylics on rice paper

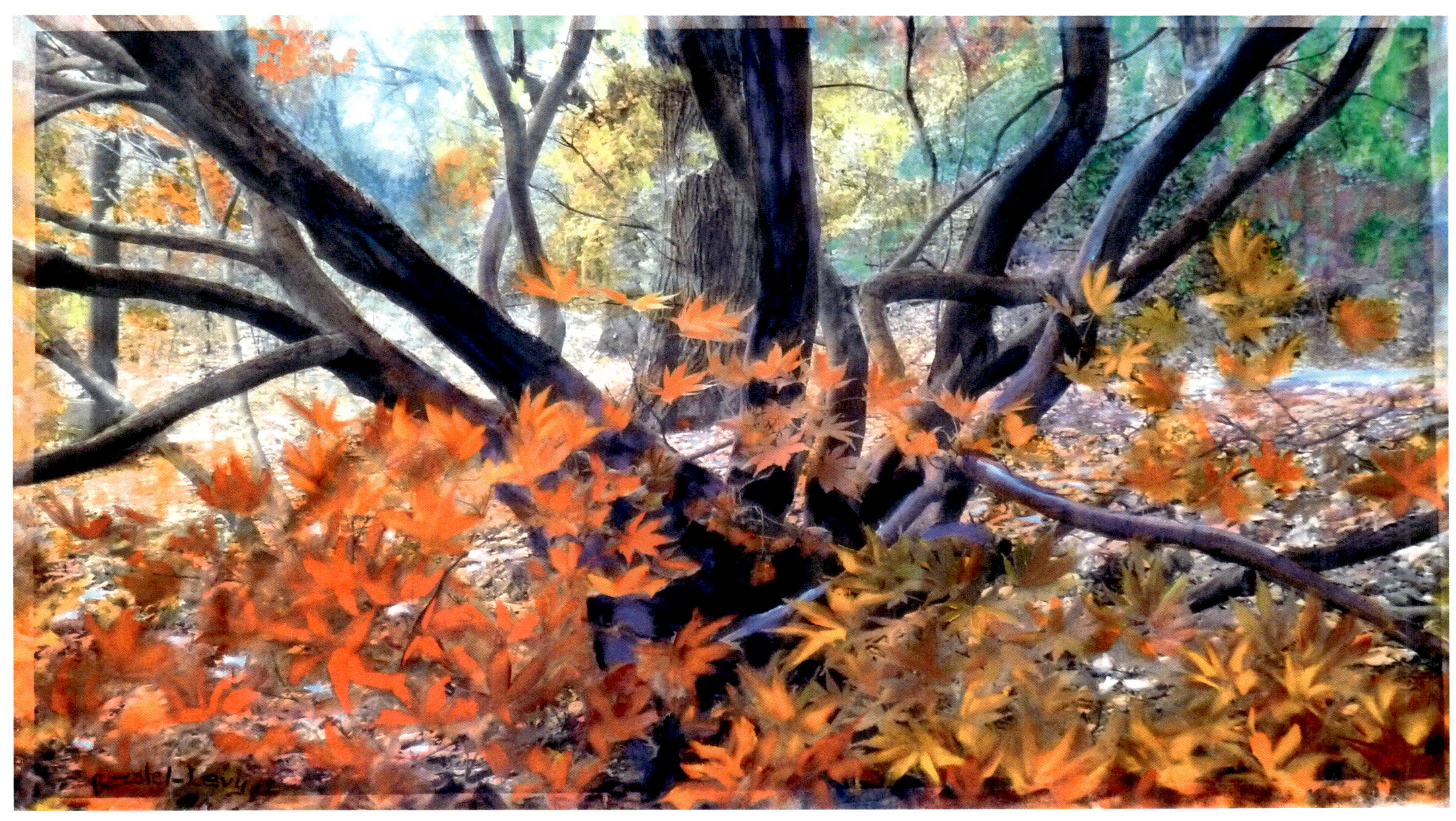

Japanese Maple, The Ramble (2010) 22 x 39 in. mixed media with photography and acrylics on rice paper

"To use the words of Park designer Frederick Law Olmsted, The Ramble is a 36-acre "wild garden." Central Park's designers imagined a tranquil spot where visitors could stroll, discover forest gardens rich with plantings, and meander along the paths. This truly is a place for the urban explorer to escape the city and get utterly lost in nature." - Central Park Conservancy website

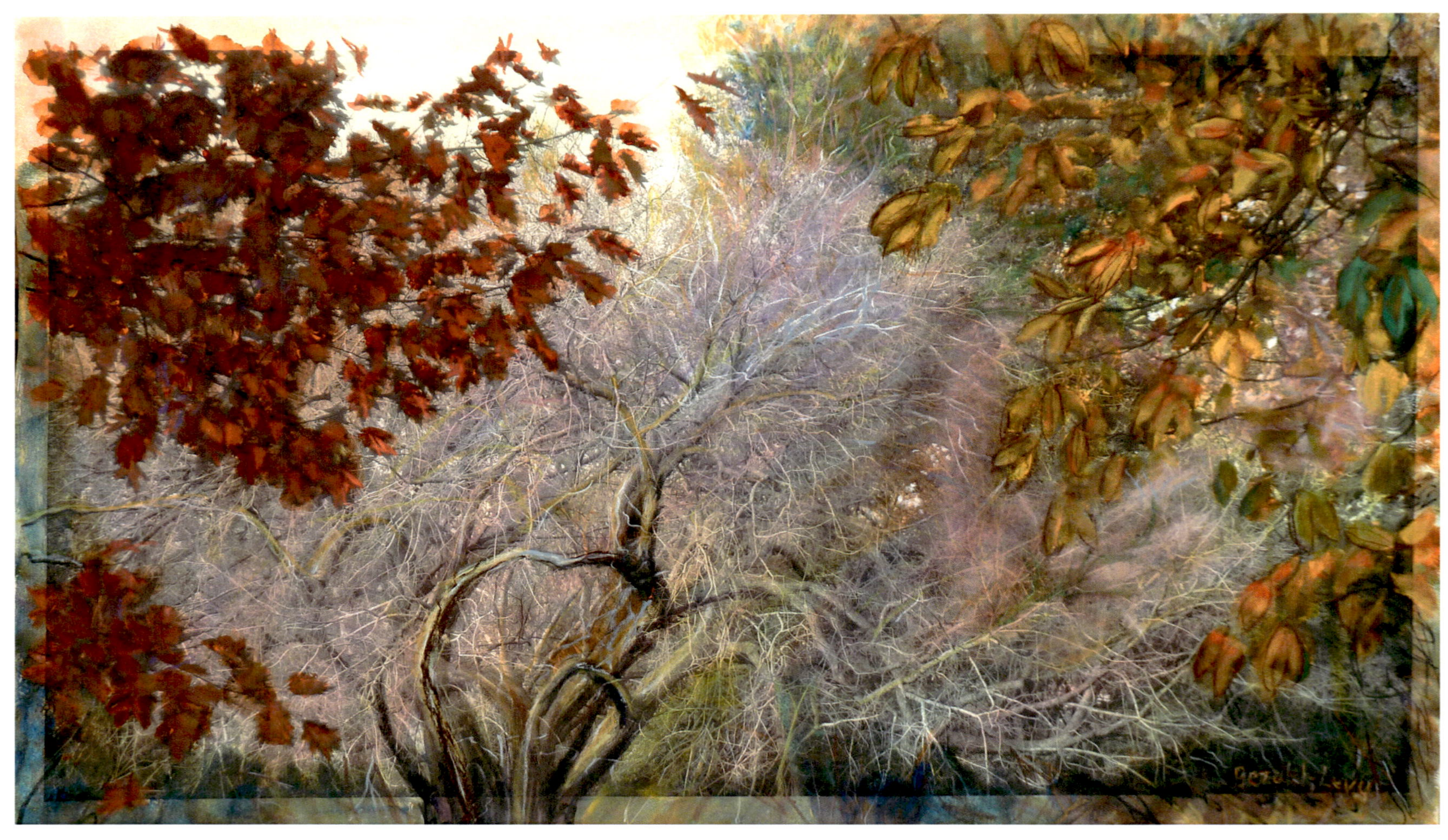

Treetops (2010) 22 x 39 in. mixed media with photography and acrylics on rice paper

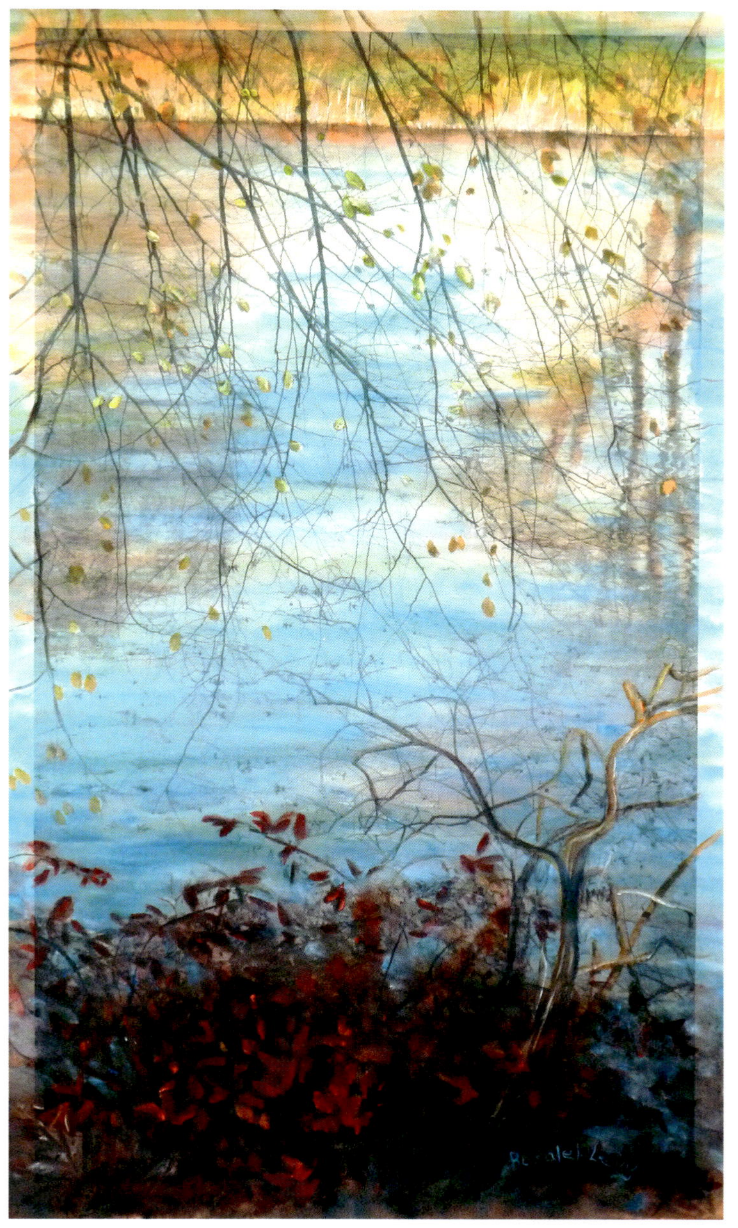

The Ramble, Central Park (2010) 39 x 22 in.

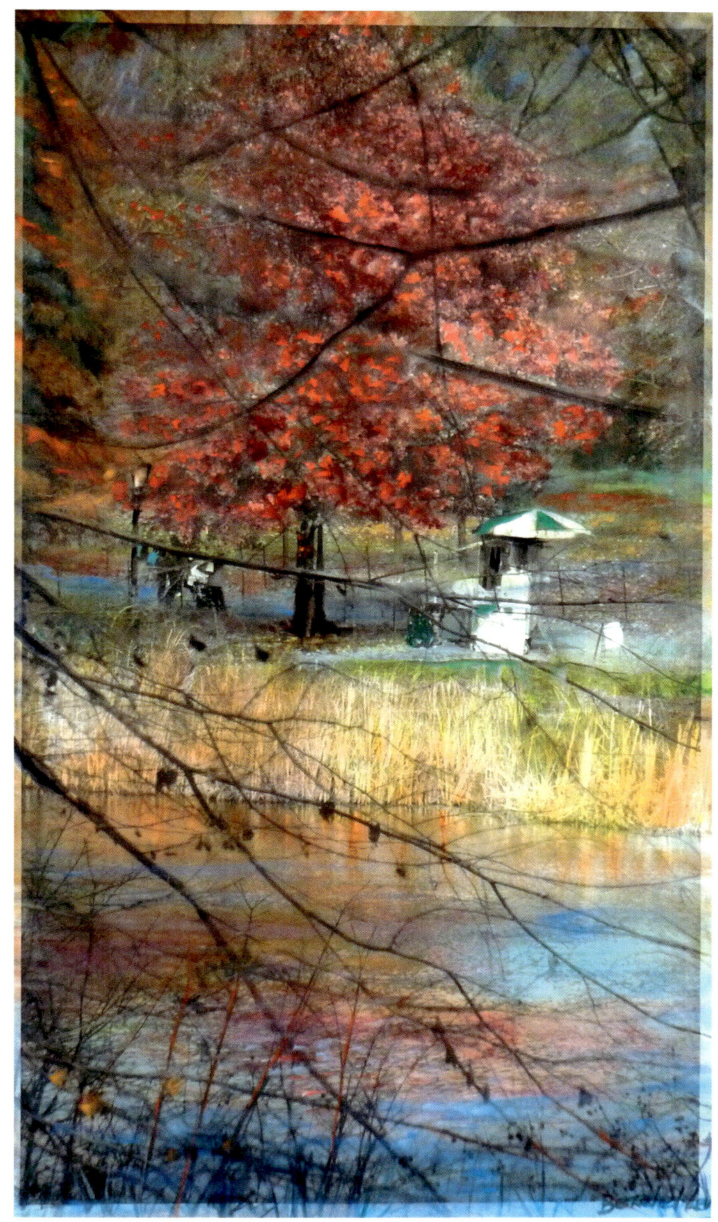

Hot Dog Stand, Central Park (2010) 39 x 22 in.

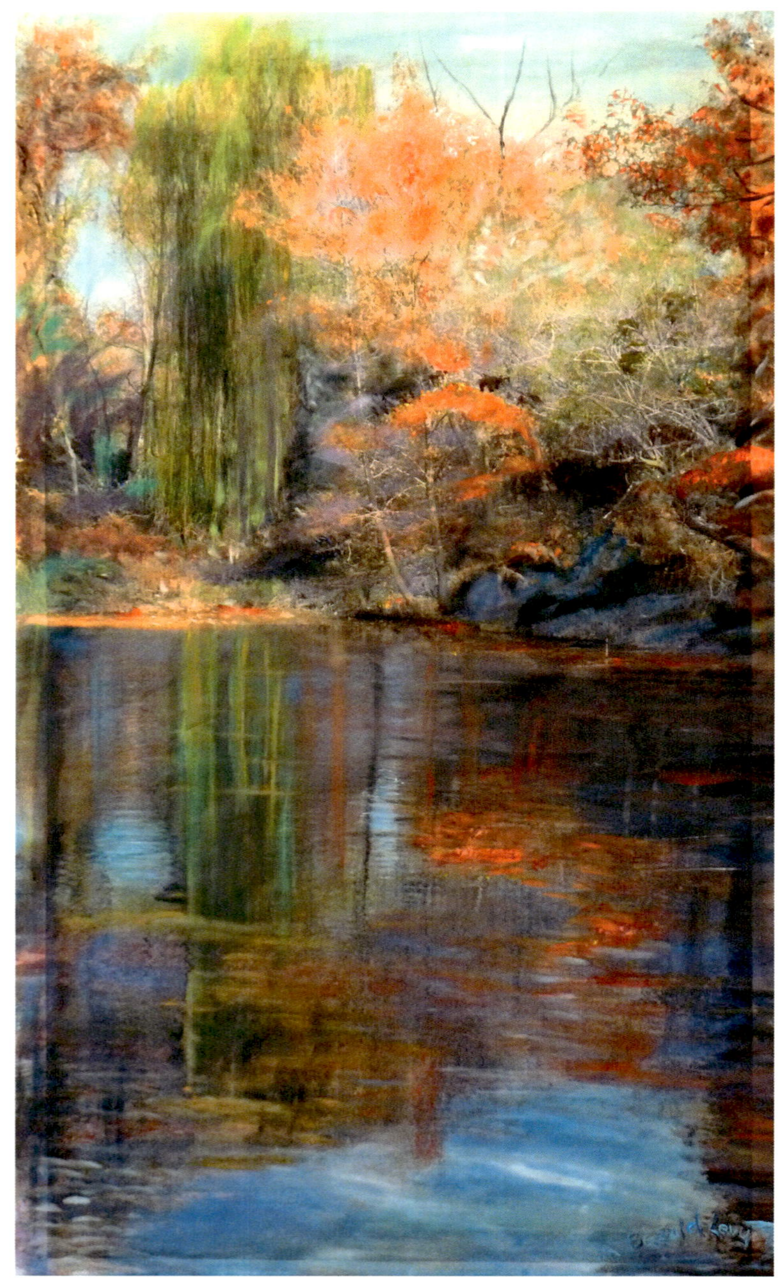

Willow, Central Park (2010) 39 x 22 in.

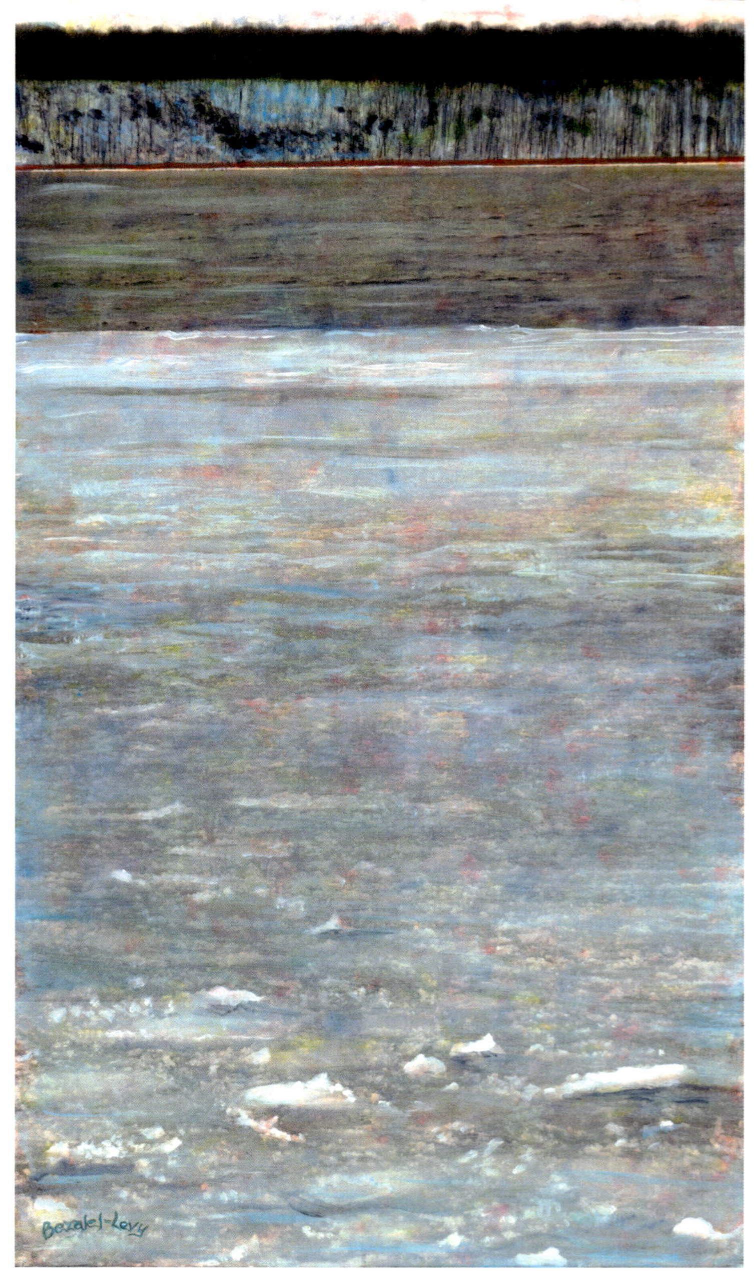

Frozen Hudson (2011) mixed-media mounted on birch, 40 x 22 in.

Pacific Scrolls

After spending a year in the Hudson Valley, we moved to Camano Island in the Puget Sound north of Seattle. Yonnah's family had roots in this region going back more than a century and together we toured the region alone, or with friends, or on organized trips. We learned on a tour with a professor of geology that as the North American plate drifted westward 200 million years ago, islands and rocks "docked on" to the continent. Thus we continued our scrolls style, seeking out compositions reminiscent of classical scrolls, but on this side of the Pacific Rim. Most of these compositions are mixed media with photography and acrylics on rice paper mounted on linen with rice paste. Exceptions to this technique are specified as such. This section is the largest in the book simply because this is where we live.

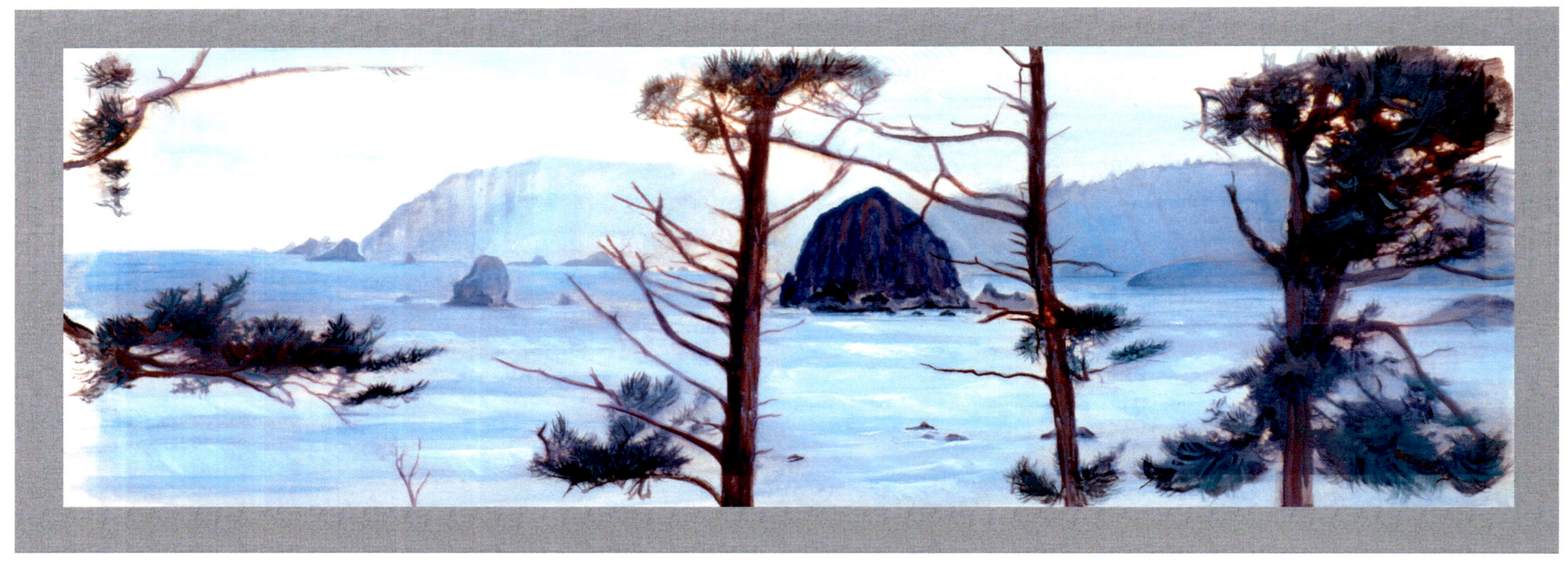

Haystack Rock, Oregon (2001) 24 x 60 in.

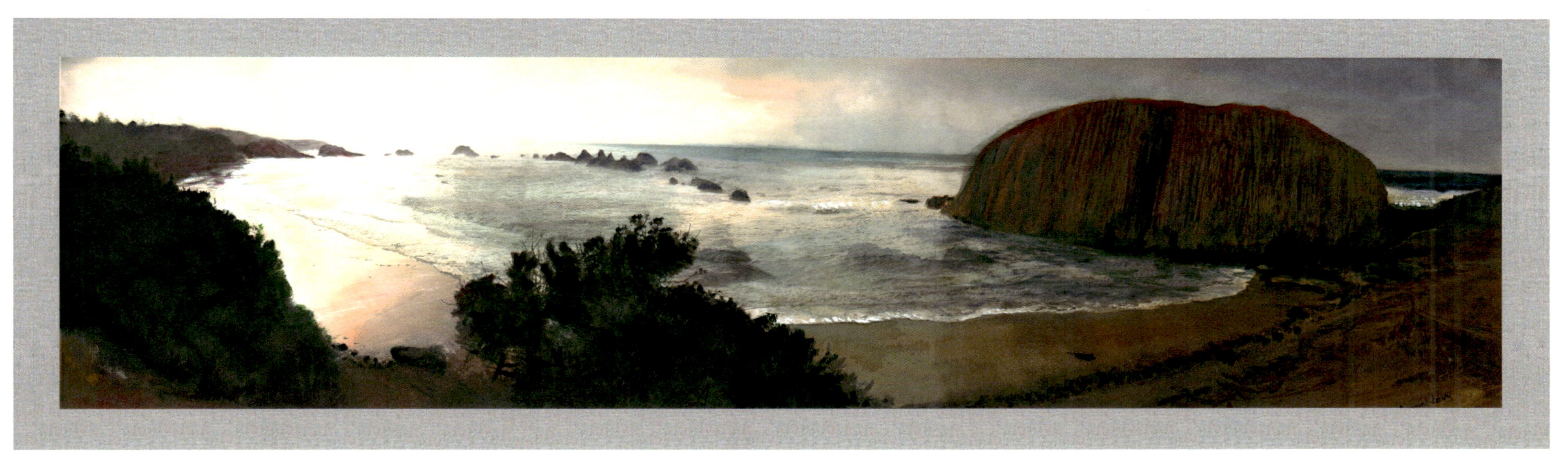

Seal Rock, Oregon Coast (2004) 22 x 72 in.

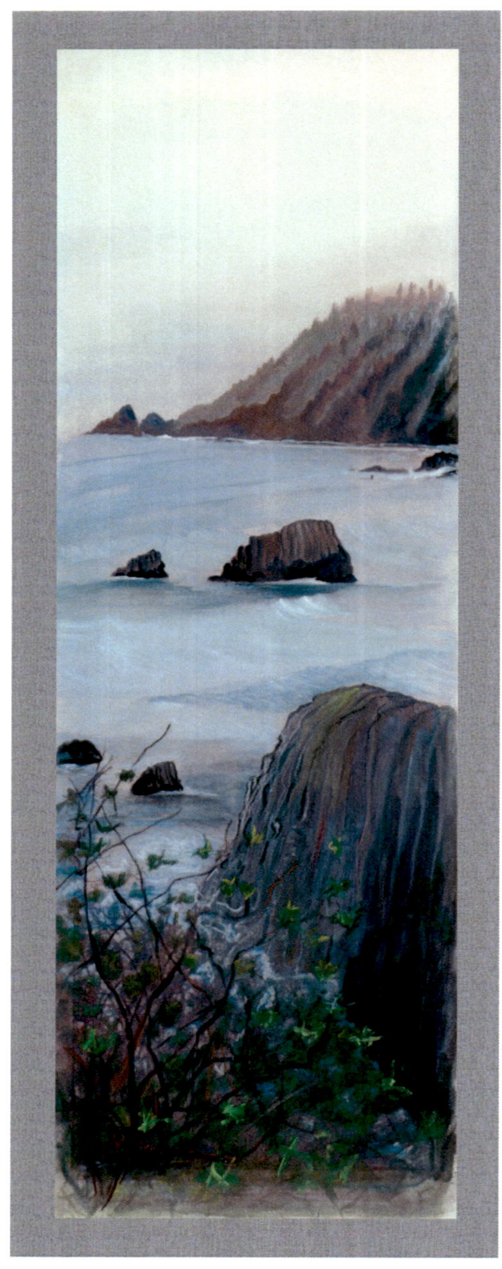

Cannon Beach (2002) 60 x 24 in.

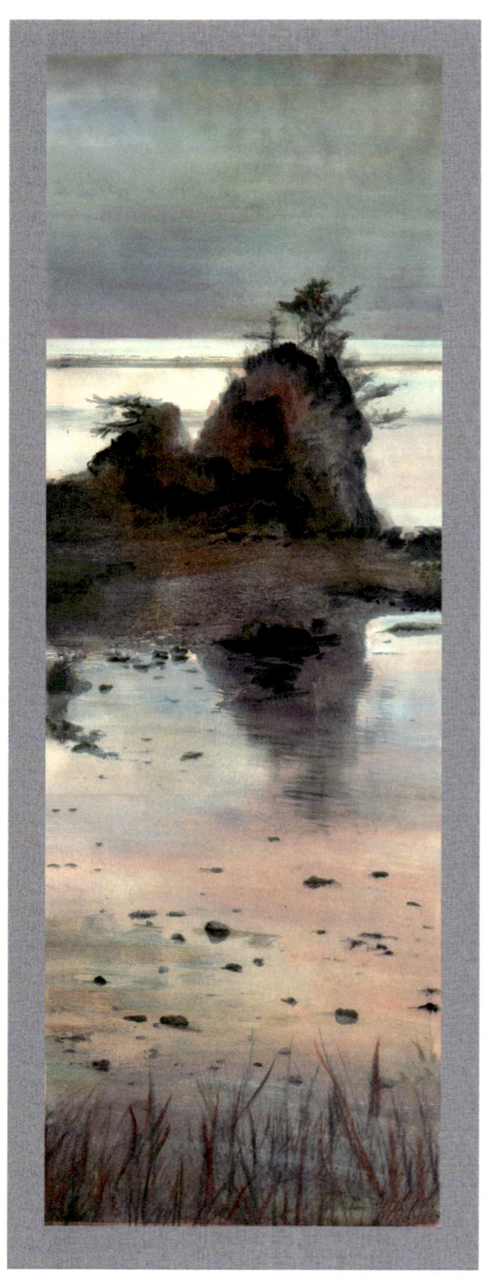

Lincoln City (2004) 60 x 22 in.

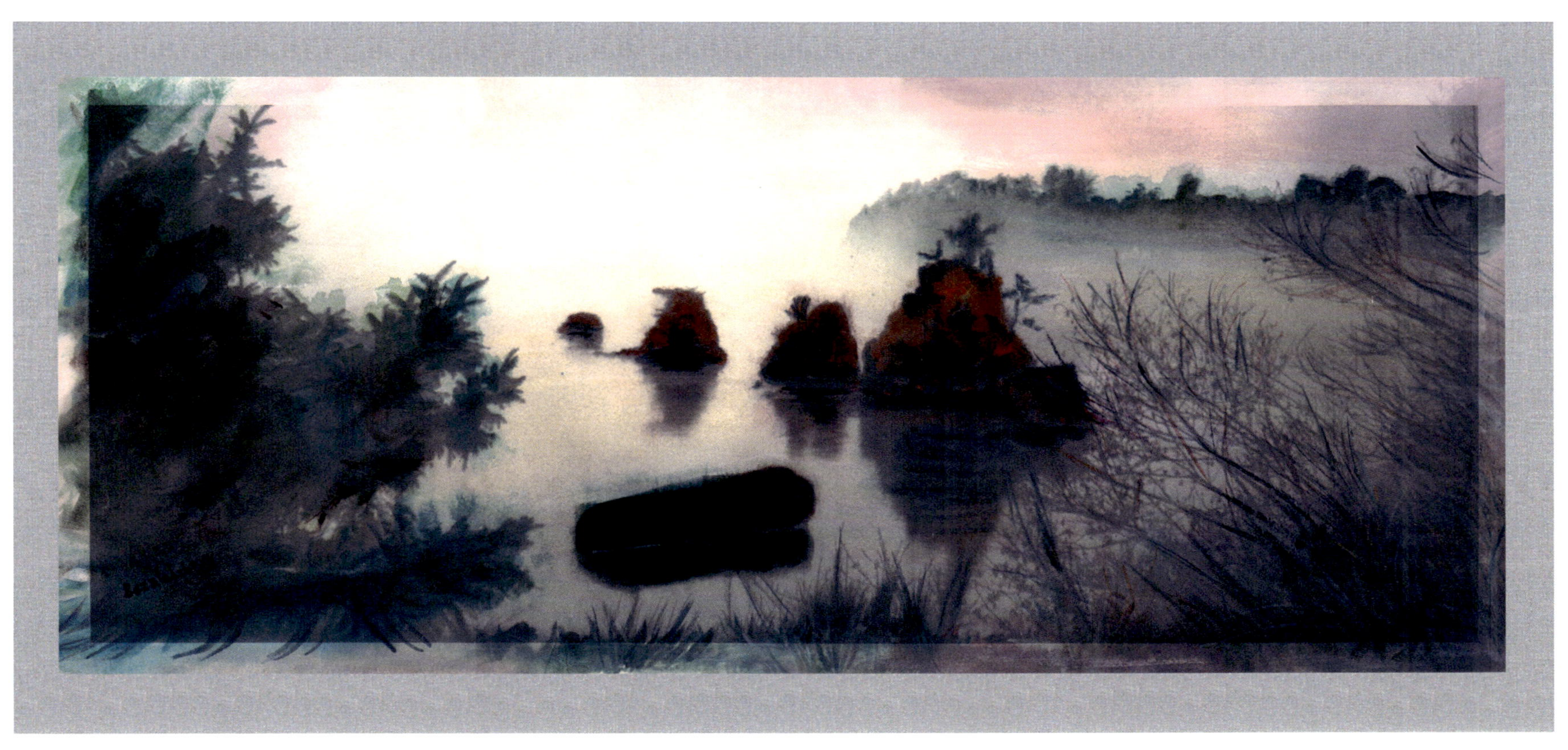

Pacific Scene (2004) 20 x 44 in.

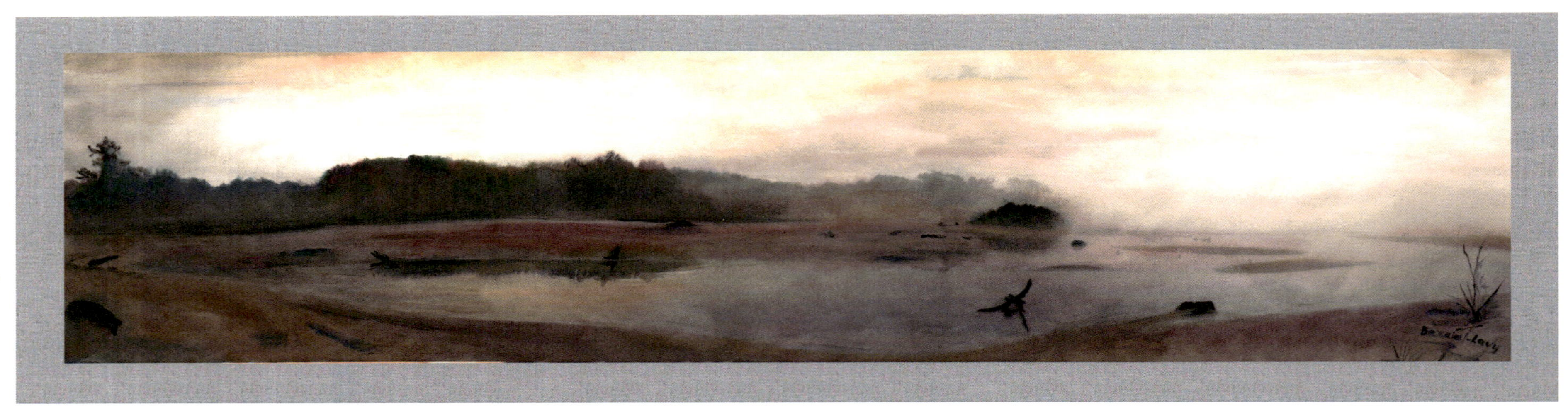

Rolling Mists, Oregon Coast (2004) 20 x 72 in.

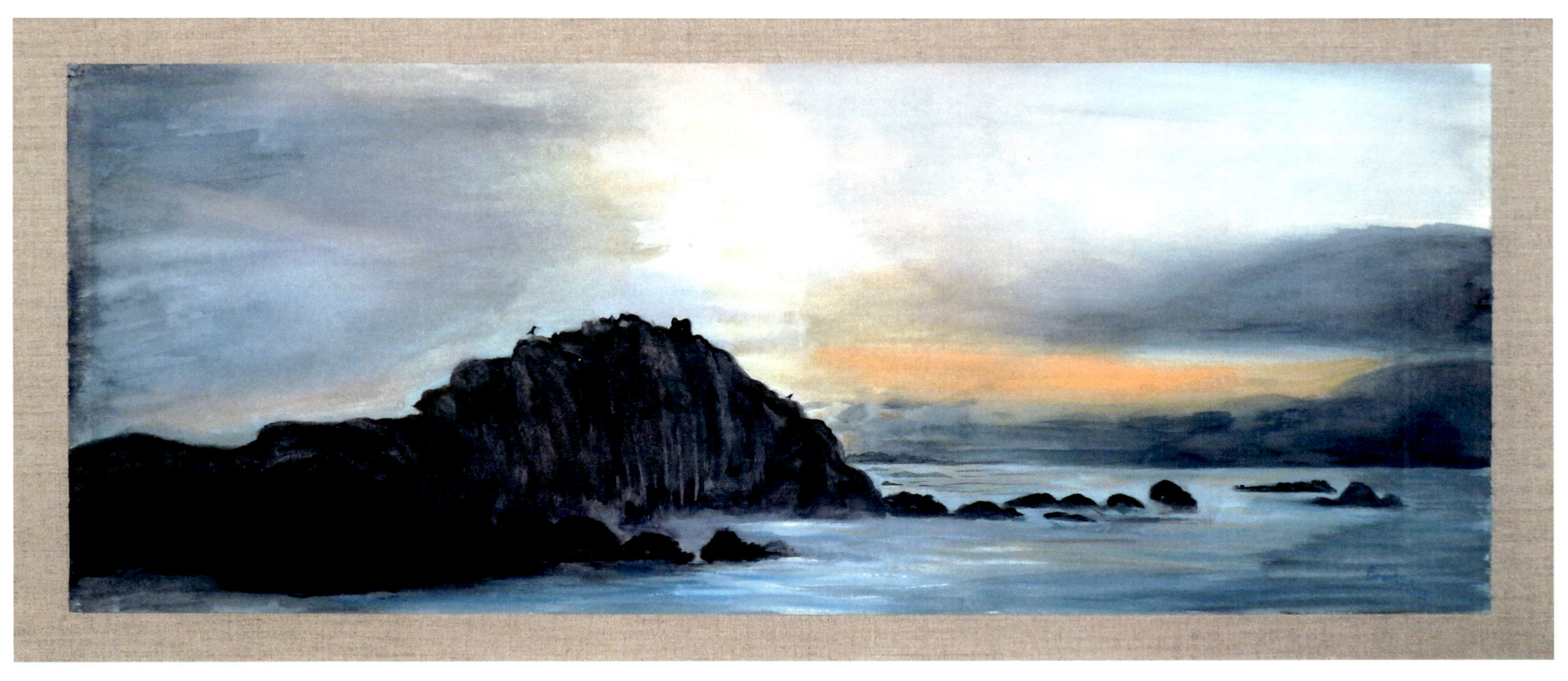

Rocky Coast I, Newport Beach (2001) 21 x 44 in.

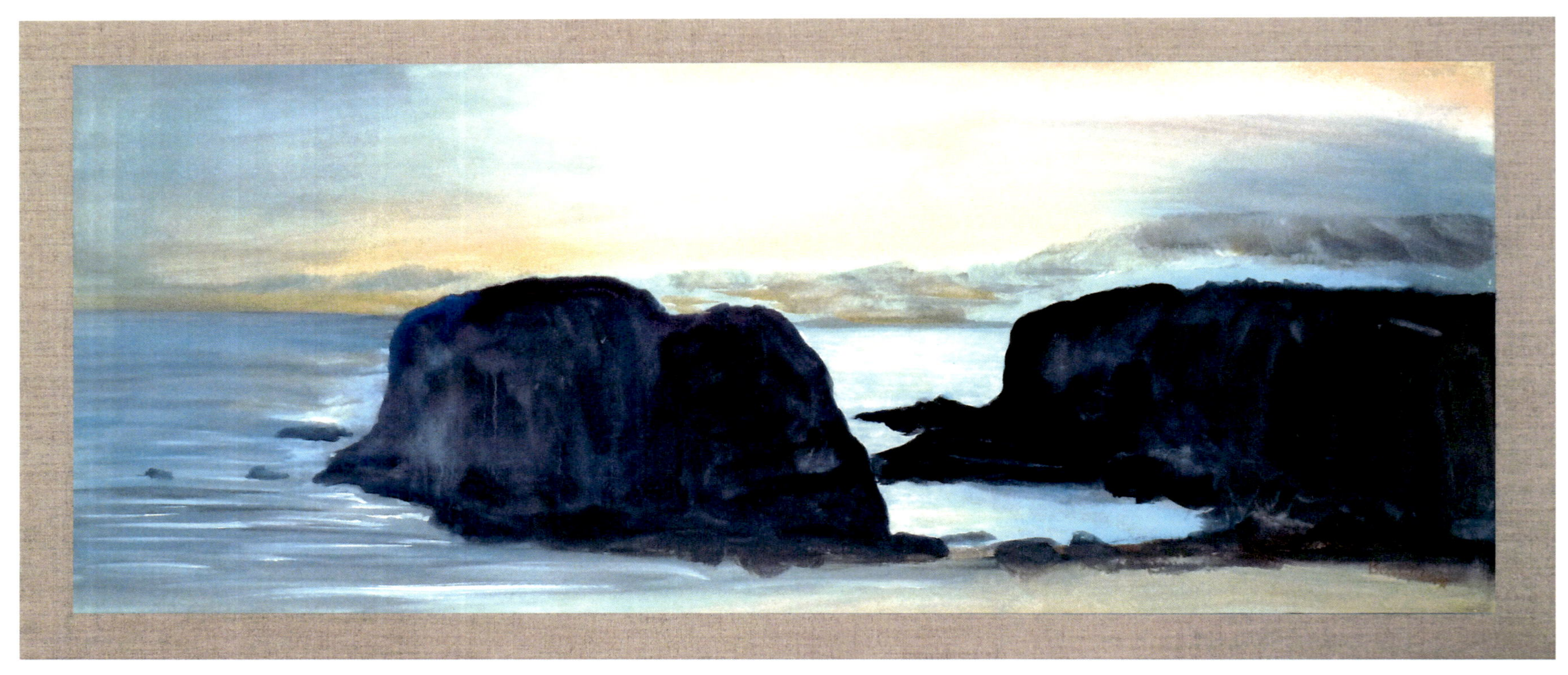

Rocky Coast II, Newport Beach (2001) 21 x 44 in.

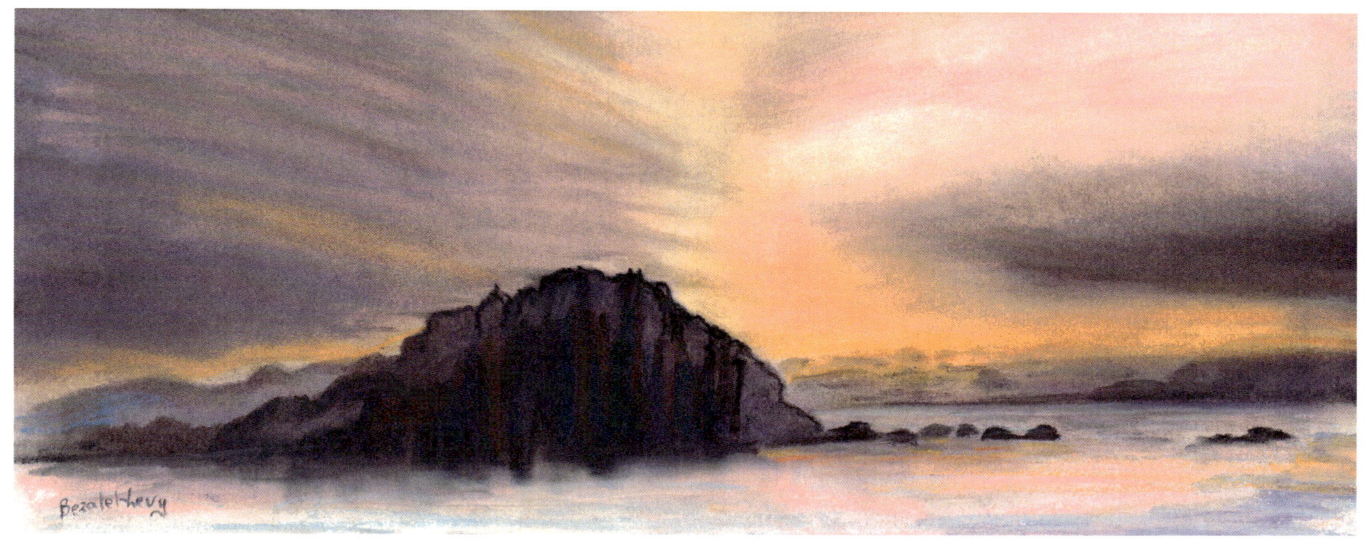

Study for Rocky Coast I (2000) photography and pastels on rice paper, 7 x 17 in.

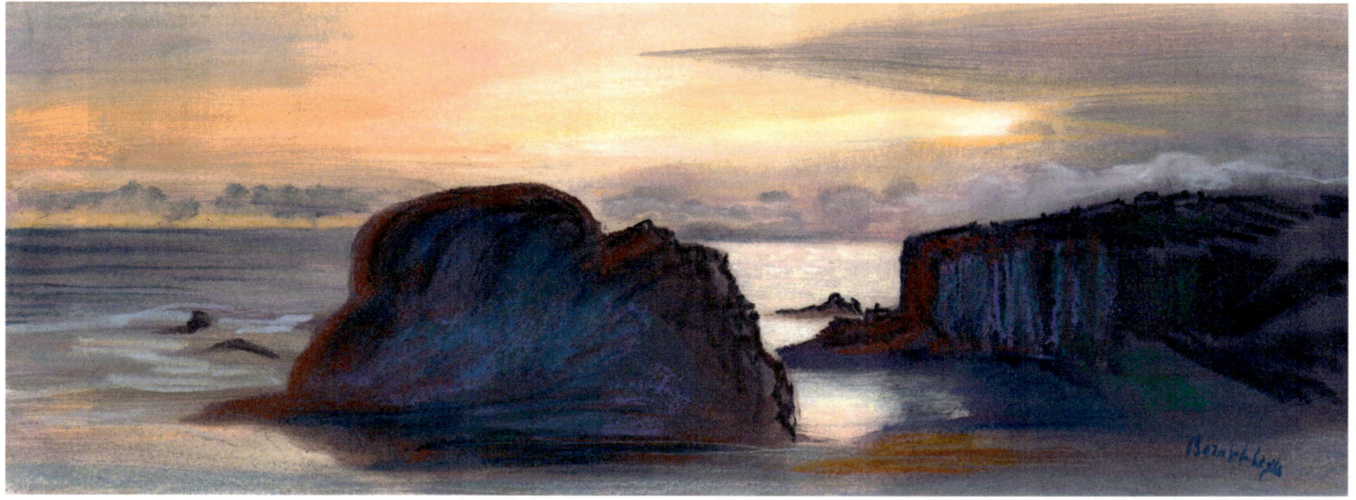

Study for Rocky Coast II (2000) photography and pastels on rice paper, 7 x 17 in.,

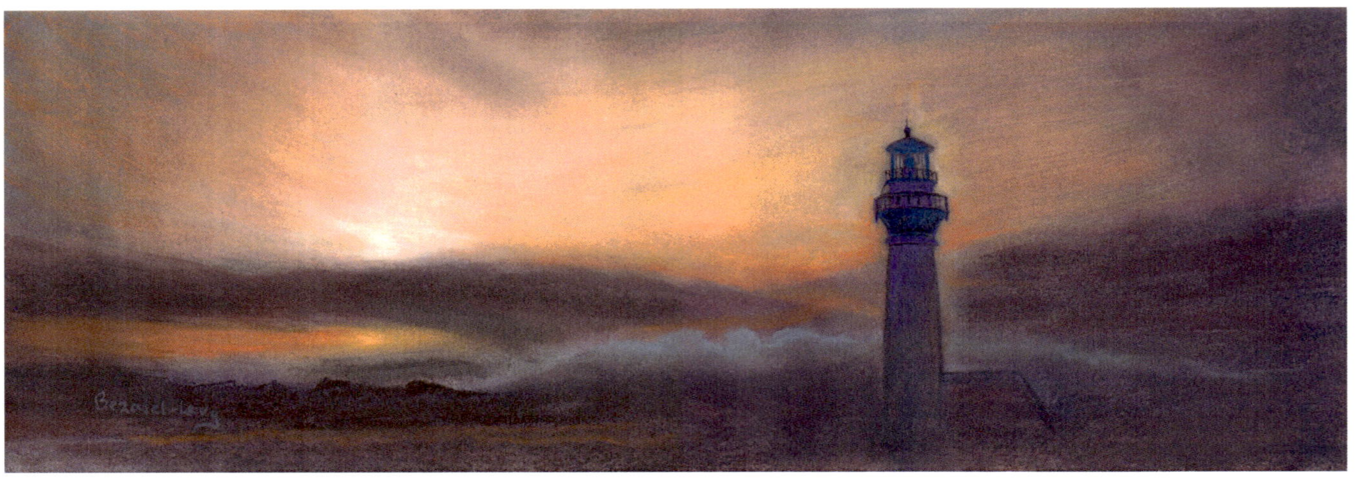

Yaquina Head Lighthouse (2000) photography and pastels on rice paper, 6 x 17 in.

Made in Paris in 1868 and shipped to Newport, Yaquina Head Light was first lit August 20, 1873, and automated in 1966. It is active with an identifying light characteristic of two seconds on, two seconds off, two seconds on, and 14 seconds off. The lighthouse still uses its original French-made, 1st order, Fixed Fresnel lens, visible 19 miles out to sea. In 1993, the lighthouse was listed in the National Register of Historic Places.

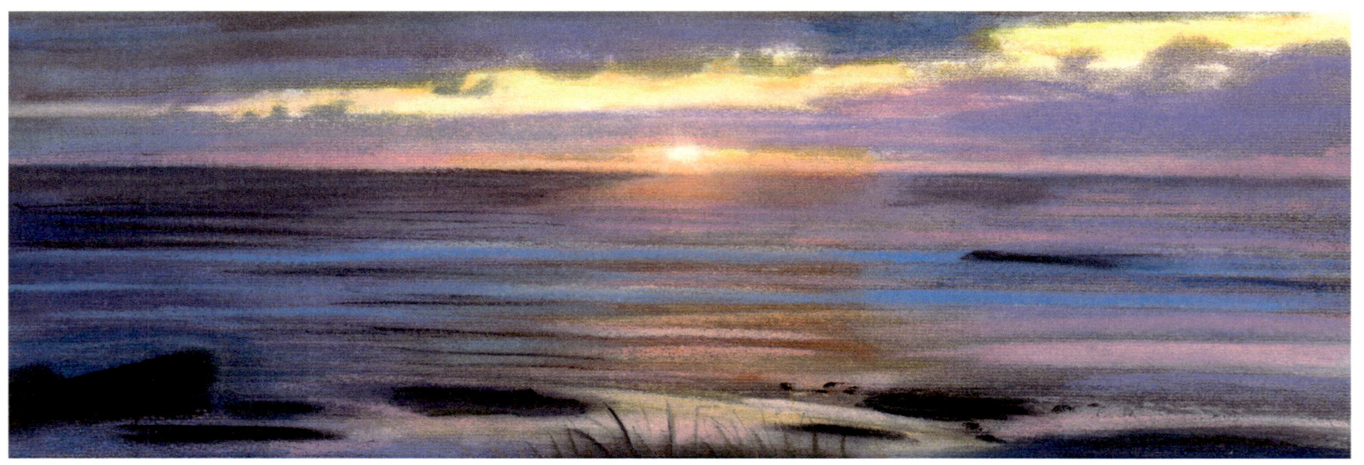

Sunset, Newport Beach (2000) photography and pastels on rice paper, 6 x 17 in.

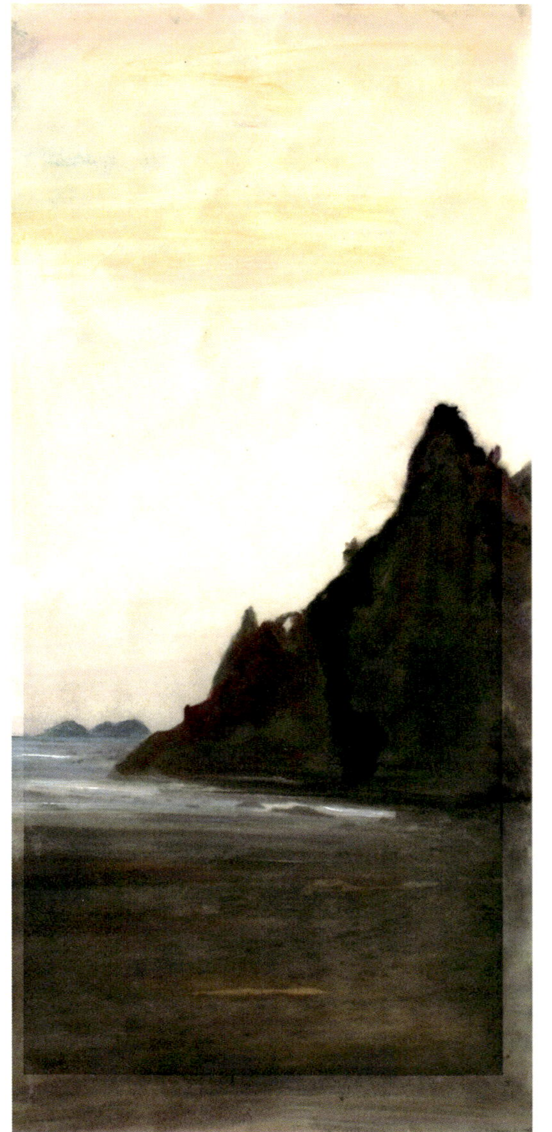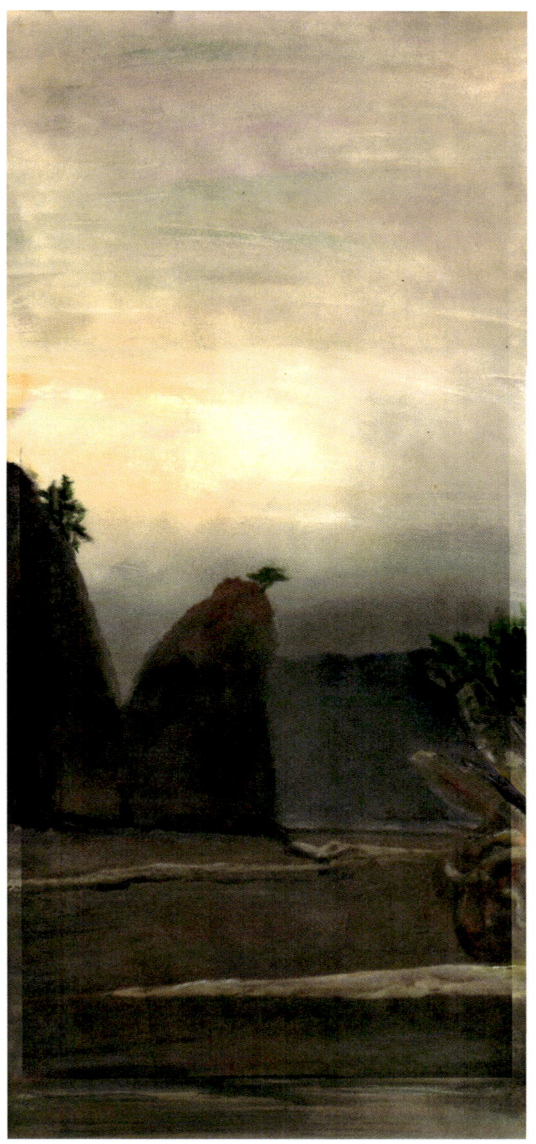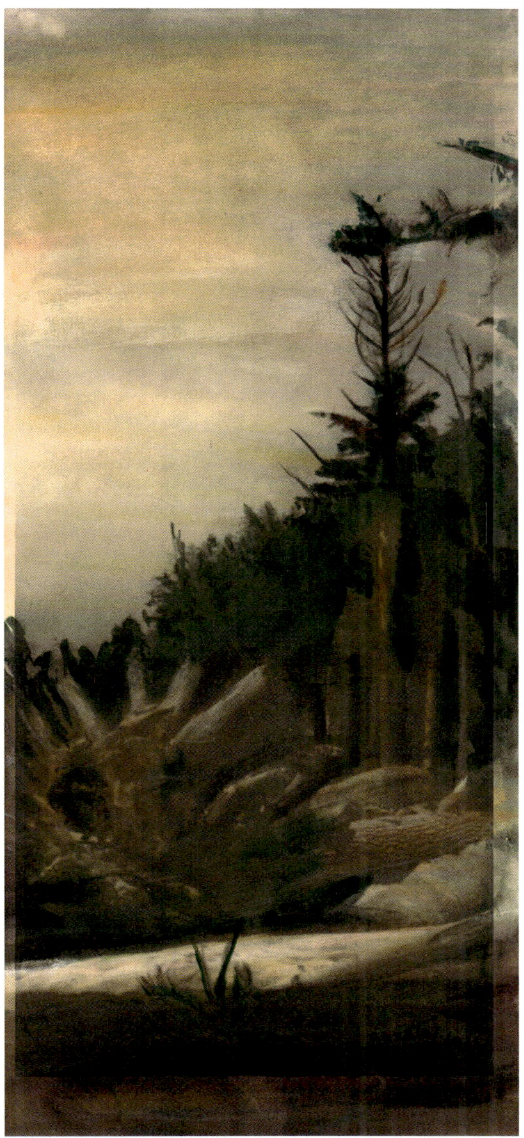

Olympic Triptych *(2004) 40 x 18 in. each panel*

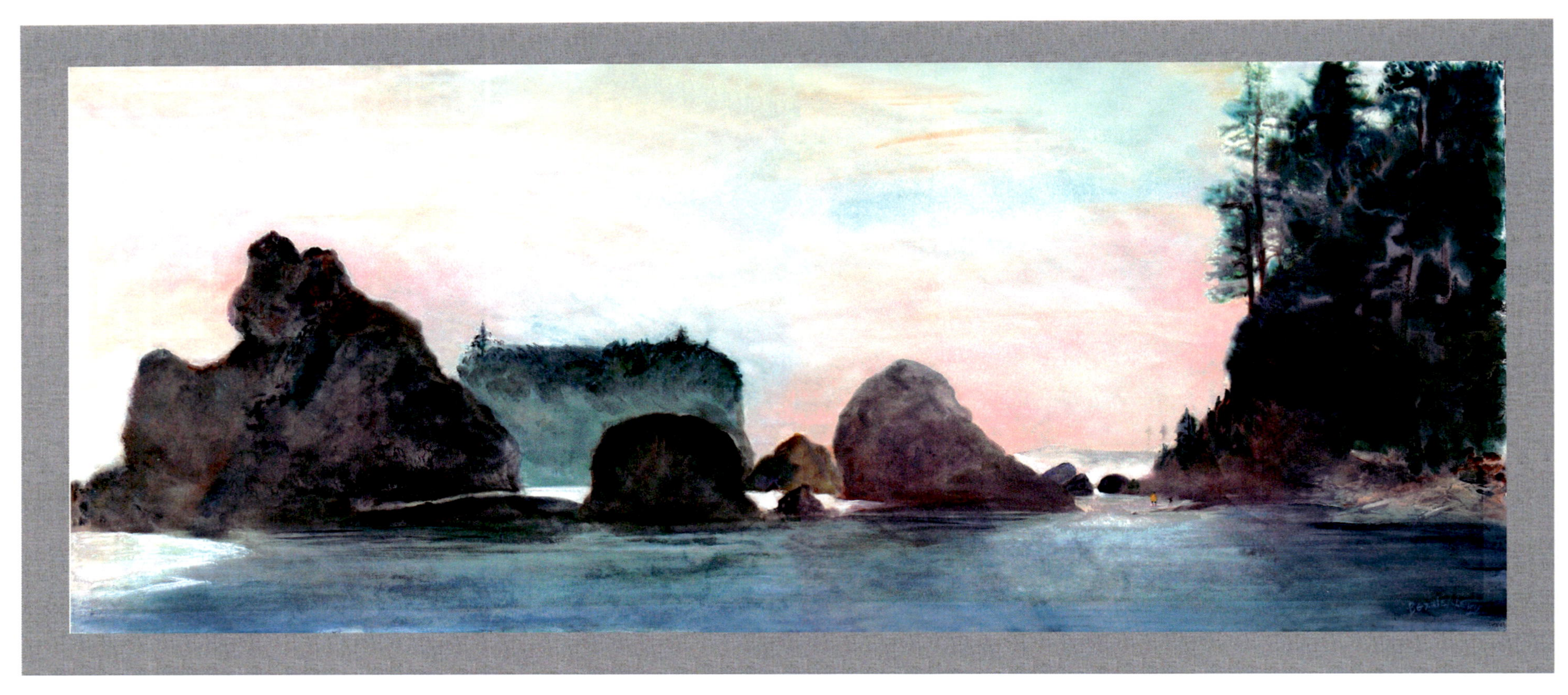

Ruby Beach *(2005) 50 x 72 in.*

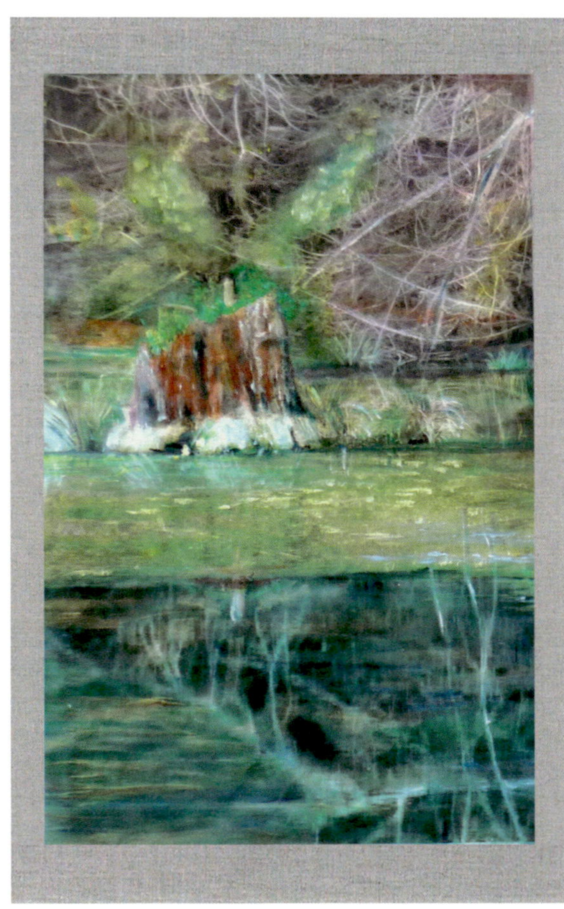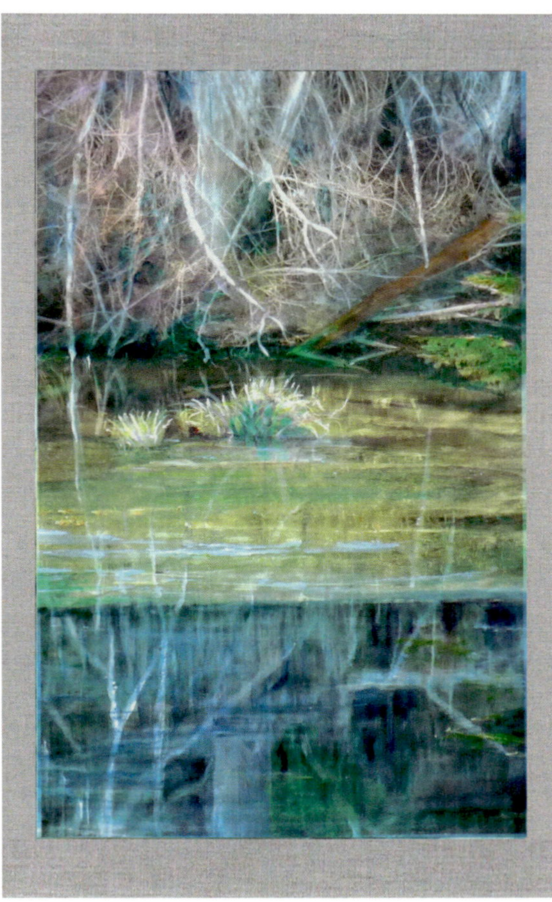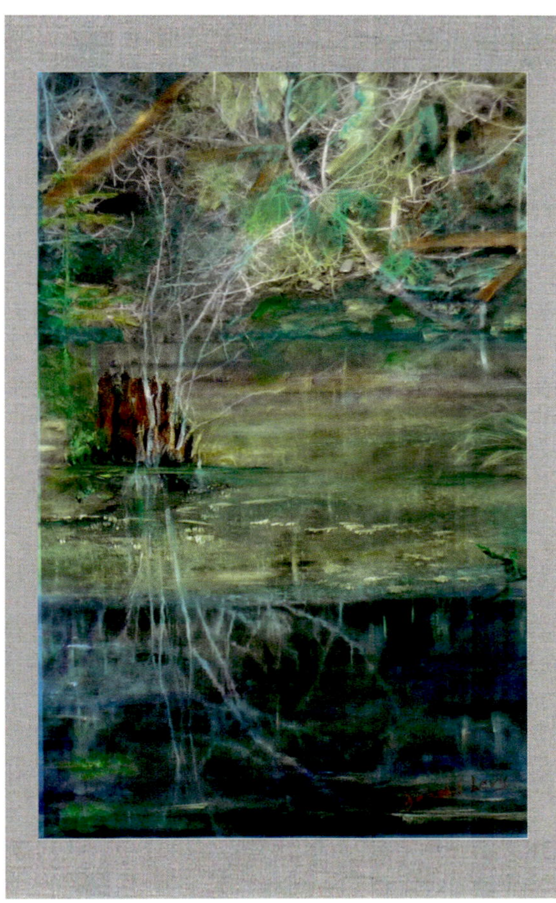

Hoh River Triptych (2009) 33 x 20 in. each panel

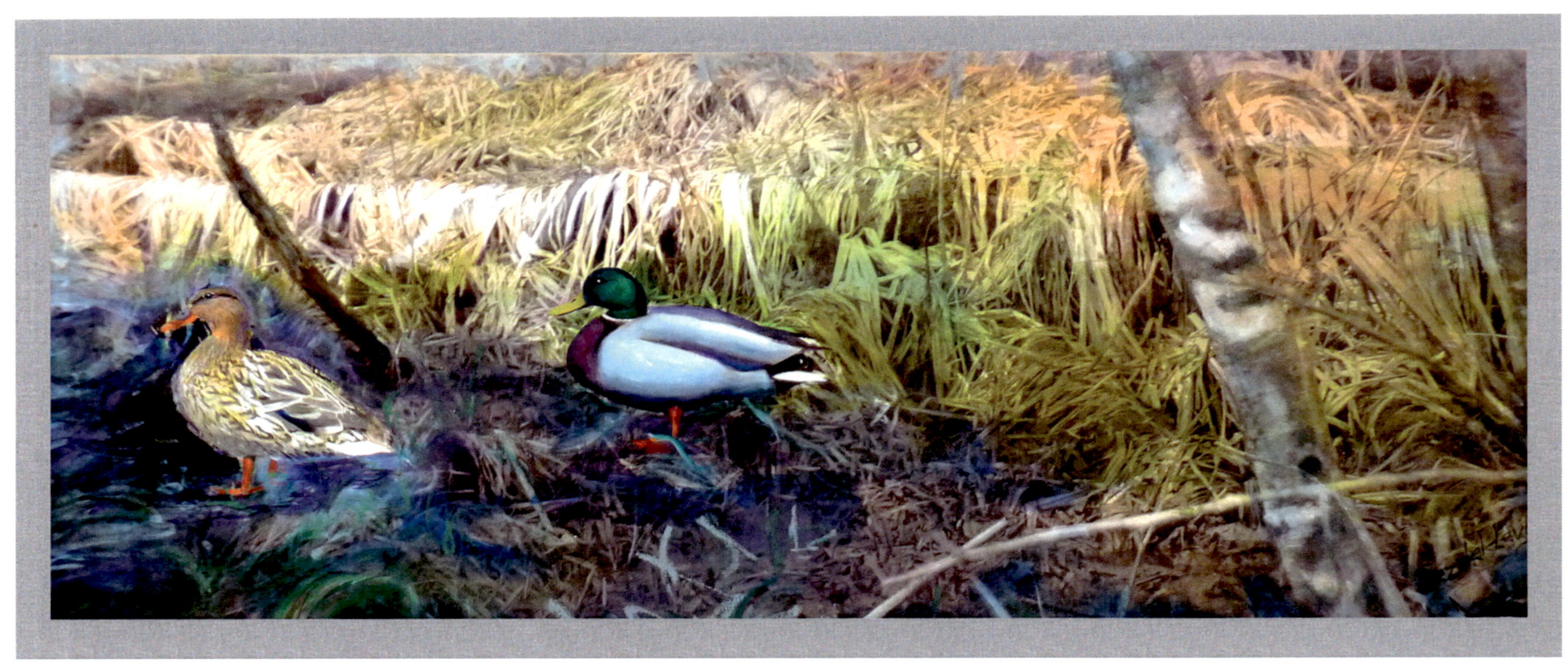

Duck and Drake, Hoh River (2011) 18 x 40 in.

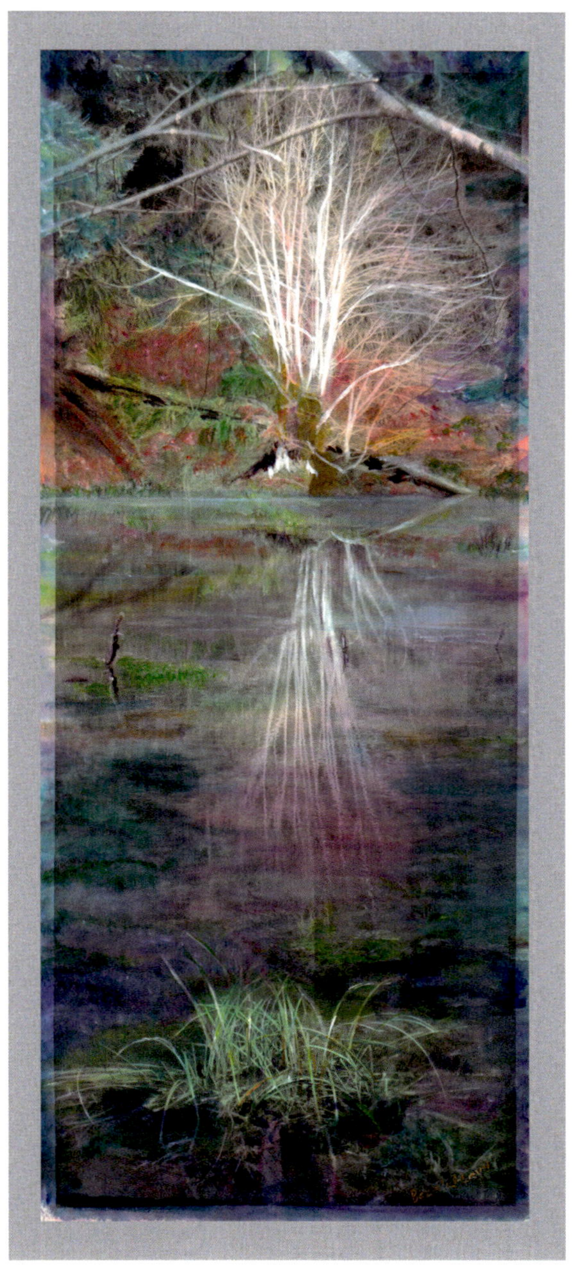

Wetlands, Hoh River (2009) 52 x 24 in.

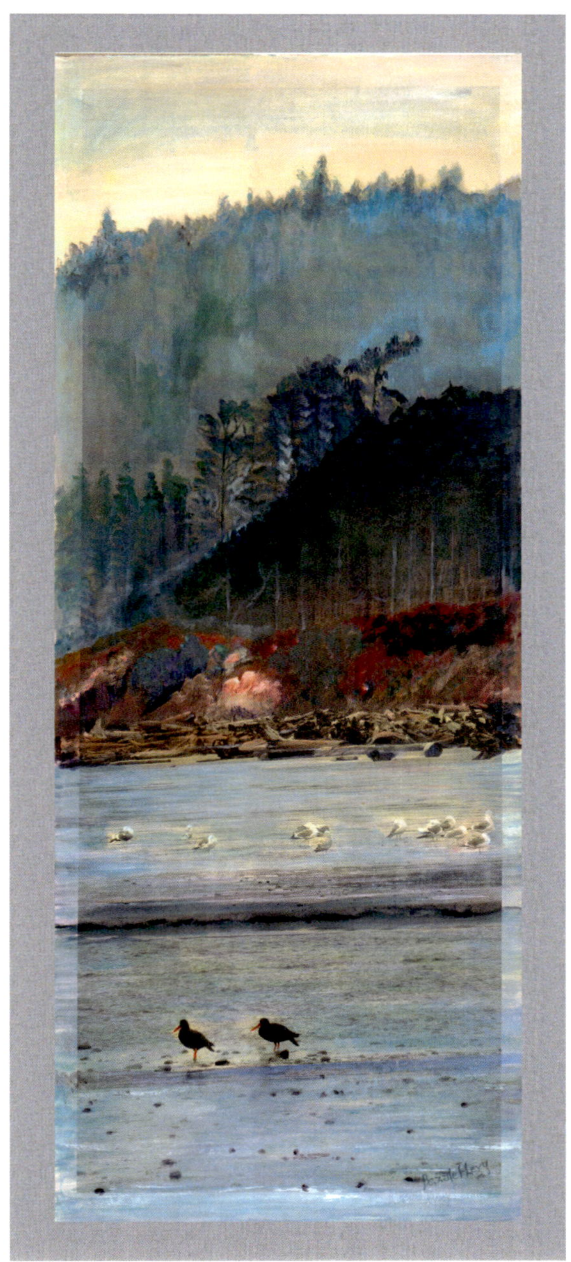

Kalaloch Beach (2009) 56 x 24 in.

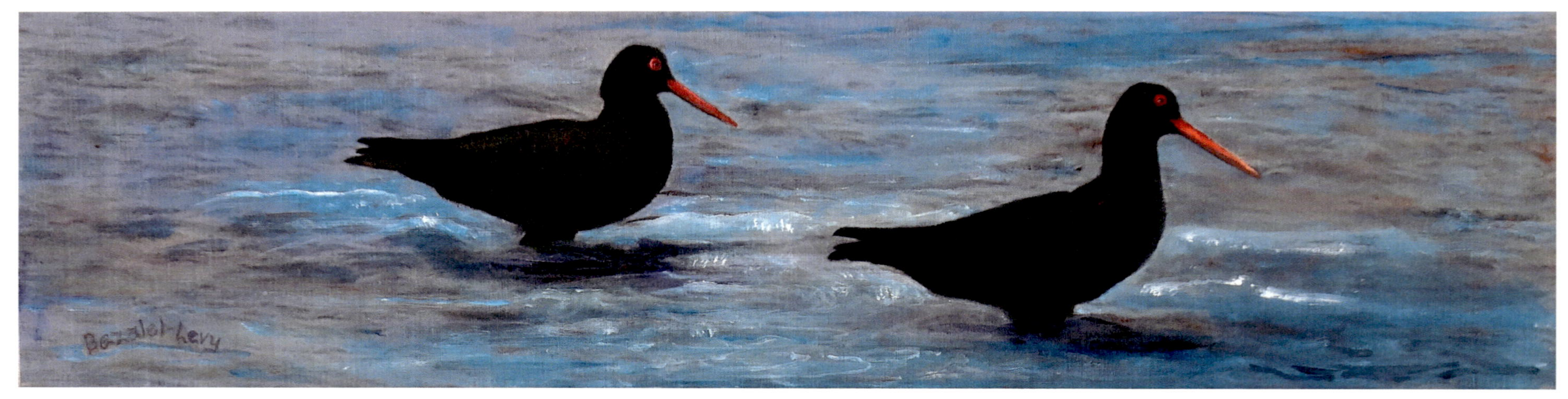

Oyster Catchers (2009) (2013) 11 x 44 in. photography and acrylics on linen mounted on birch

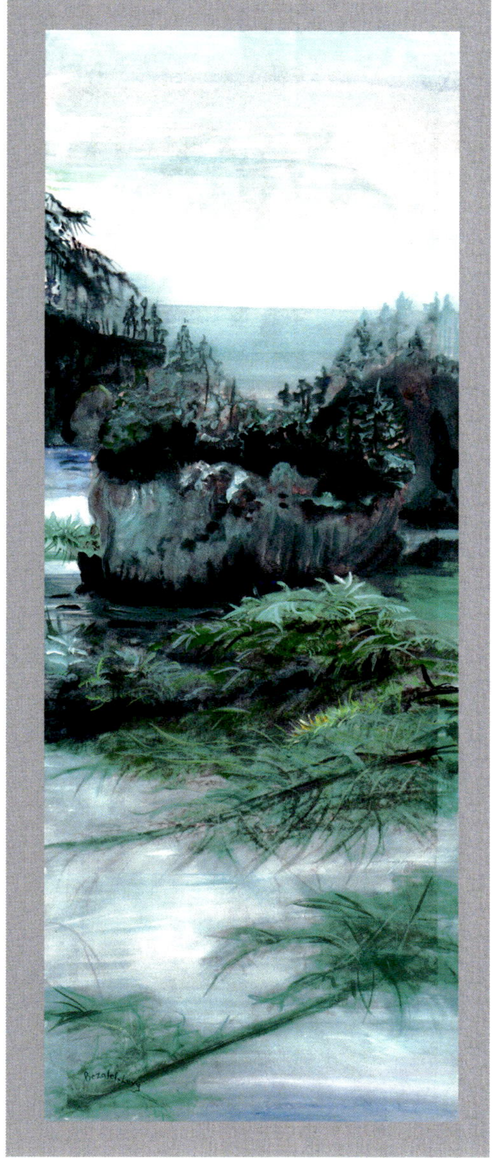
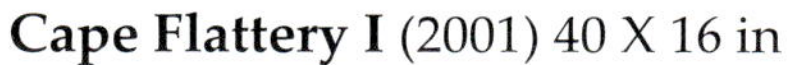

Cape Flattery I (2001) 40 X 16 in

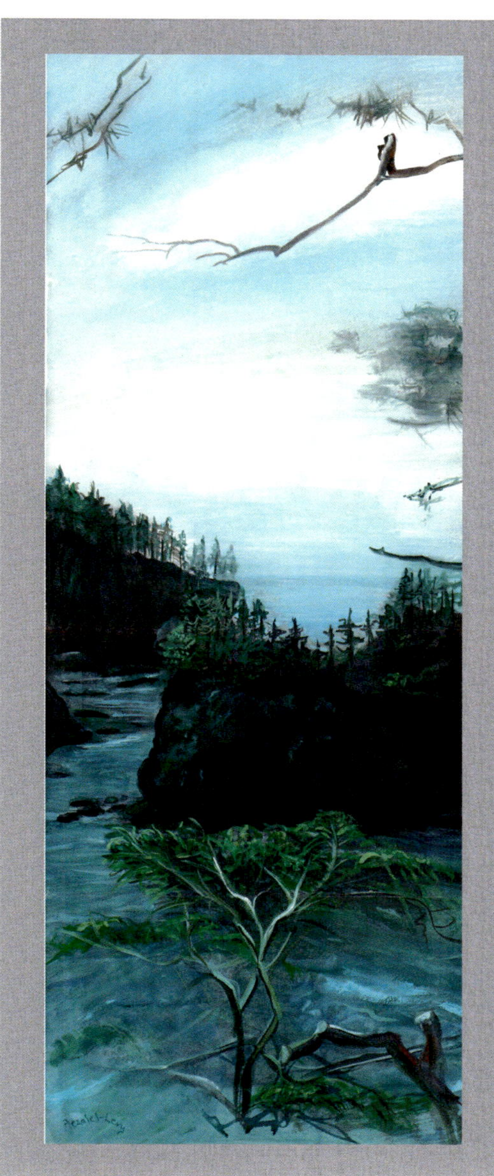

Cape Flattery II (2001) 40 x 16 in.

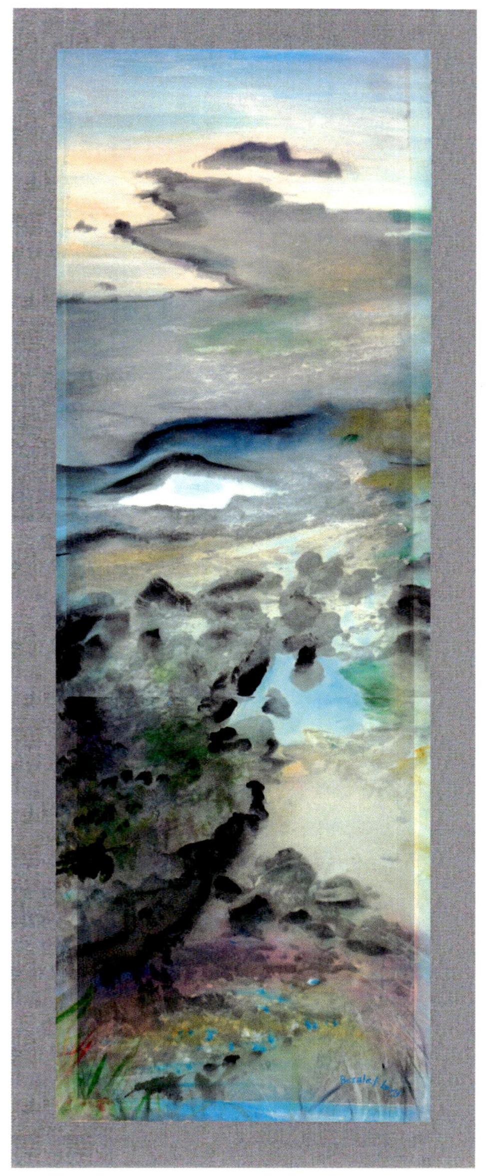

Cape Flattery III (2013) 60 x 24 in.

"This point of land and the bush that grows upon it is the most north and west point on the contiguous landmass of the continental United States (the "lower 48") - a sort of Northwest's northwest. It is located on Cape Flattery, between the Strait of Juan De Fuca, and the Pacific Ocean, on the Makah Indian Reservation." - Center for Land Use Interpretation

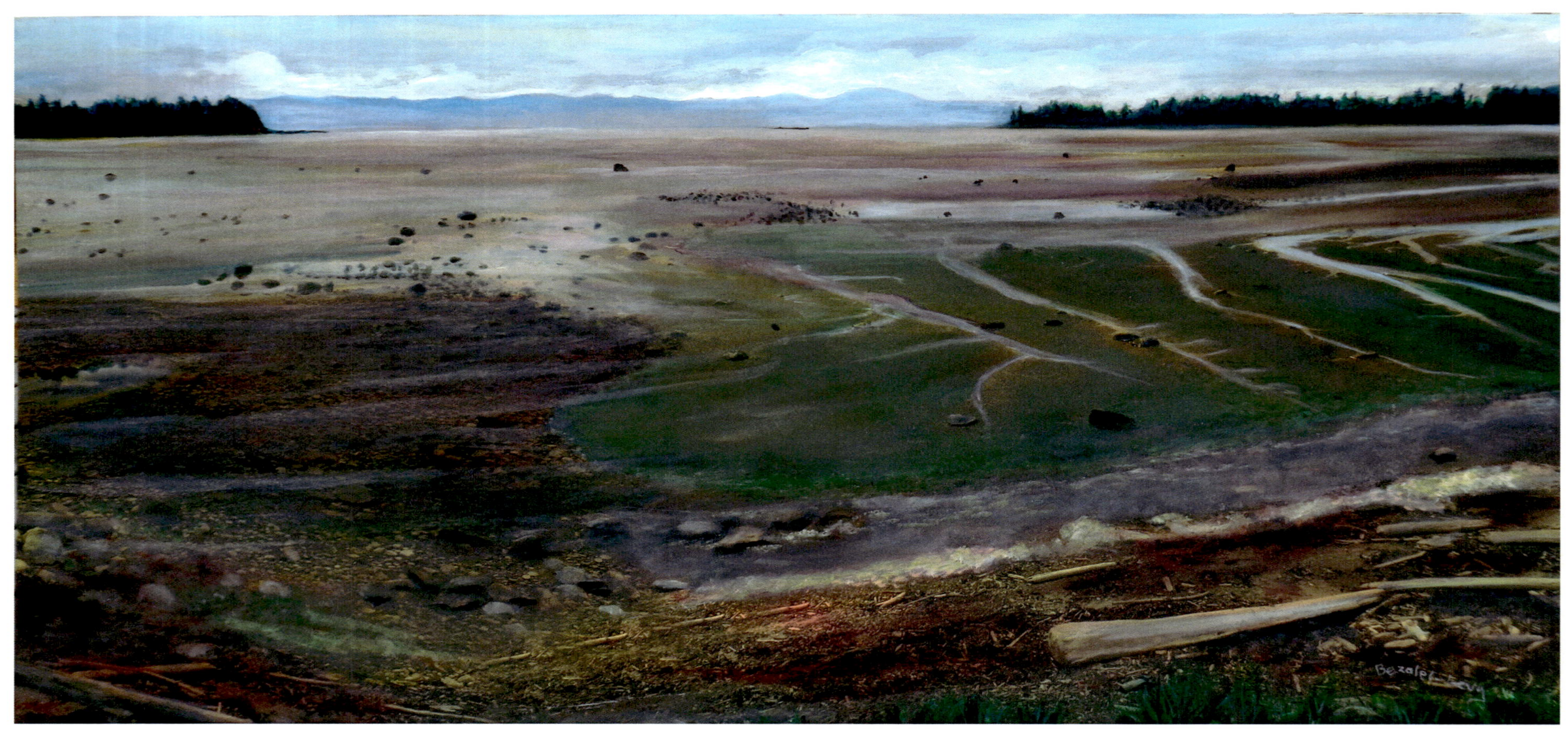

Low Tide at False Bay, San Juan Island (2016) 28 x 59 in. photography and acrylics on paper mounted on birch

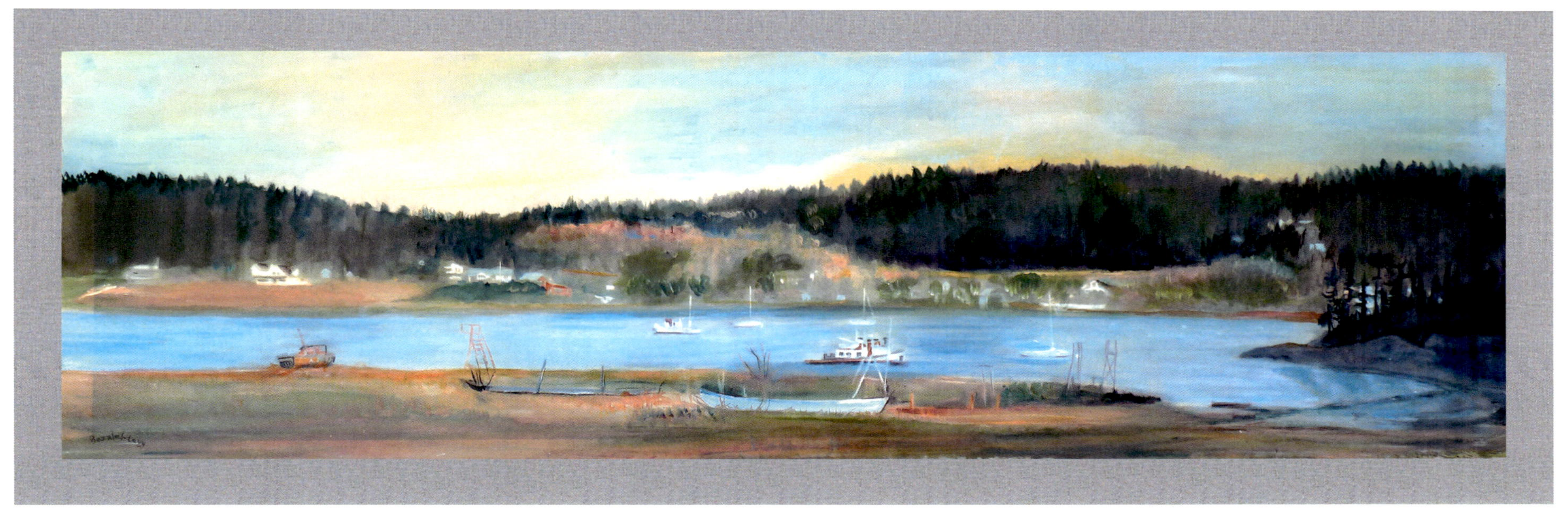

Harbor, Lopez Island (2011) 16 x 64 in.

While playing guitar in the South End String Band during our "Island Tour" of the San Juan Islands, an archipelago in the upper Puget Sound, we performed our renditions of Old Time music, including many reels and songs from the 1800's, at a community center on Lopez Island. The San Juan Islands stretch into Canada where they become the Gulf Islands.

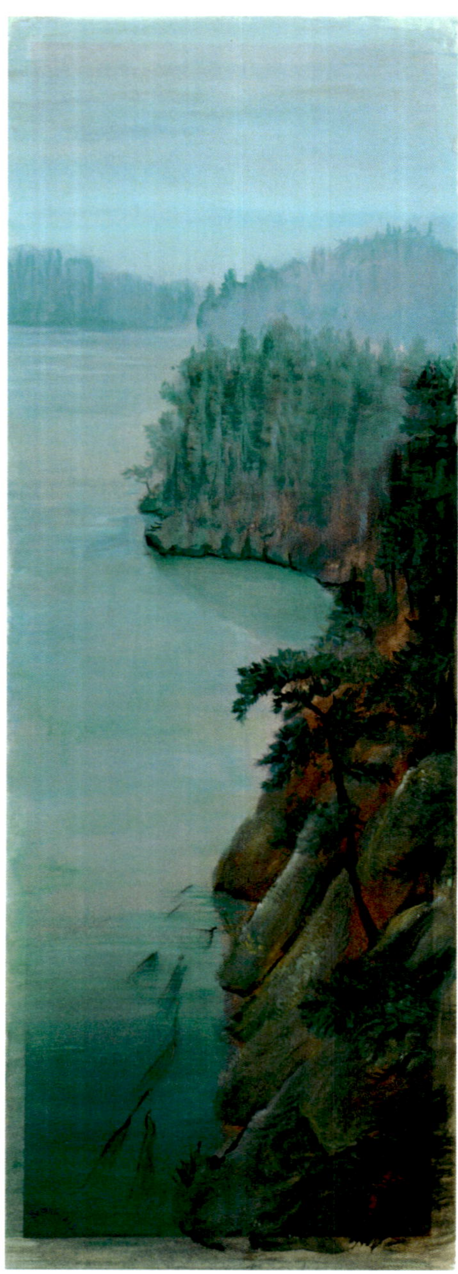

Deception Pass I (2000) 60 x 24 in

Ode to Deception Pass

Grey mists of pearly clouds
 meet the swimming whales -
 swirling tides of rushing water
 ebb and flow around my heart
 as I stare into the narrow passage
 between Puget Sound and
 the Straits of Juan de Fuca
My spirit casts out far beyond this
 end of the earth isle
 through whirlpools and kelp beds
 Wondering if these same waters reach the
 shores of Ashkelon on the Mediterranean,
this other far off home.
 We live there and here,
 stretched between two harbors
 like sailboats rising and falling
 on wind catching waves
 our little ships tack back and forth
 through the passages and shoals
 of inner and outer waters
What great portents
 and adventures lay ahead
 like curious eyes peeking
we plot the next journeys
 around the far horizon

-Yonnah Ben Levy

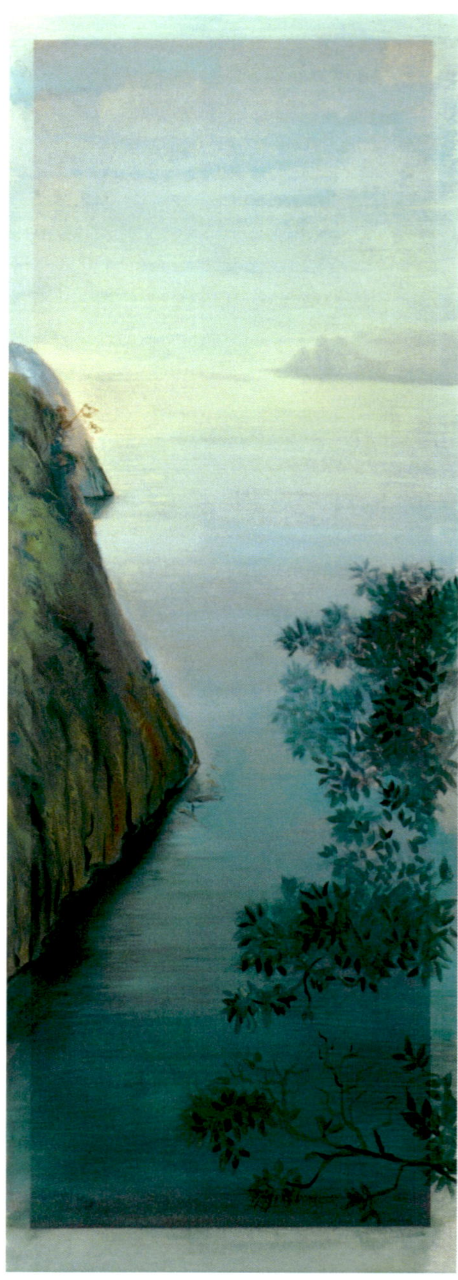

Deception Pass II (2000) 60 x 24 in.

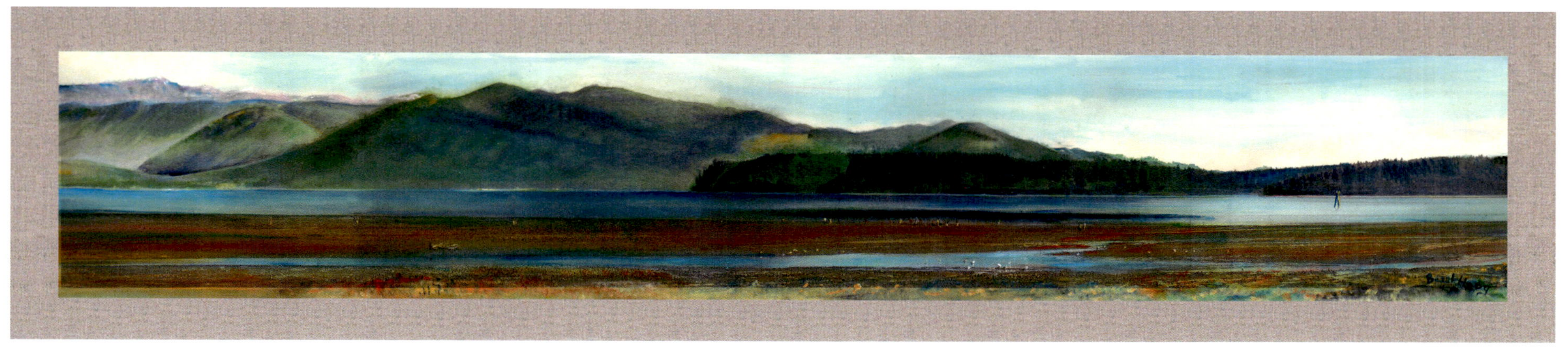

Oyster Pickers on the Hood Canal (2005) 12 x 72 in.   Detail below actual size

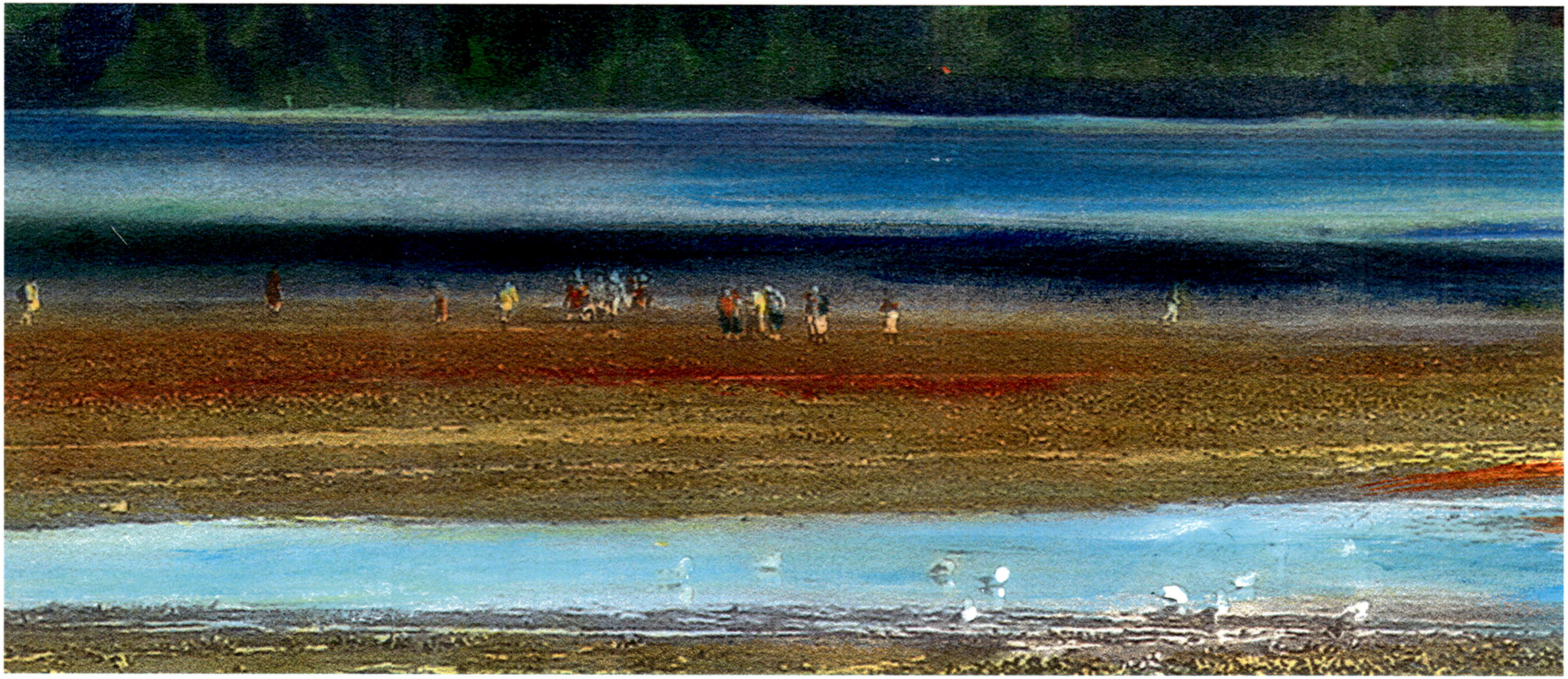

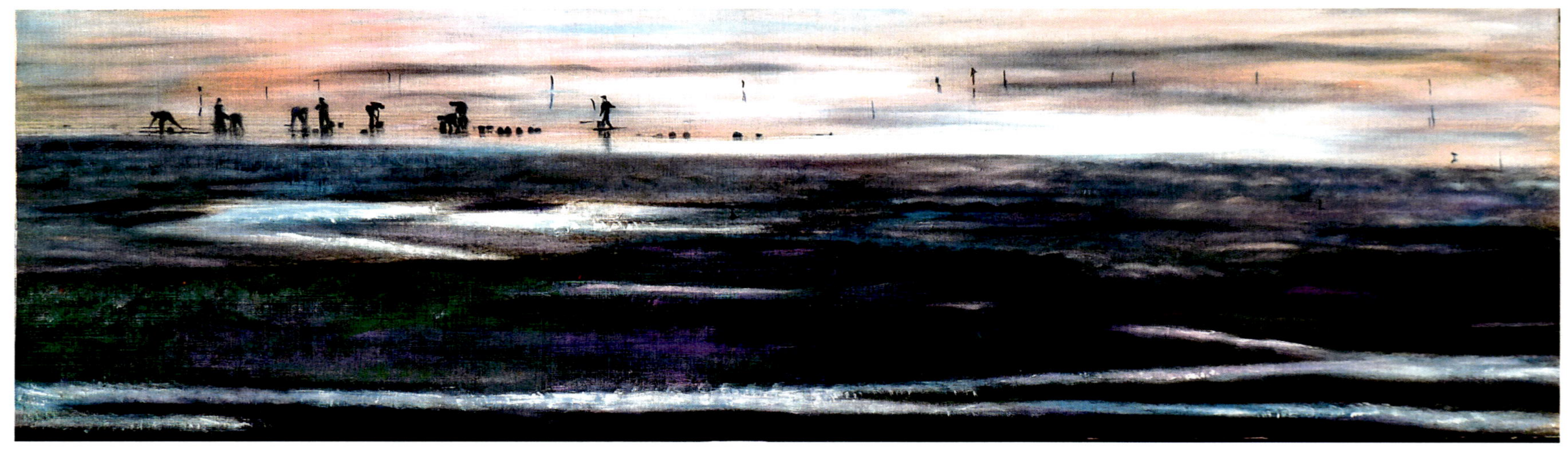

Clam Diggers, Bellingham Bay (2012) 15 x 51 in. photography and acrylics on linen mounted on birch

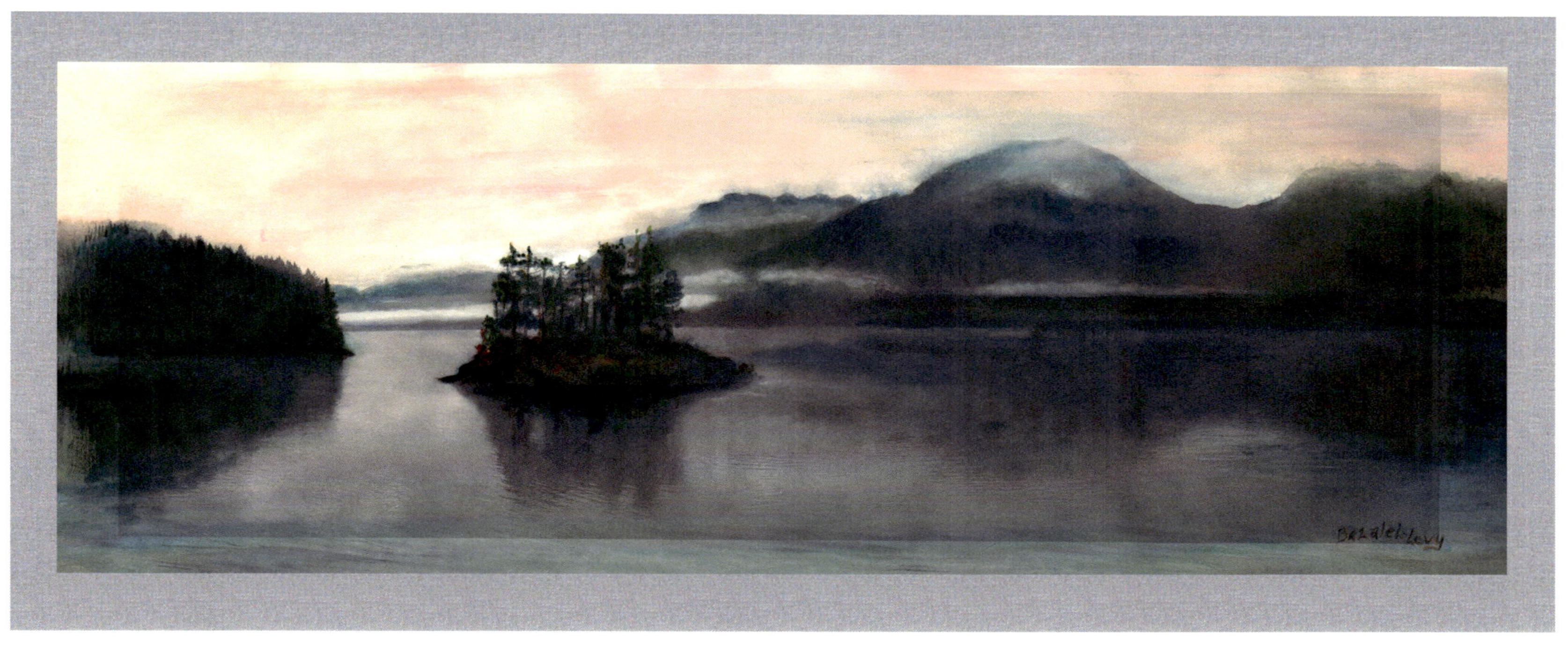

Malibu Camp, British Columbia (2004) 17 x 44 in.

The upper portion of the Puget Sound and the coastal waterways that continue into British Columbia are known as the Salish Sea. The Coast Salish are the indigenous peoples who live in southwest British Columbia and northwest Washington along the Salish Sea and share a common linguistic and cultural origin. The related tribes speaking twenty-three separate languages were encountered by Lewis and Clark on their expedition. Malibu Camp, where Yonnah spent some time as a teenager, is located on the Princess Louise Inlet, a narrow finger of water extending from the upper portion of the Salish Sea. We hope Canadians will not object to our including several paintings from over the border among the American Scrolls, but North American Scrolls didn't have the same ring to it.

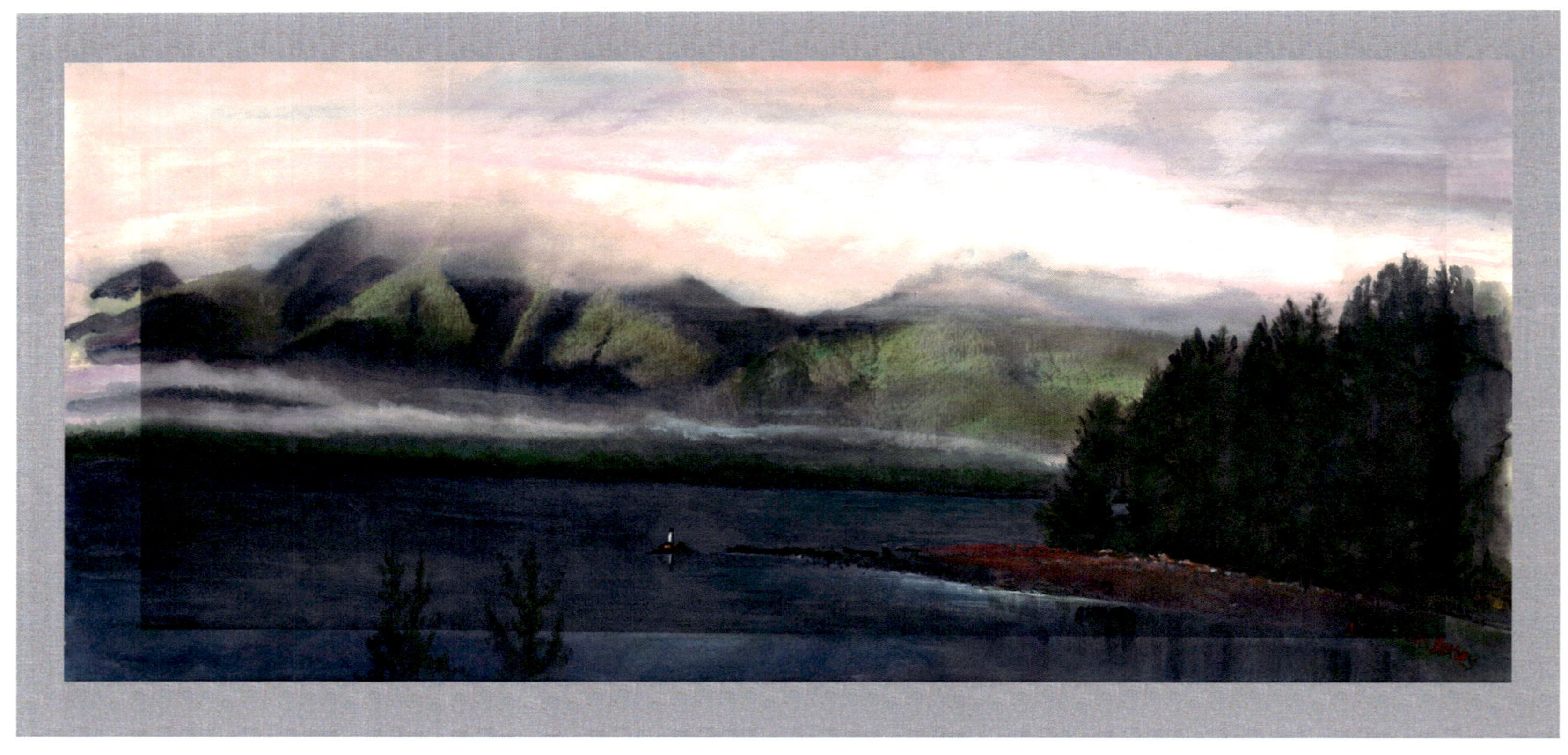

Lighthouse, Princess Louise Inlet (2004) 20 x 42 in.

Camano Island

   The landscapes on this page and the following one are from our home on Camano Island, Washington which we owned from 1999 until 2016. The view across the Saratoga Passage of the Puget Sound to Whidbey Island is unspoiled. The Victoria Clipper passed every morning on its route to Vancouver Island. Once a year, native tribes from Washington, Alaska, and British Columbia pass in ocean going canoes carved from tree trunks as they visit local tribes on their way to the host destination.

   Camano Island is named for the Spanish explorer Jacinto Caamaño. The original name of the island was Kal-lut-chin which in the language of the indigenous Snohomish tribe meant "land jutting into a bay". They used the island as a base during the fishing and shellfish gathering expeditions.

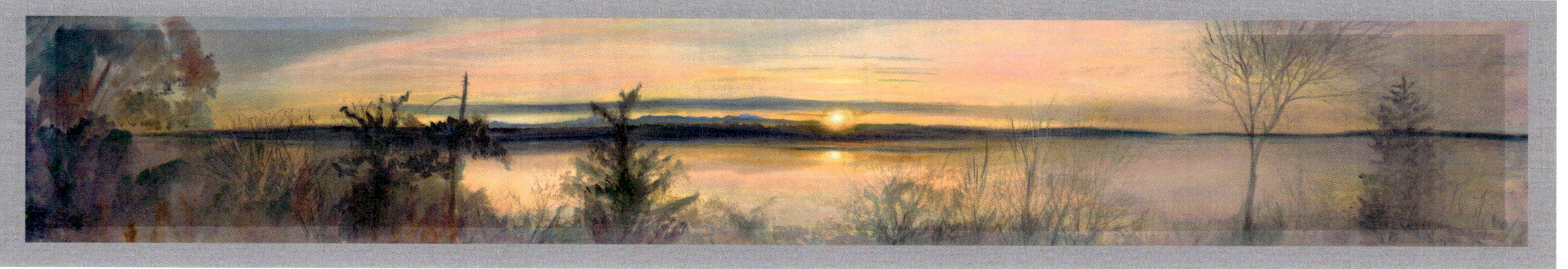

Saratoga Passage, Puget Sound (2006) 16 x 72 in.

Eagle

there is an eagle
sitting over me
his watchful eye
signals as his head cocks
downward
not missing
my raspberry fleece

Ah I'm reminded
there is not a day
I have missed
being cared for
from far above
worldly cares
and the lonely abyss

His cries
fill my ears
and I stop my work
to gaze back in wonder
at his stately strength
and his incredible size
I'll take this sentinel
who guards the earth around me
and the wide open skies

-Yonnah Ben Levy

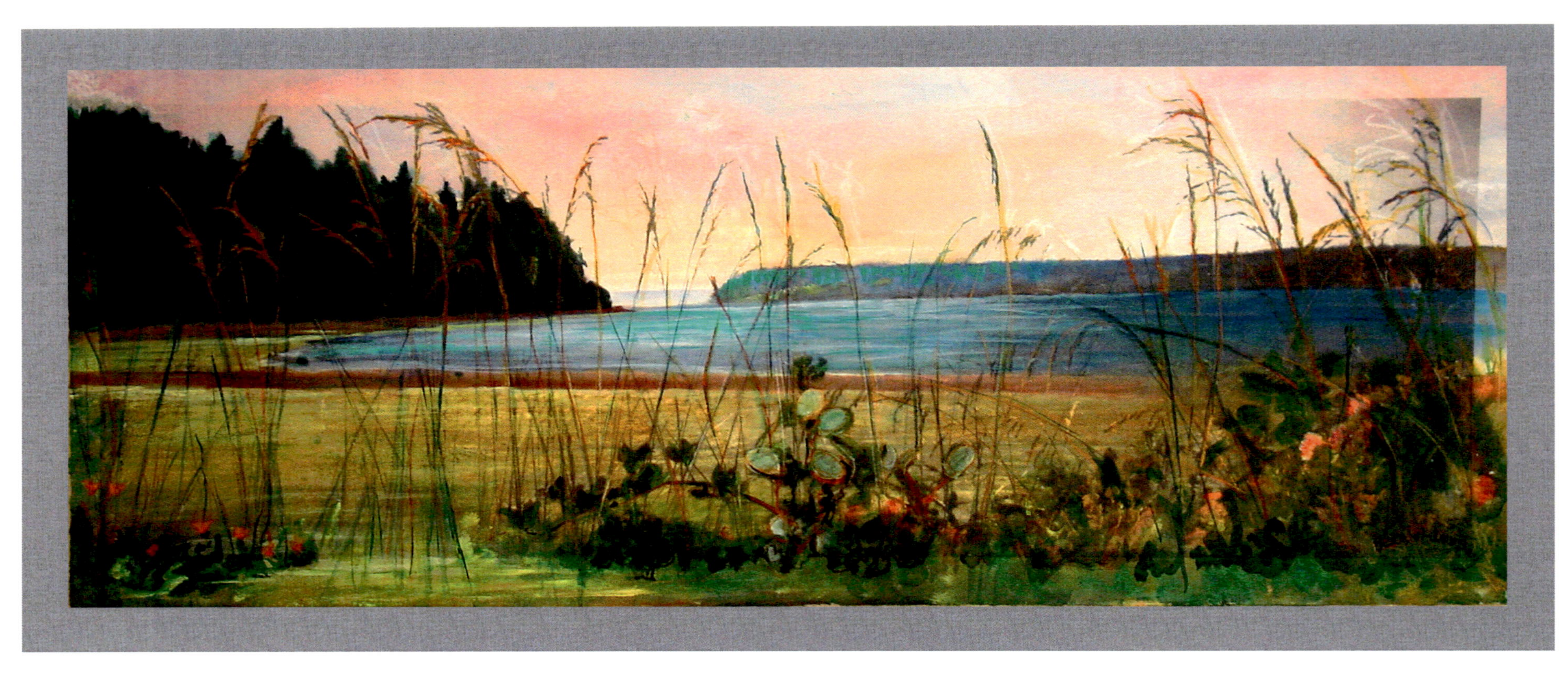

Low Tide, Summerland (2009) 24 x 53 in.

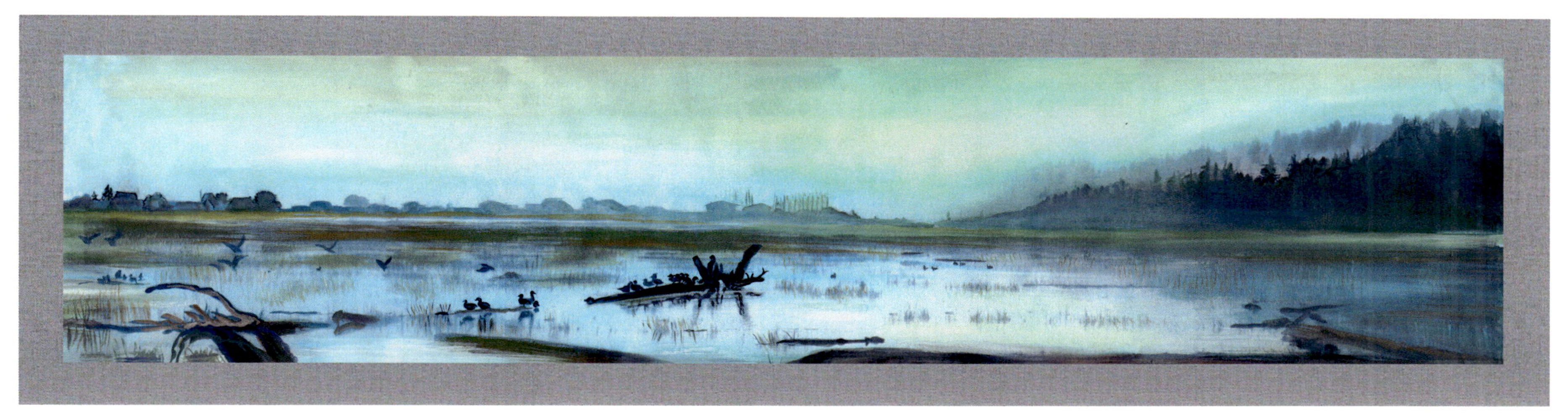

Triangle Cove (2002) 12 x 42 in.

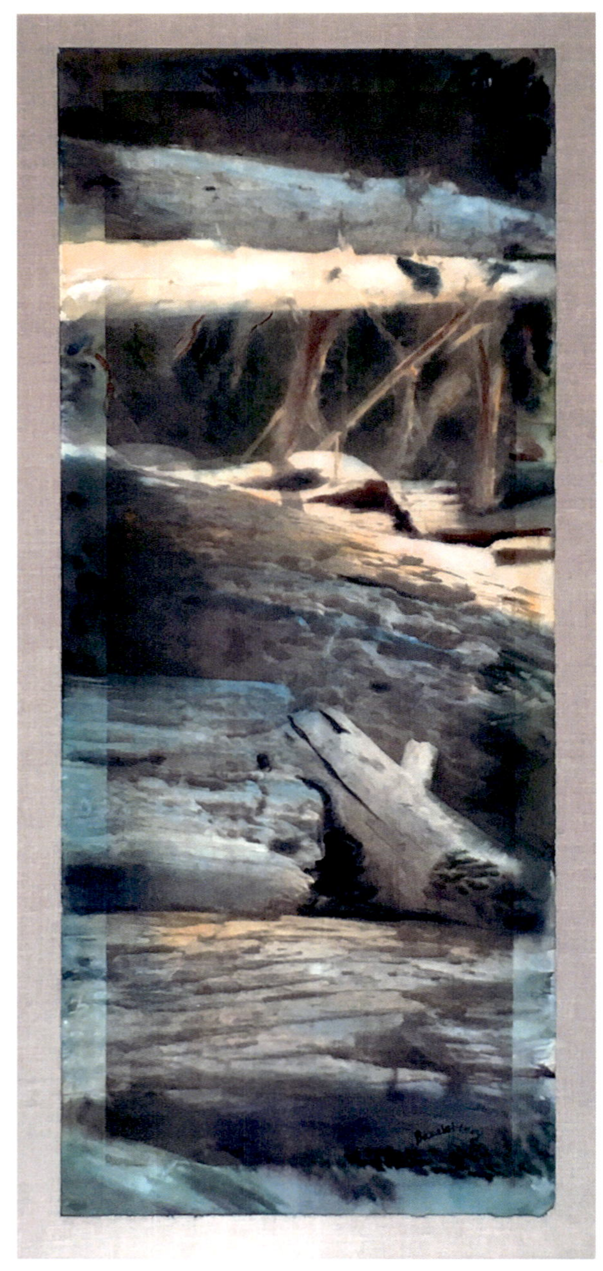

Driftwood (2004) 60 x 24 in.

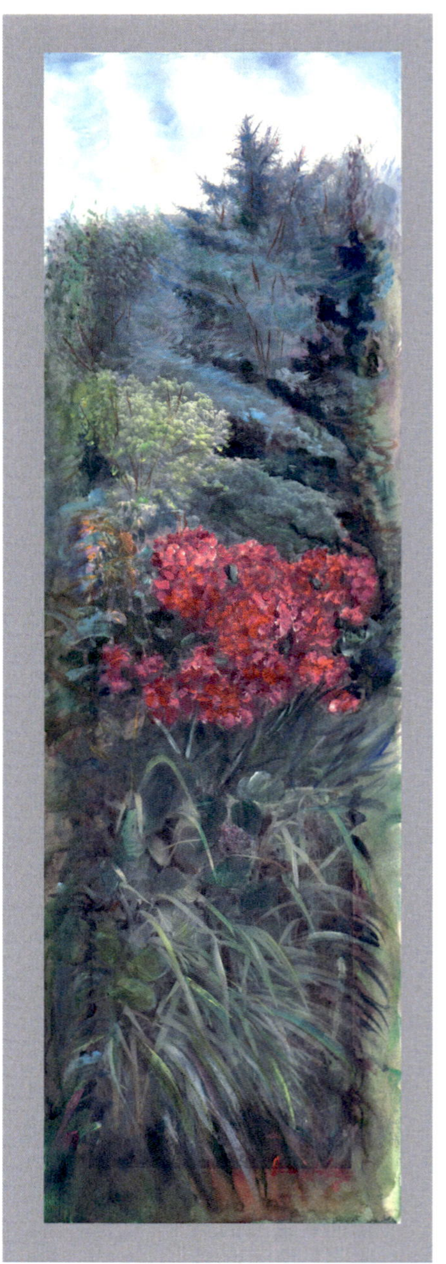

Rhododendron Scroll (2003) 59 x 17 in.

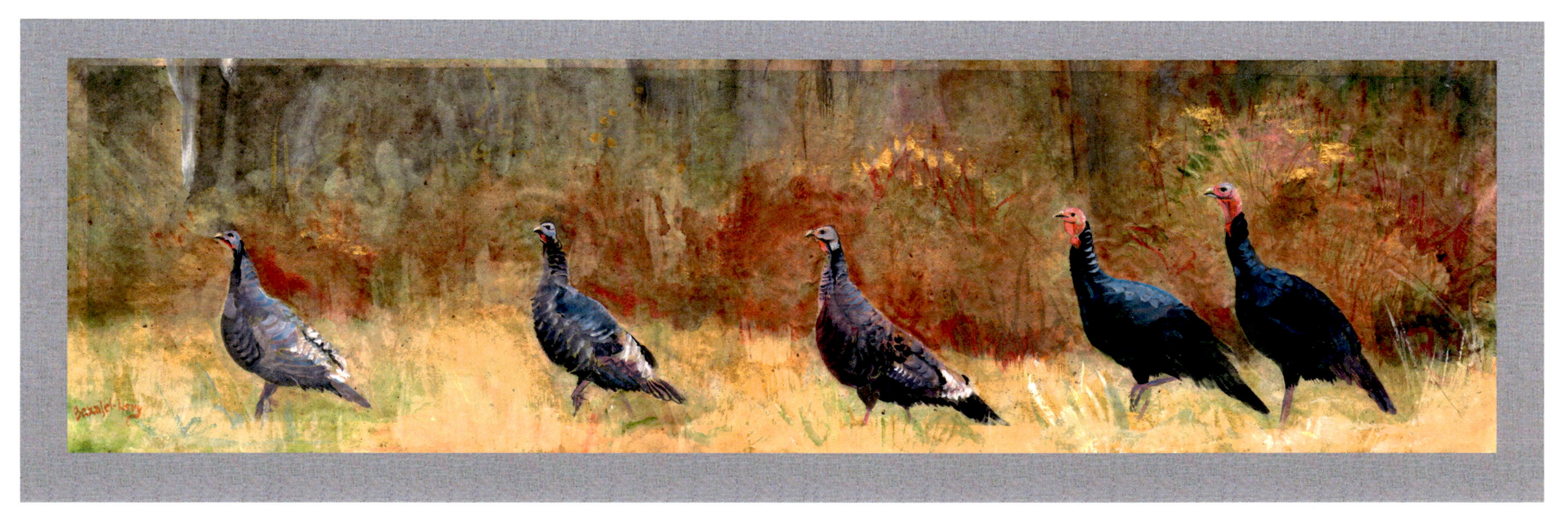

Wild Turkeys (2006) 16 x 50 in.

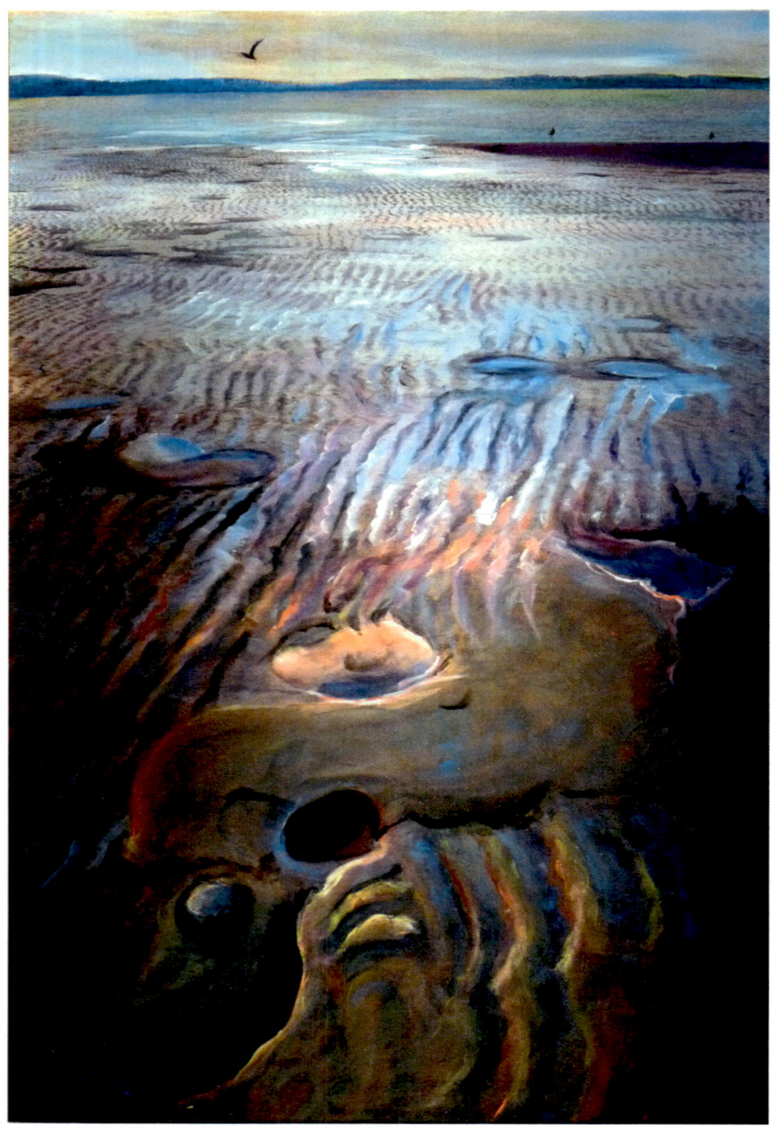

Low Tide of the Year (2011) mixed-media with acrylics, 36 x 24

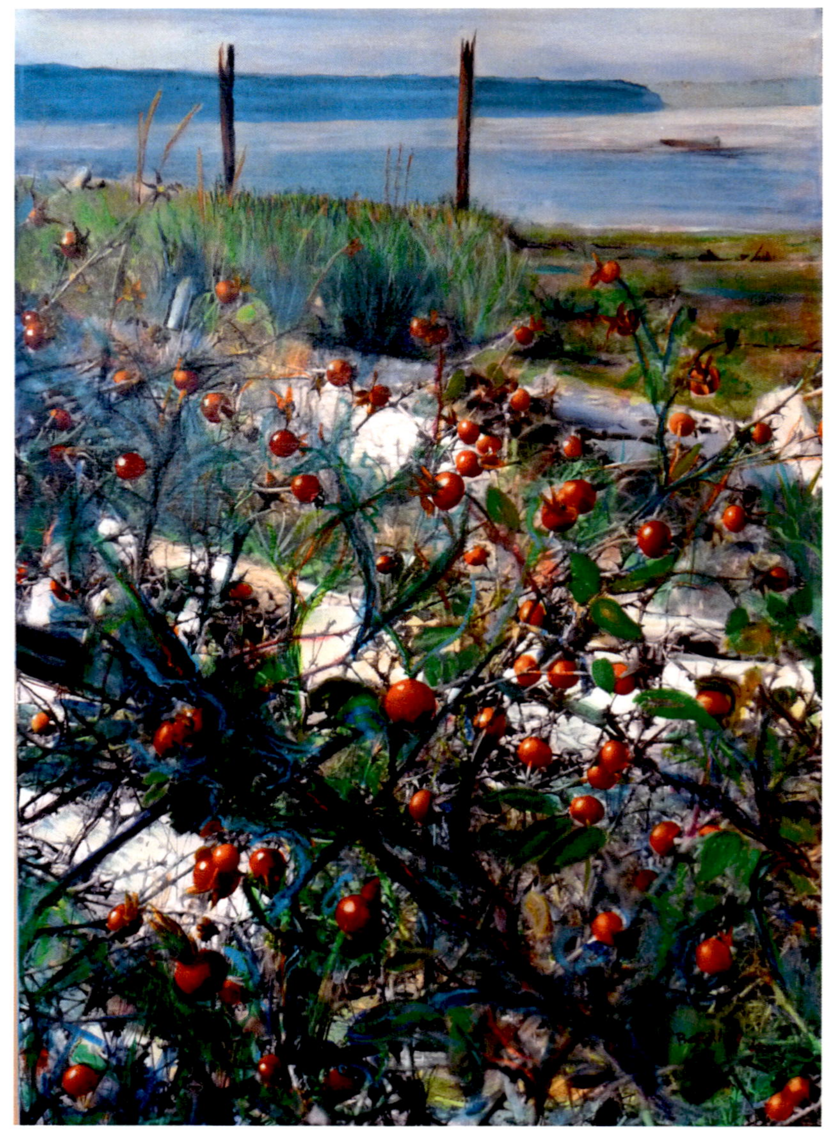

Rosehips at English Boom (2011) mixed-media with acrylics, 24 x 17 in.

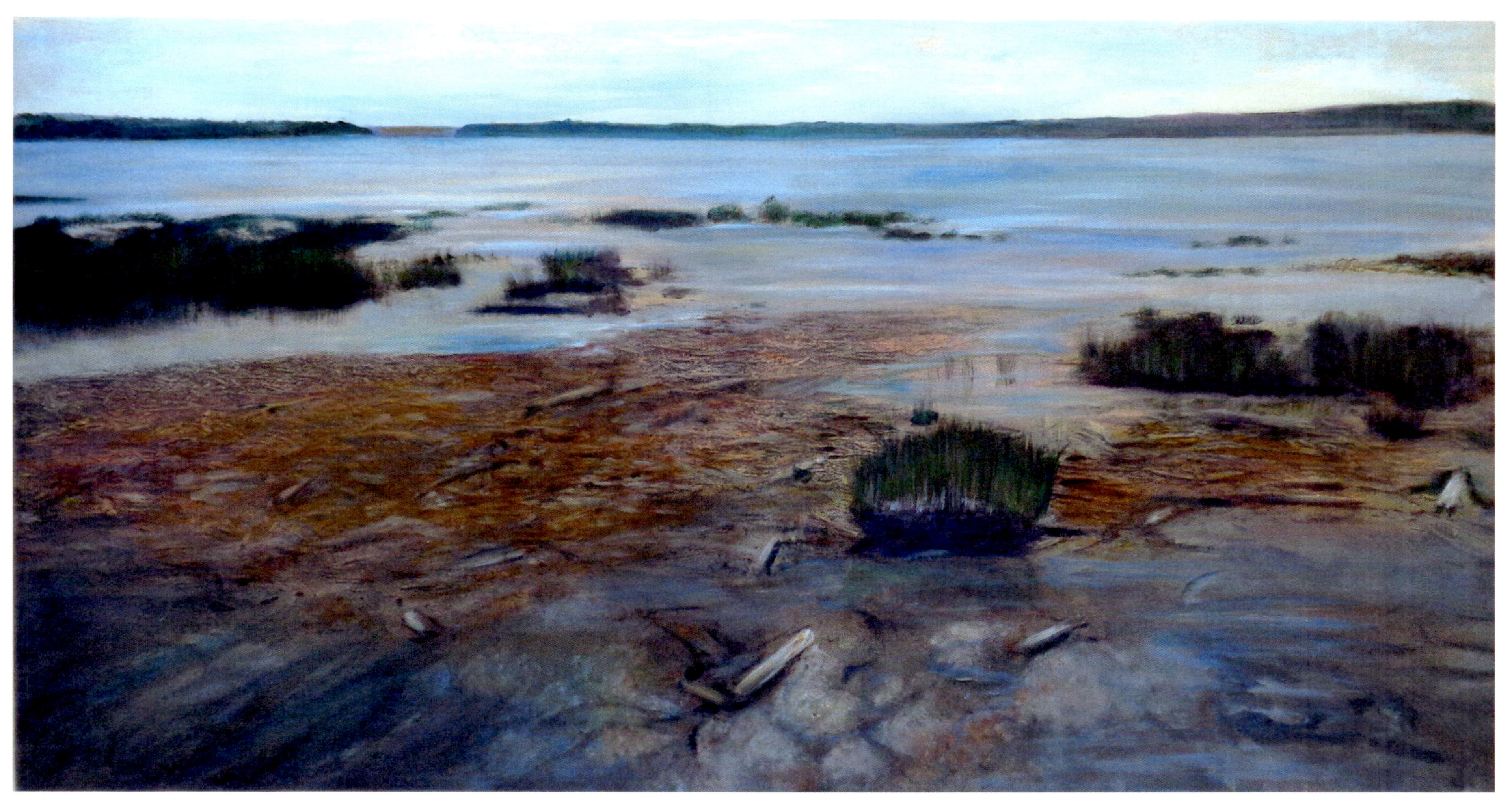

Juniper Beach (2016) 27 x 54 in. photography and acrylics on canvas

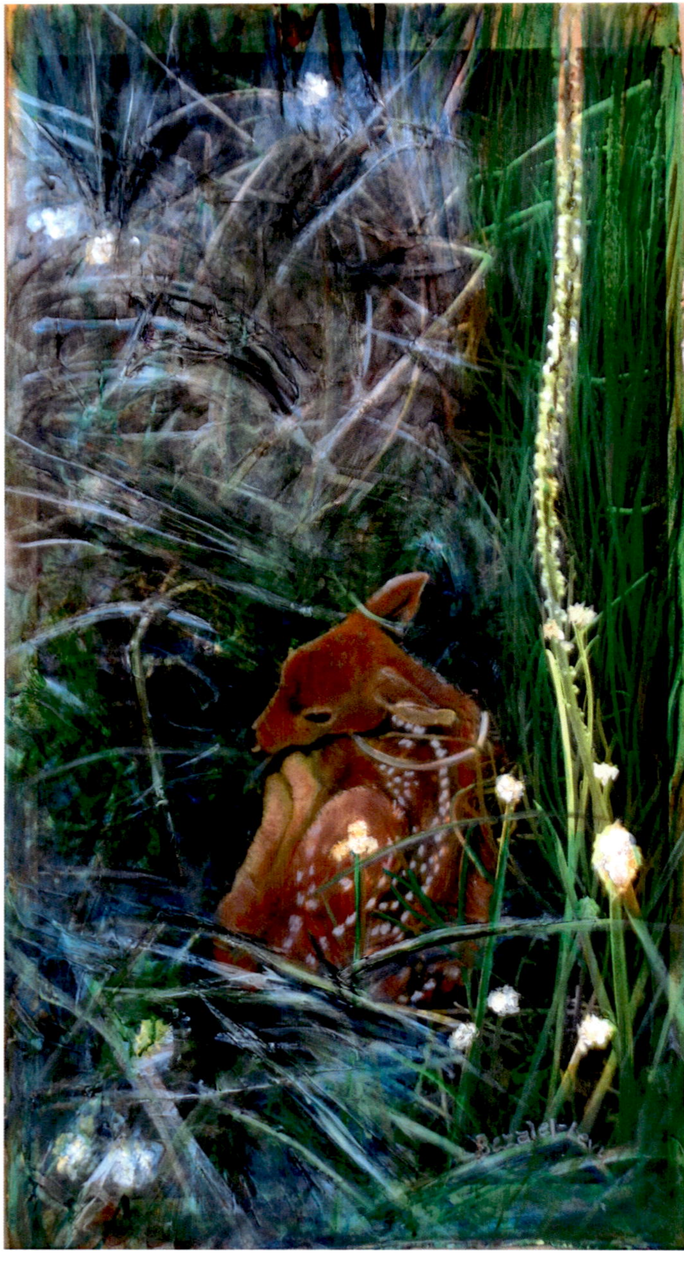

Afternoon of a Fawn (2016) photography and acrylics on rice paper, 18 x 34 in.

In 1999, after driving across the country in a U-Haul truck, we arrived at the last leg of our journey, the seventeen miles from the northern to the southern end of Camano Island. We had not expected to remain in the States. While visiting earlier, we had bought a trailer expecting to travel around the country using it as a temporary home and studio. We stayed in it for a few weeks as it was parked in the yard of Yonnah's oldest daughter and her husband. One morning, Judy gave her mother the real estate section of the PennySaver. "Look for owner financing," I said, since we had been out of the country for too long to have maintained any credit.

Now the trailer would be used as an extra bedroom as it sat parked next to the house we had bought, the one house with owner financing, at the end of the island. For a short time, little more than a year, all six children of our hopefully consolidating family were in the Pacific Northwest, but we didn't realize that it would be so short.

As we drove down the island, under a canopy of trees, we noticed signs announcing an art studio tour that was taking place on this Mother's Day weekend. Stopping the U-Haul at one of the venues, we realized that this island, once known as a place for fishing, farming, or retirement, was attracting artists. As I write this, we will be returning soon to our American home to participate in the twentieth annual Camano Island Studio Tour for this, our nineteenth year.

Chris, one of our fellow artists also runs a dance studio on the island. Yonnah, who has been dancing for many years, is one of his students. One afternoon we received a call from him. Come quickly, a newborn fawn was lying in the grass. Camano Island still is a place of natural beauty as well as fishing, farming, retirement, and now, though it may be a long one, commuting. On the opposite page is a painting of the peach tree that is planted in front of where the trailer used to stand when we lived there.

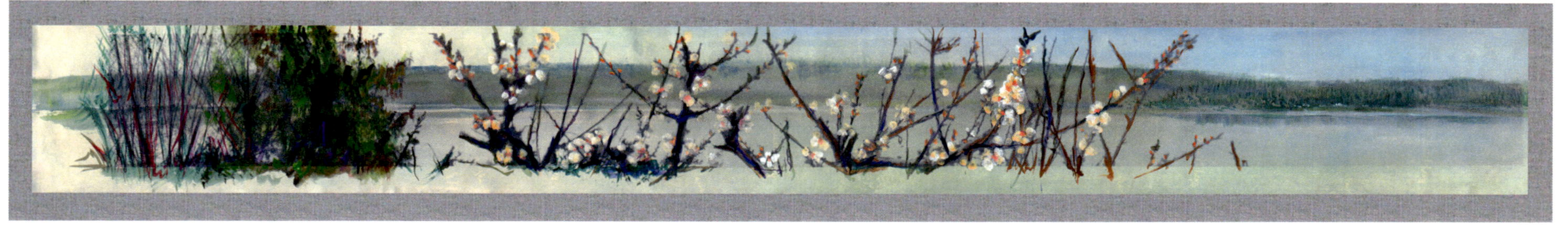

Peach Blossoms, Saratoga Passage (2002) 12 x 72 in.

An Interlinear Poem

There is a kind of peace
distilled like old wine
ruby red and smooth.
I have that in my island home
 perched over an embankment
 closer to the edge
 than today's permits will allow

Where I sit eagle-like.
The Northwest wind blows
an even, warming breeze that
will decrease gradually to a whimper
as the summer's highs lodge off
the Washington coast.
However today the spirit can
soar along with the sailboats
as they unfurl their brightly colored
spinnakers catching the waves and wind
to reach their destination on
the opposite shore

I perceive my Grandmother's voice
in the wind as I dream her
softness comforting me deep down
into the fathoms of loss and despair
which have risen to the surface
like the the green clumps of eel grass
floating on the water
pulled one way and another under
the moon's sway and tow.
Her apparition looms over the day
reminding me of the White Lilac perfume
on white lace handkerchiefs
tucked inside her blue suits with pockets

How can she be present
if she has died and gone so many years ago?
but in the soothing breeze her empathy echoes
as I remember she too had a Mother pass away early,
leaving her too soon before puberty.
Like a life giving umbilical chord between
mother and child her spirit floods my soul
with peace beyond reckoning.

-Yonnah Ben Levy

Rivers and Watersheds

The Pacific Northwest has often been referred to as Cascadia because of the rivers, which contain rapids and waterfalls in the mountains where they have their sources. As they empty into the Sound they form wetlands, sloughs, and rich farmland. According to the Mirriam-Webster Dictionary, a slough is a swamp, an inlet on a river; also a backwater, a creek in a marsh or tide flat.

Most of these rivers are named after the local tribes, such as the Stillguamish, which means simply, people of the river. The Stillaguamish River, sometimes called the Stilly, branches and empties into the both the Puget Sound at Port Susan to the south and Skagit Bay to the north, both off Camano Island, near the town of Stanwood, where we now live. All of these converging waterways create a flood plain, a flyway and winter home for migrating birds including snow geese and swans. In the book *Public Works* (Dekel Press, 2018), I mentioned some issues of water use, access, and enjoyment which were addressed during my tenure as a planning commissioner in the City of Stanwood.

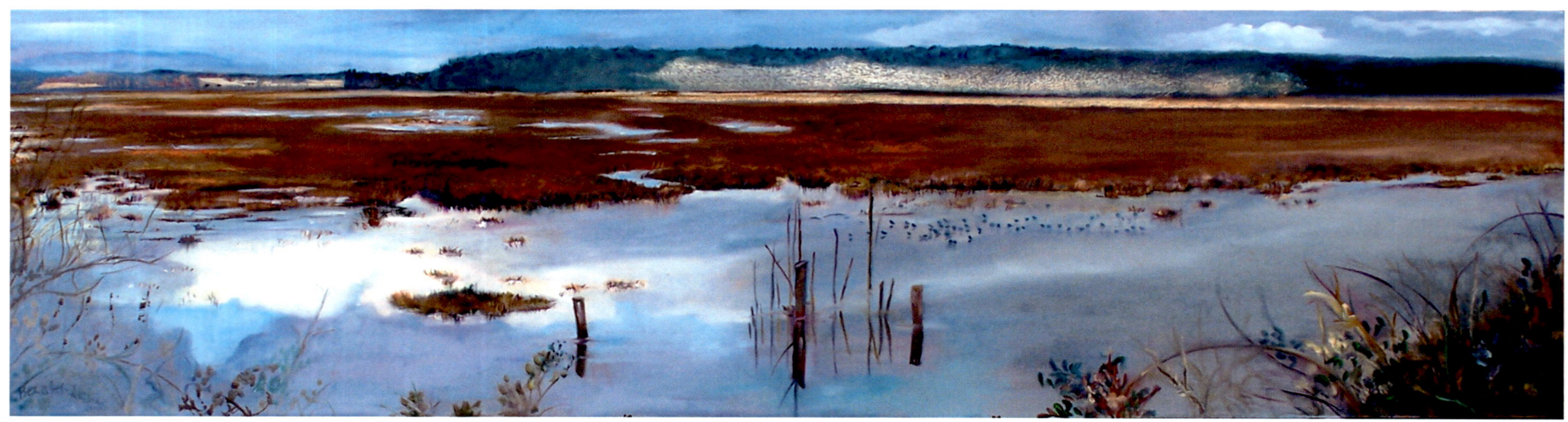

Snow Geese, Stillaguamish Watershed (2007) photography and water based oils on paper mounted on hardboard

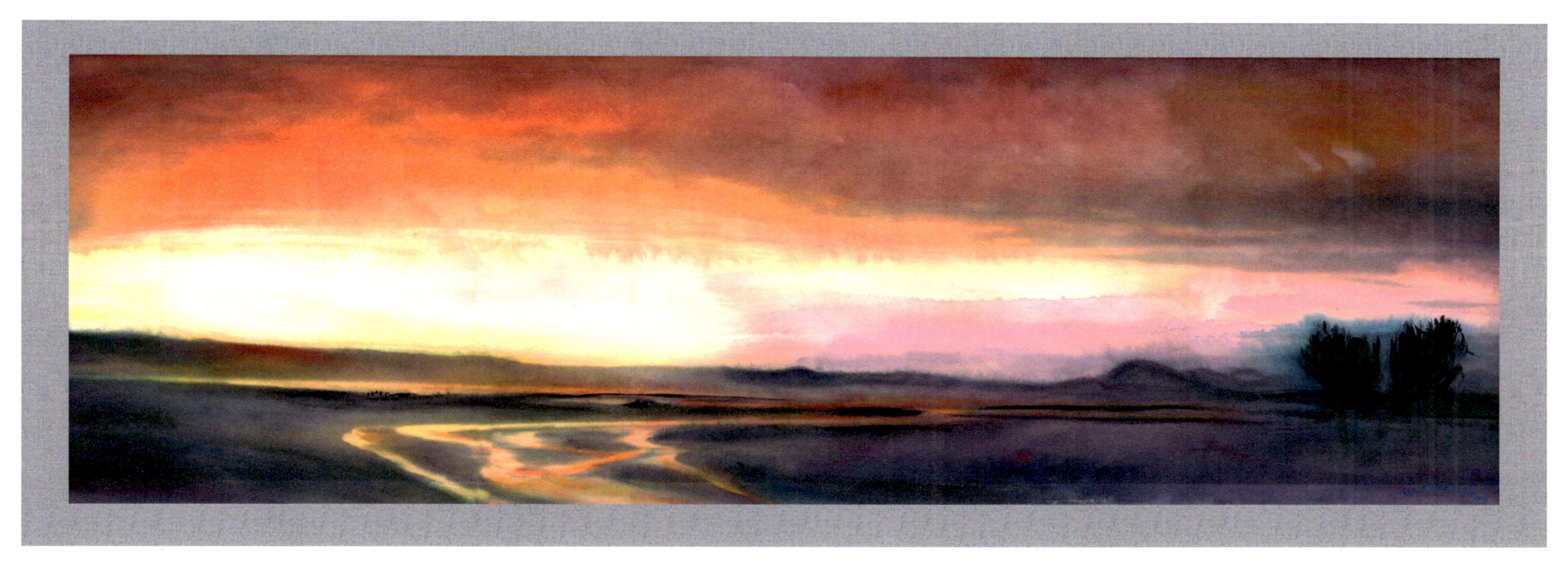

Red Stilly (2004) 24 x 67 in.

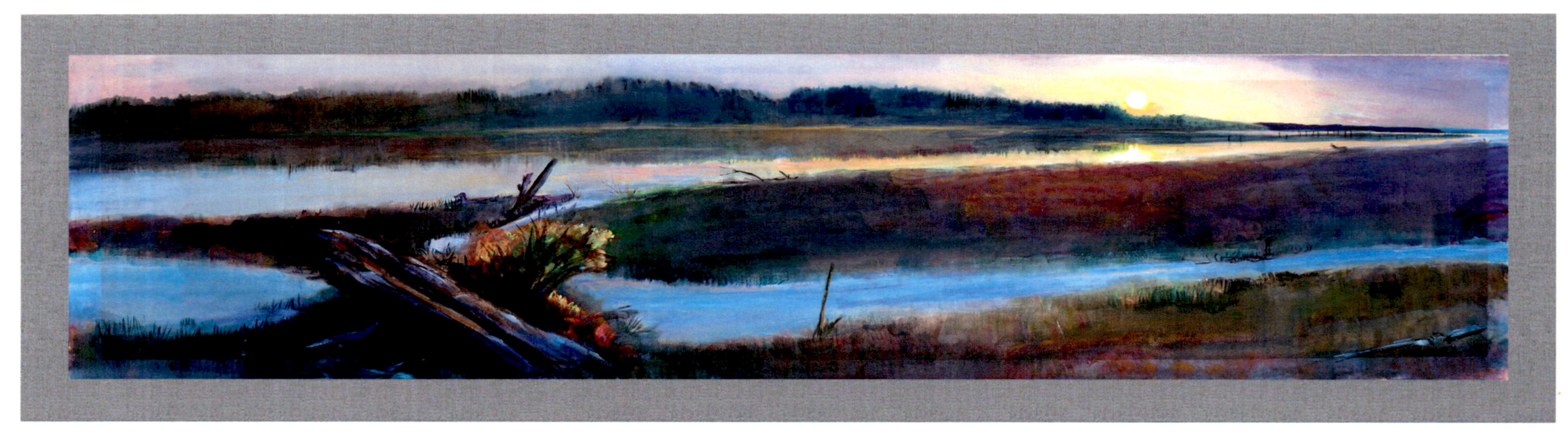

Stillaguamish Sunset from the Johnson Farm (2005) 21 x 72 in.

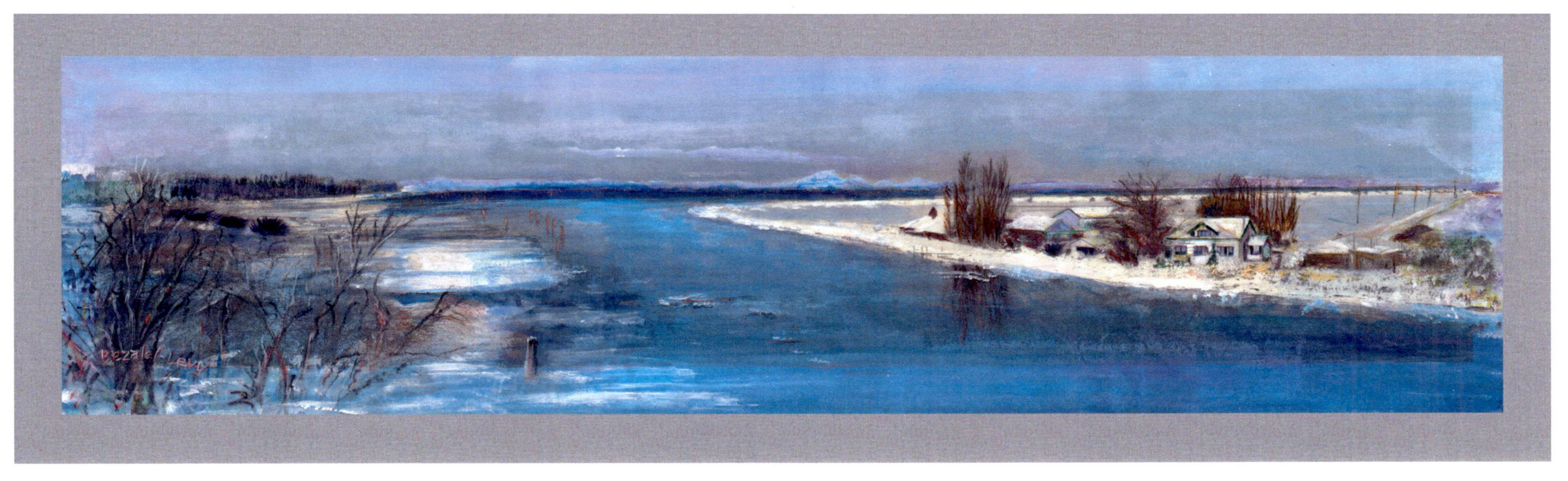

Johnson Farm in Winter (2006) 13 x 48 in.

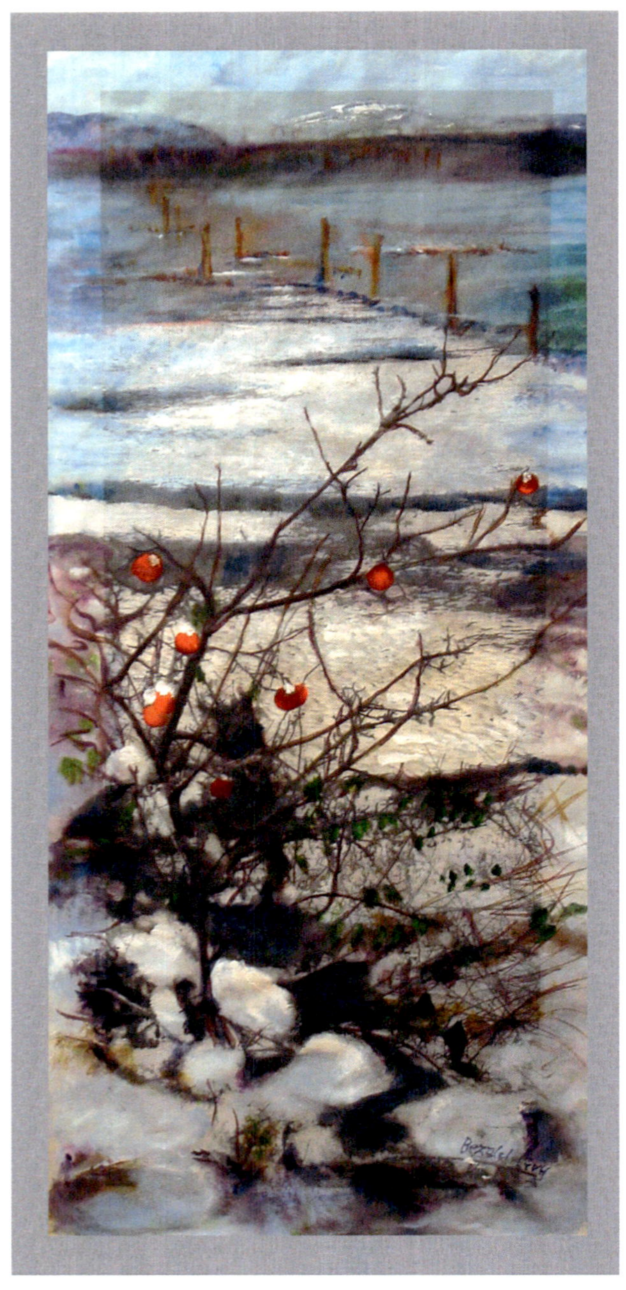

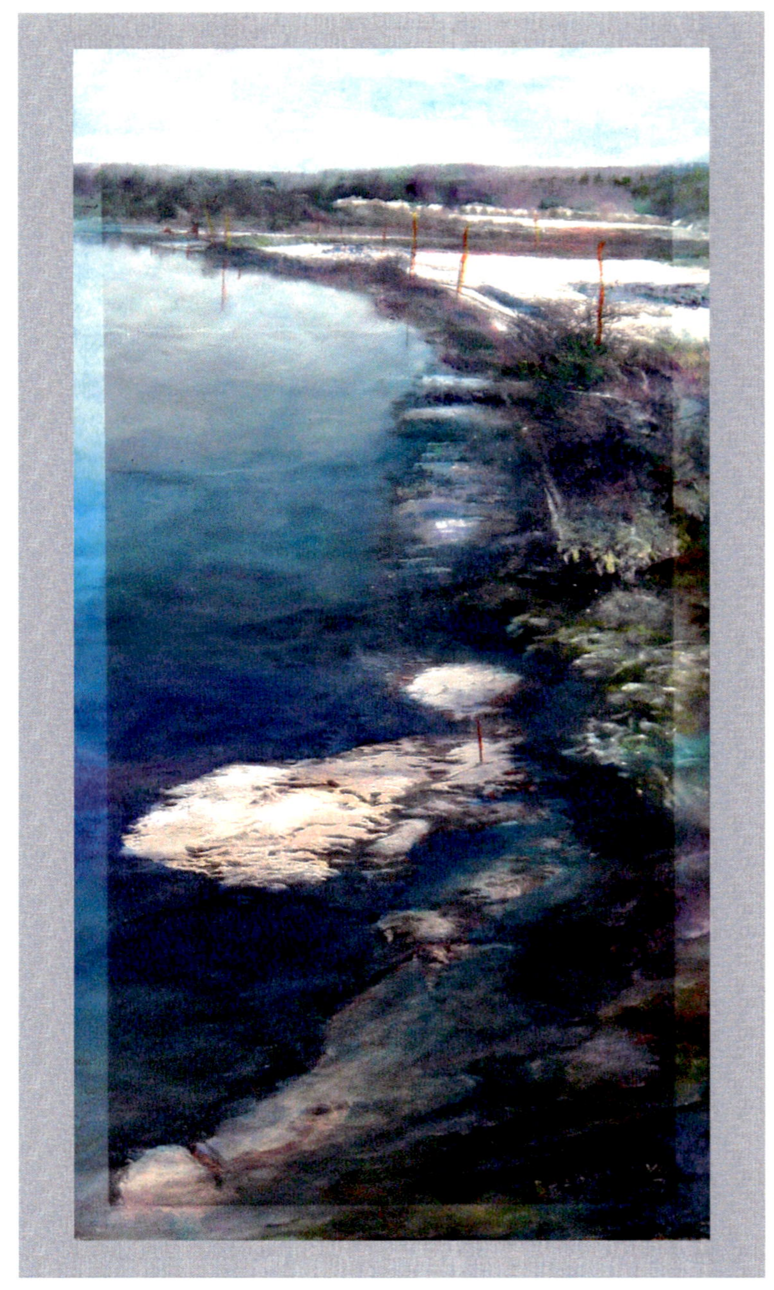

Snowfall I, Stillaguamish River (2006) 44 x 22 in.   **Snowfall II, Stillaguamish River** (2006) 44 x 23 in.

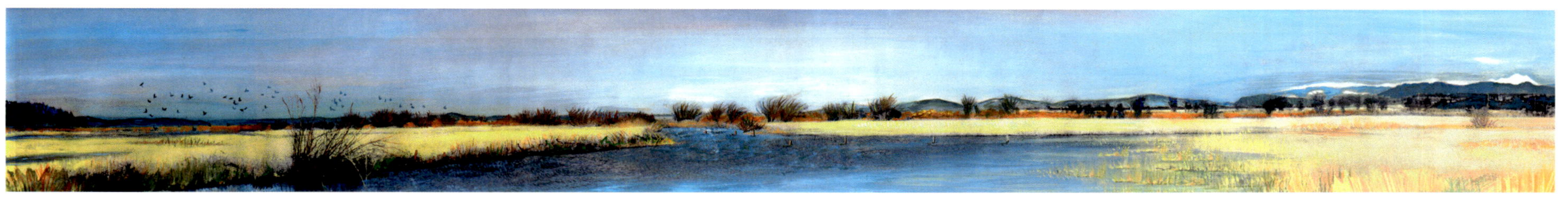

Davis Slough I (2000) 7 x 72 in. photography and acrylics on rice paper

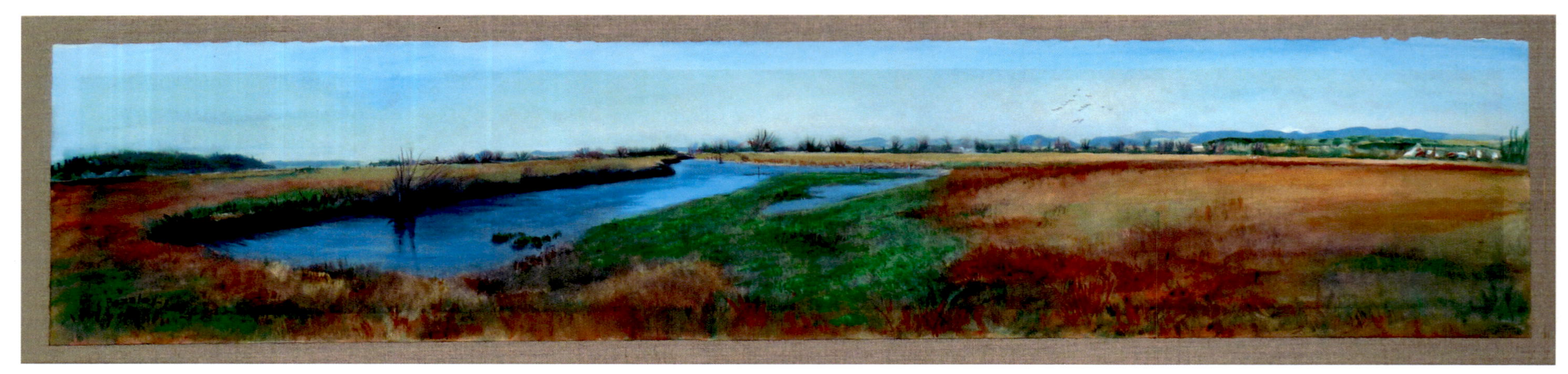

Davis Slough II (2011) 16 x 67 in.

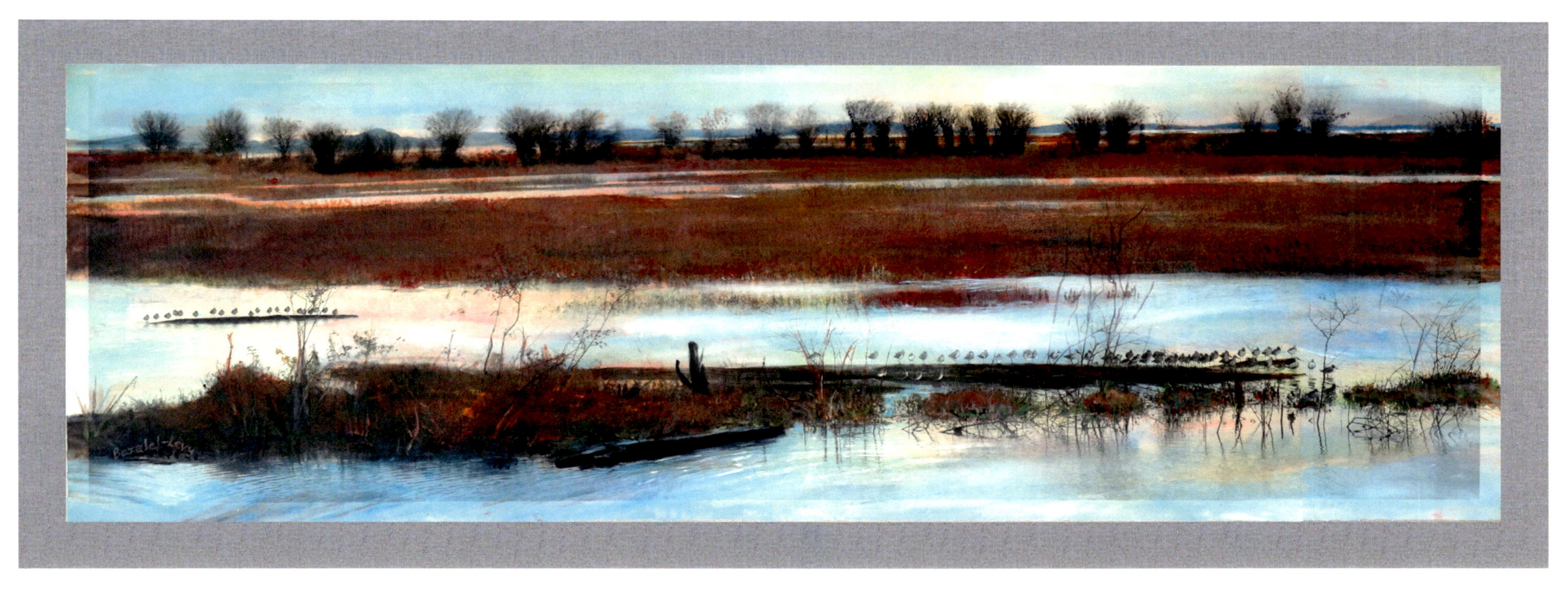

Davis Slough III (2013) 27 x 73 in.

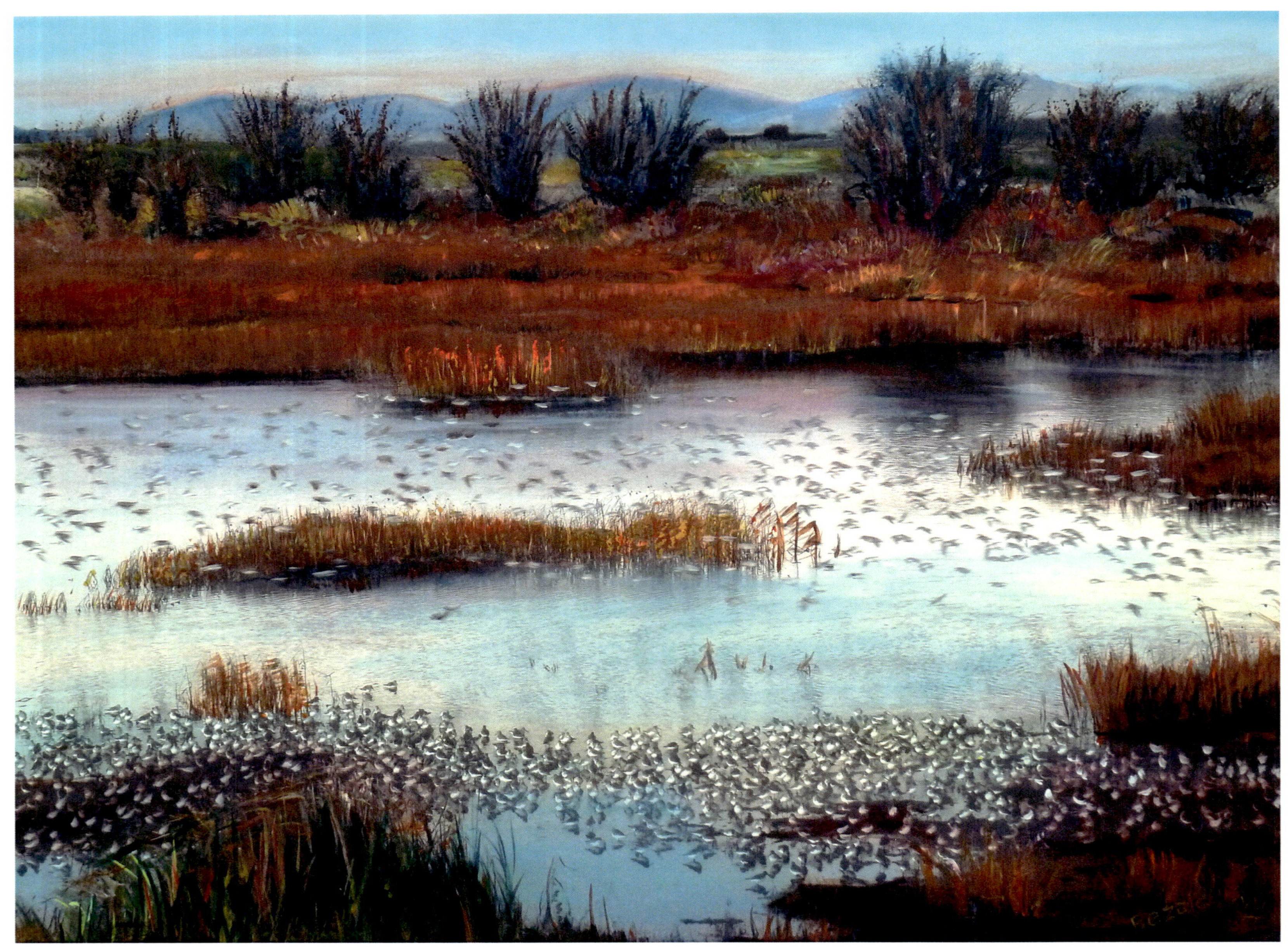

Davis Slough IV (2013) photography and acrylics on Rives paper mounted on birch, 30 x 40 in.

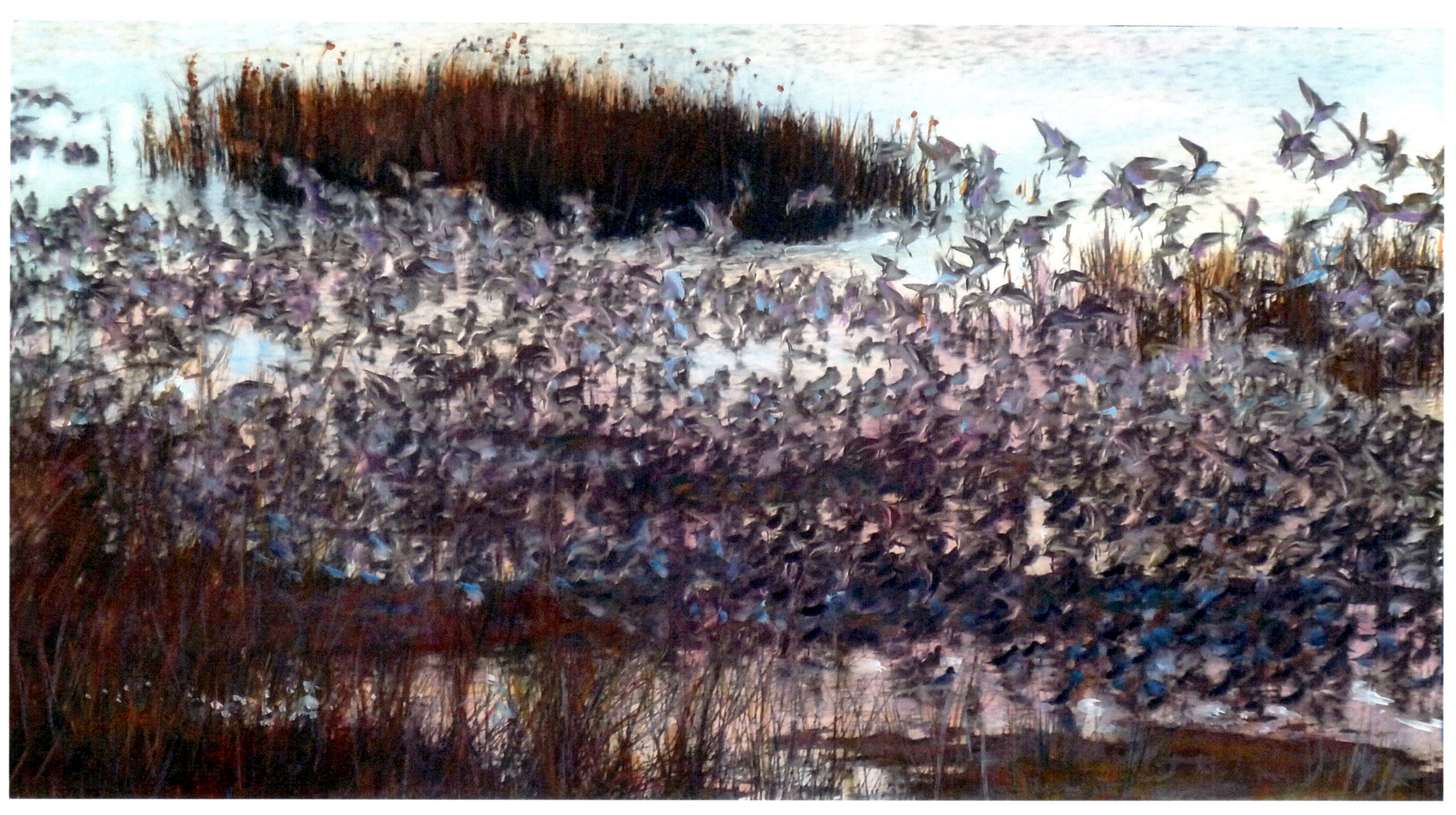

Pacific Dunlin, Davis Slough (2013) photography and acrylics on Rives paper mounted on birch, 30 x 40 in.

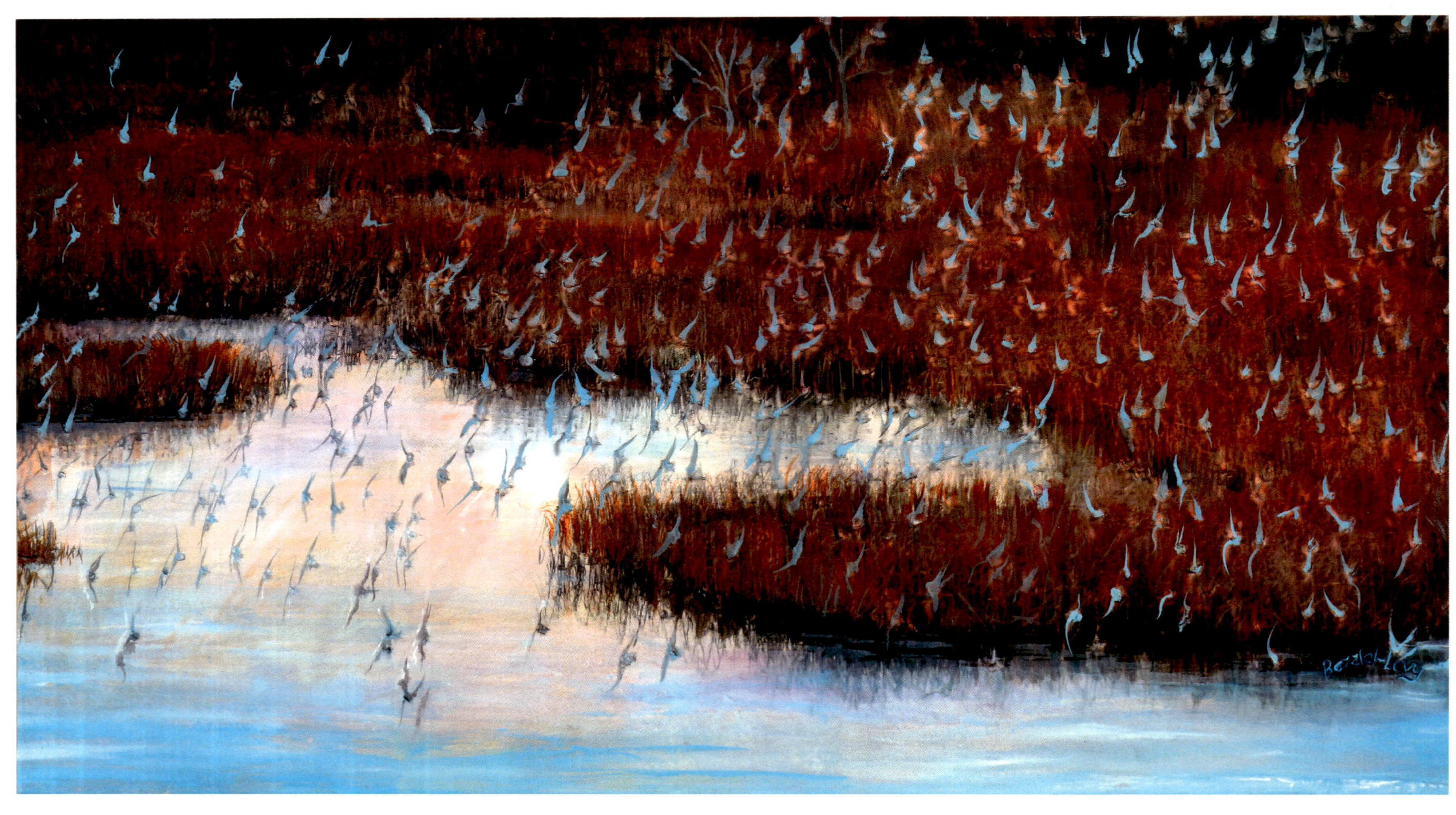

Murmuration (2013) photography and acrylics on Rives paper mounted on birch, 23 x 40 in.

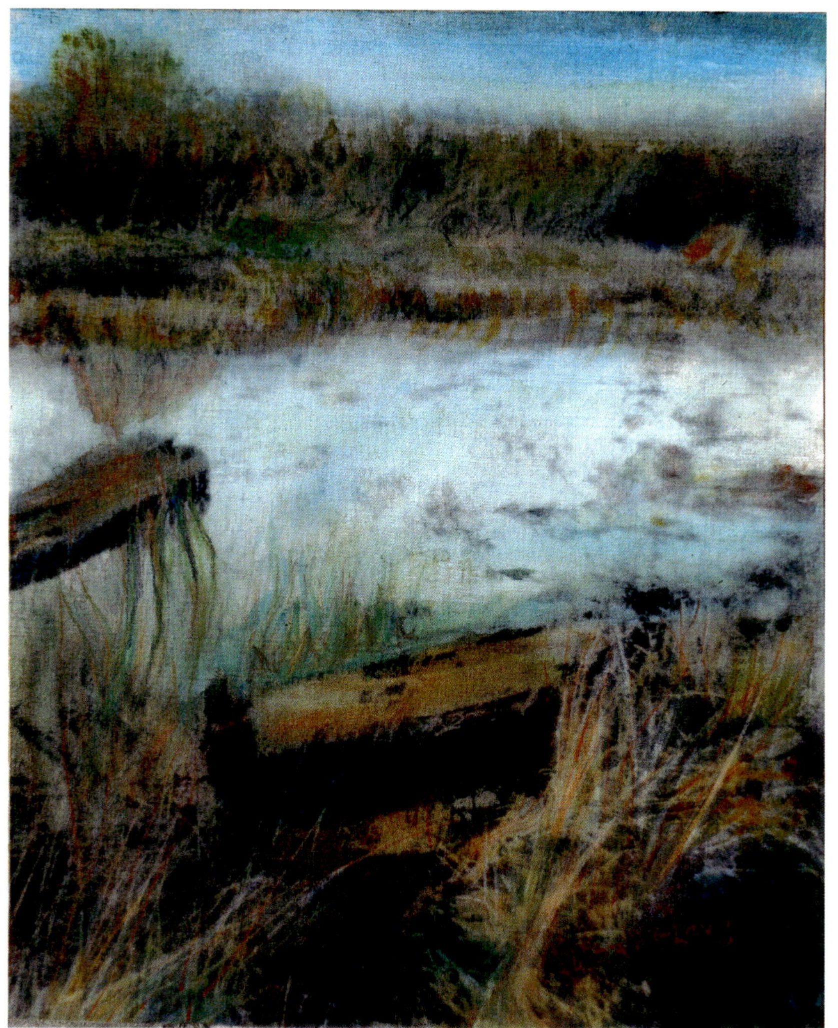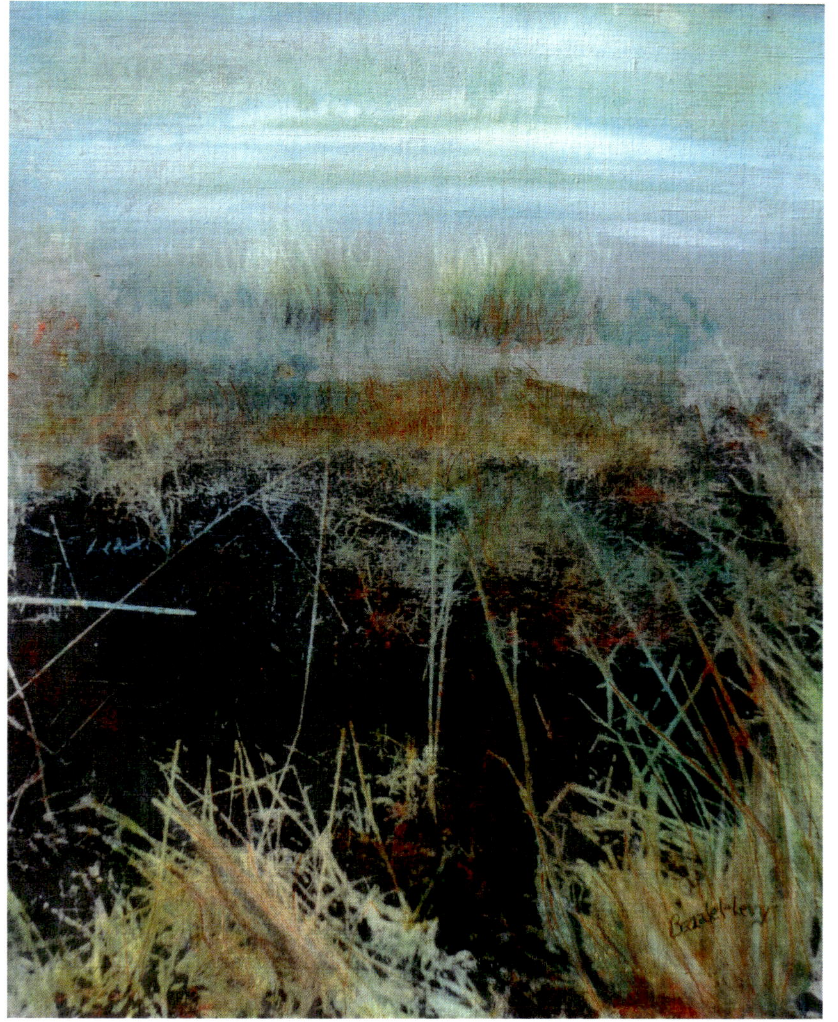

Davis Slough V & VI (2015) 26 x 20 in. each, photography and acrylics on linen

For the paintings above, black and white photographs taken with a medium format plastic toy camera were printed onto lightly gessoed raw linen and then painted over with acrylic paints.

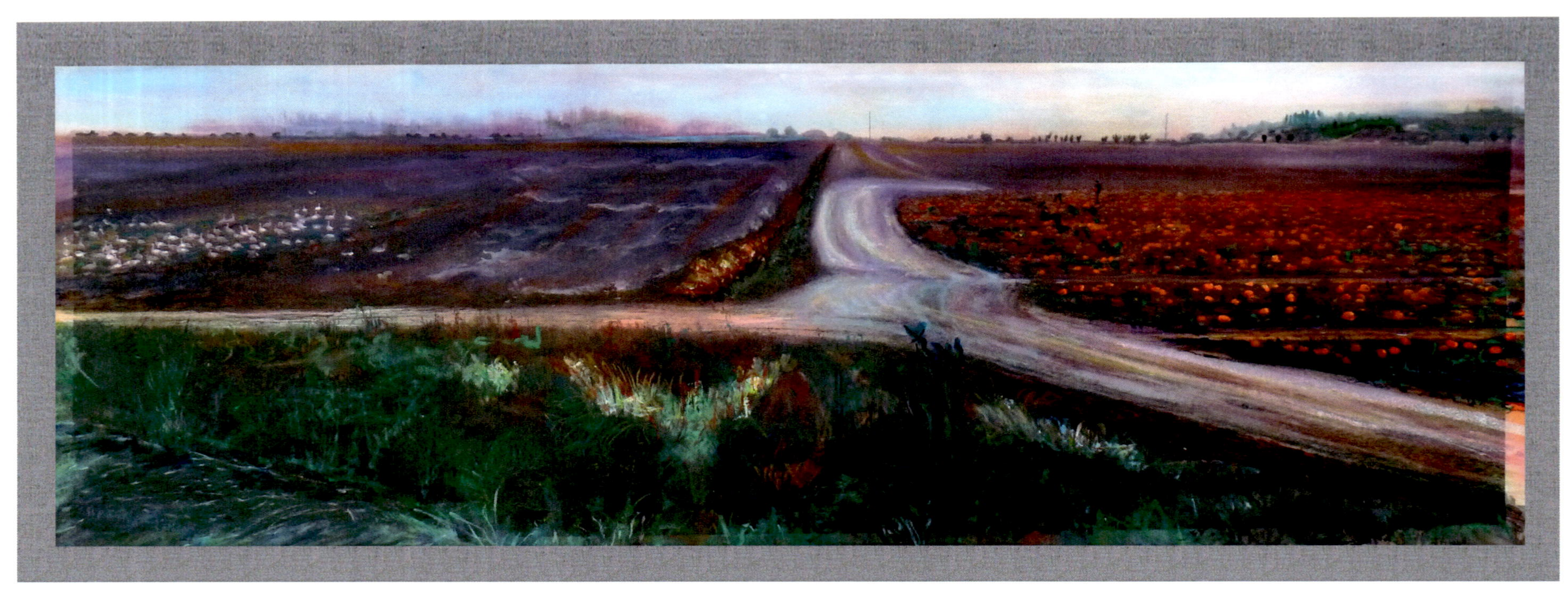

Field of Pumpkins, Field of Geese (2011) 25 x 66 in.

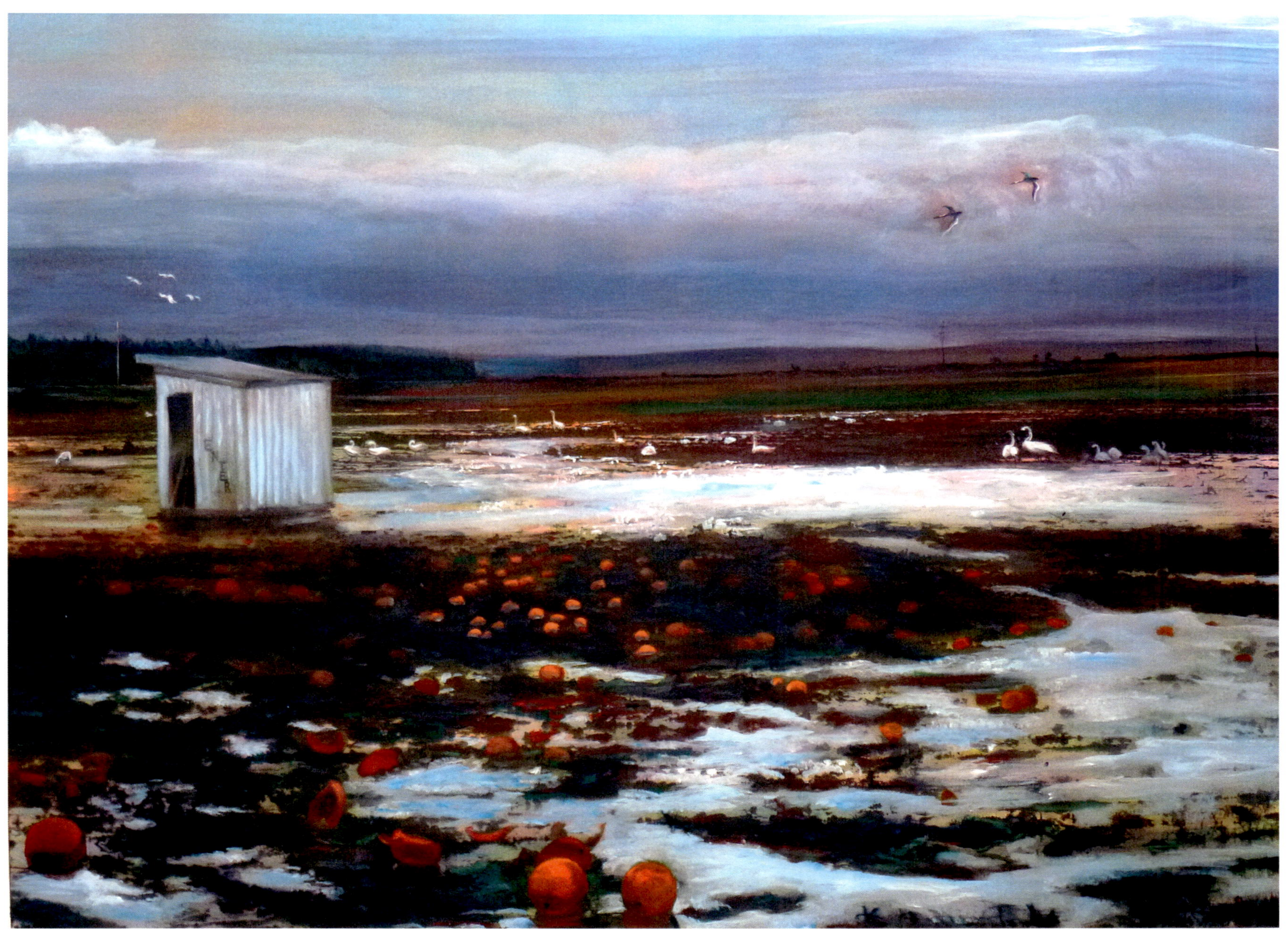

Late Autumn, the Swans Return (2011) photography and acrylics on Rives paper mounted on birch, 30 x 40 in.

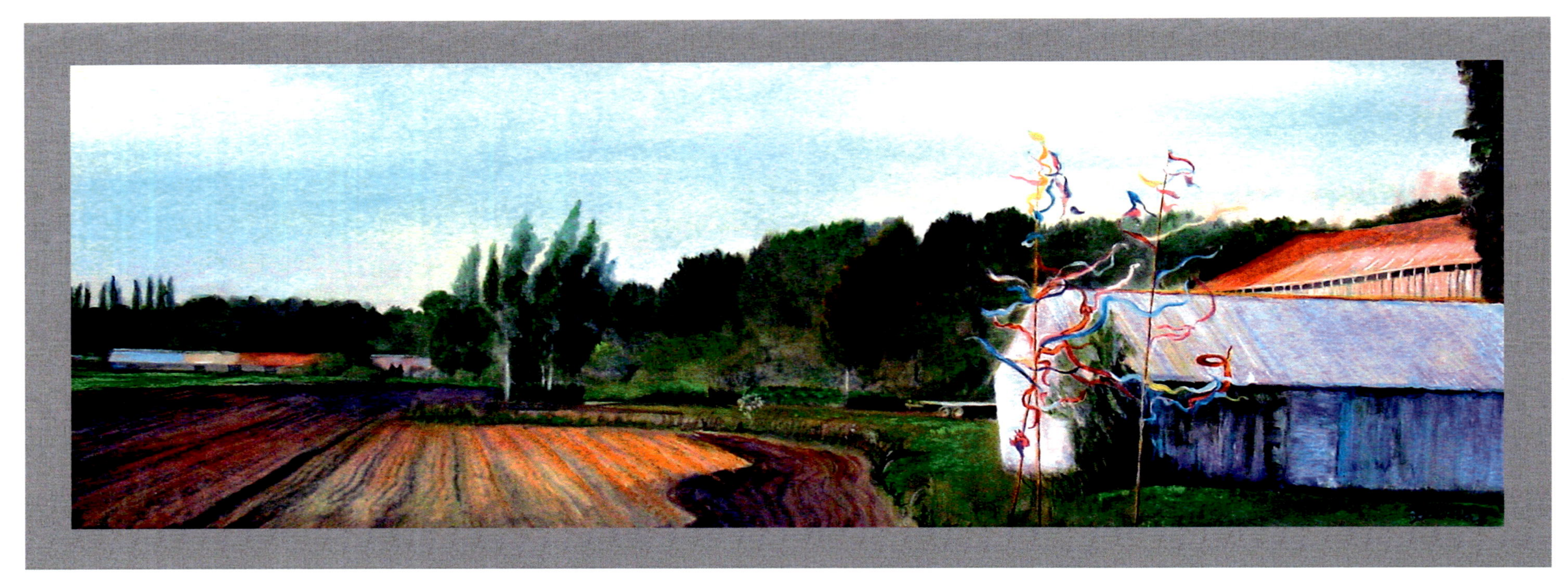

Farmland (2007) 24 x 62 in.

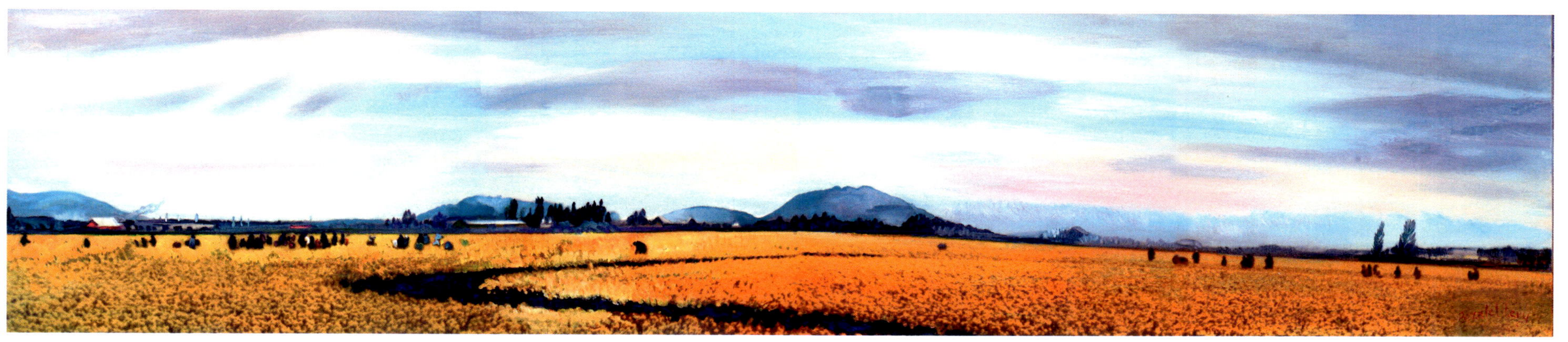

Farm Workers in a Field of Daffodils (2007) 16 x 72 in. photography and water based oils on paper mounted on hardboard

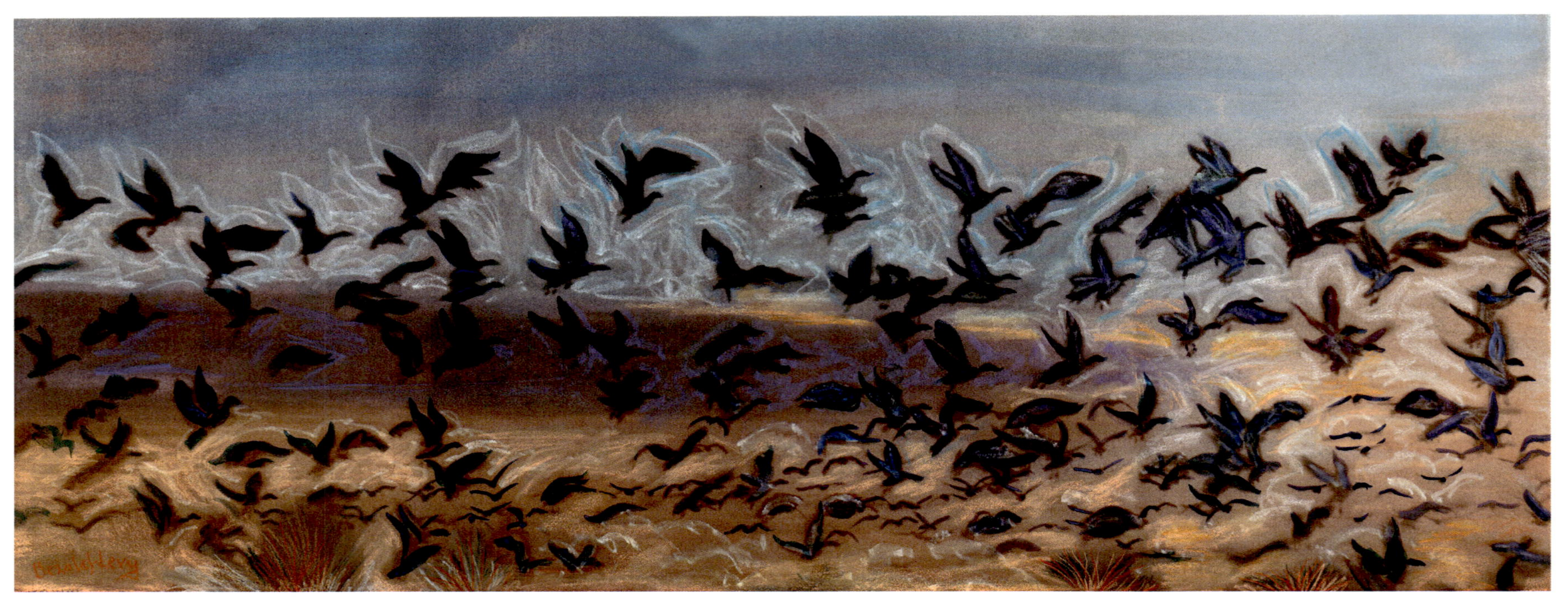

Snow Geese over Skagit Flats *(2004) 18 x 48 in. photography and pastels on rice paper*

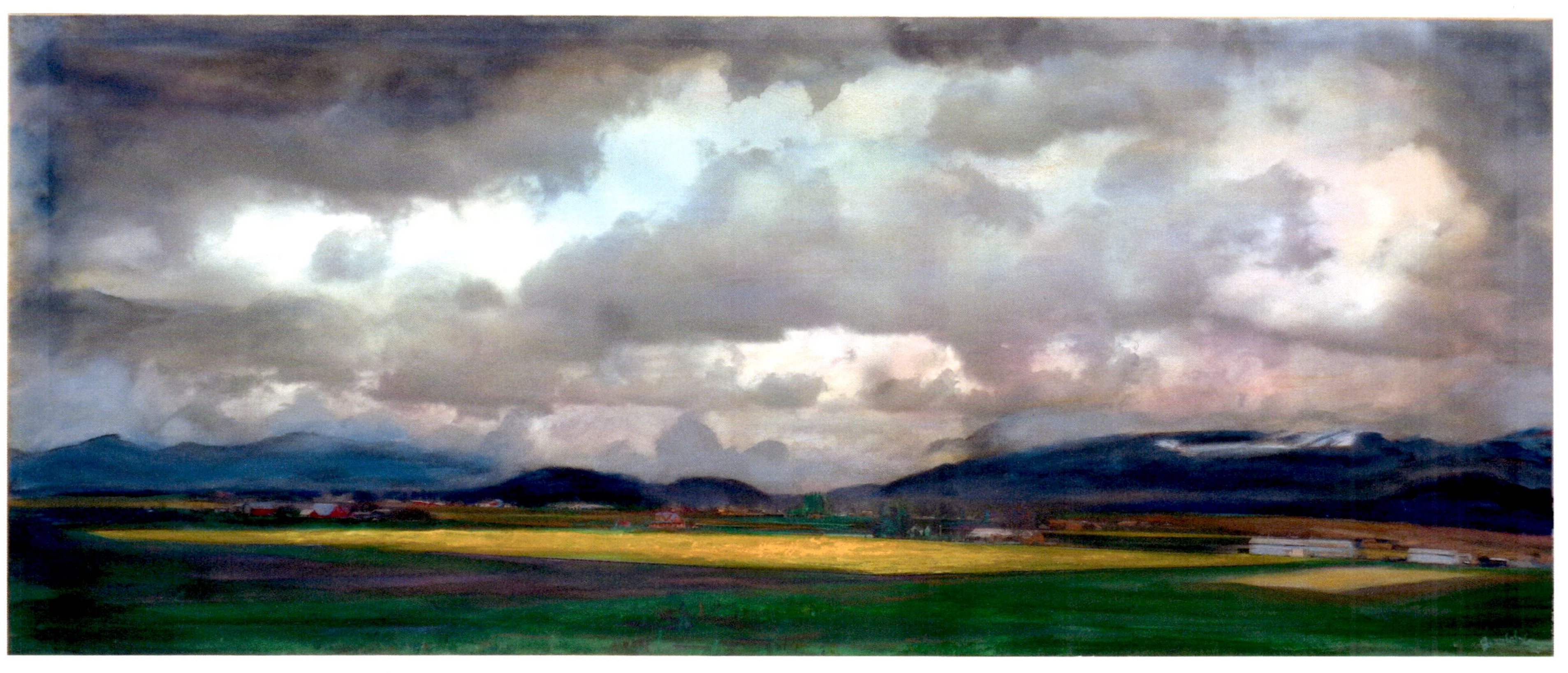

Gathering Storm (2014) 27 x 61 in. photography and acrylics on paper mounted on birch

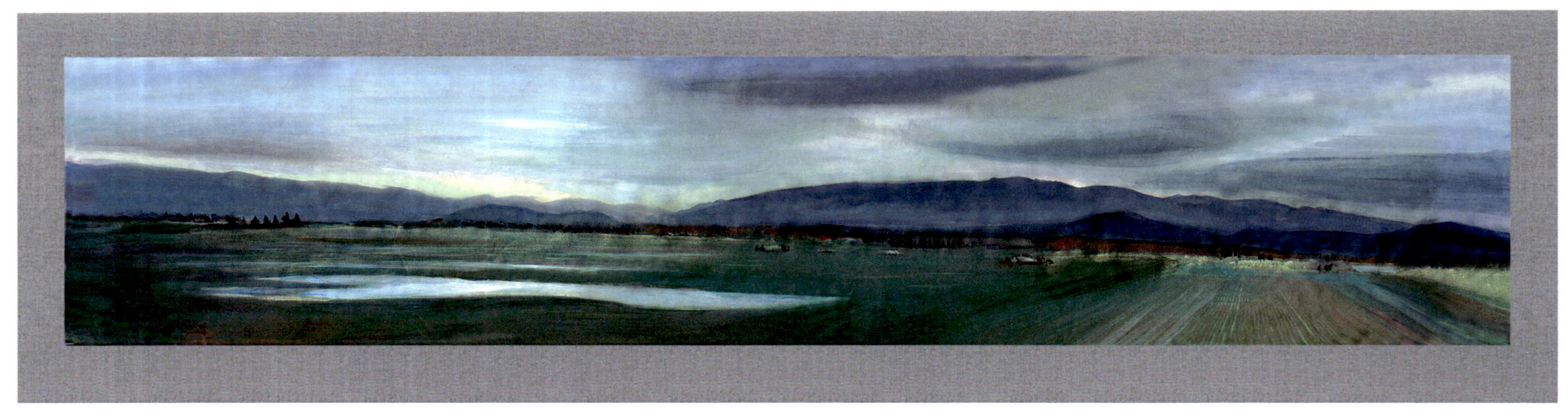

Raining on the Skagit Flats (2005) 16 x 64 in.

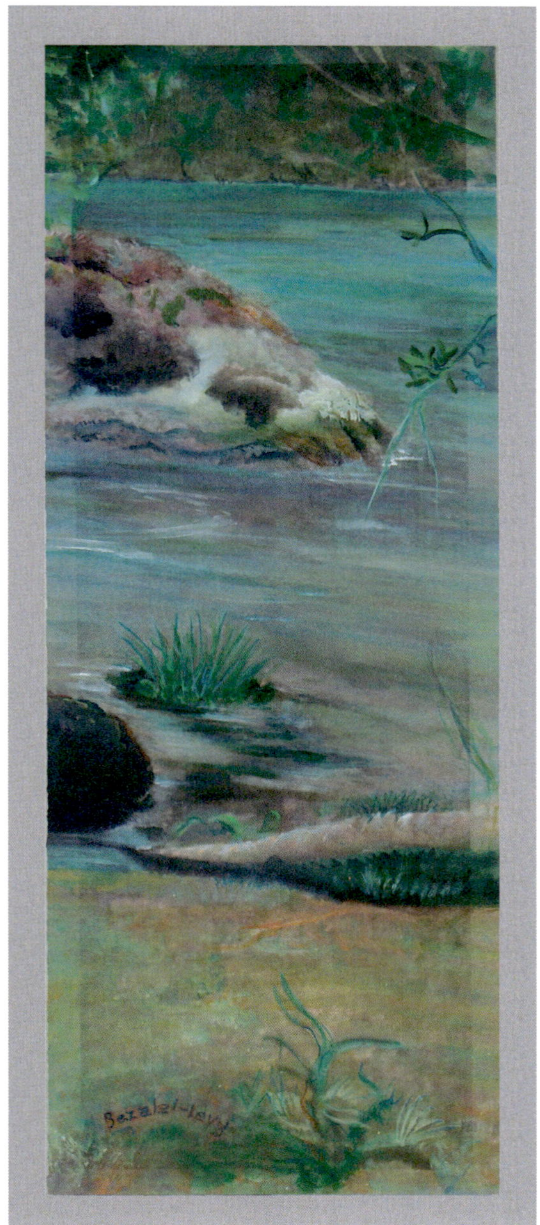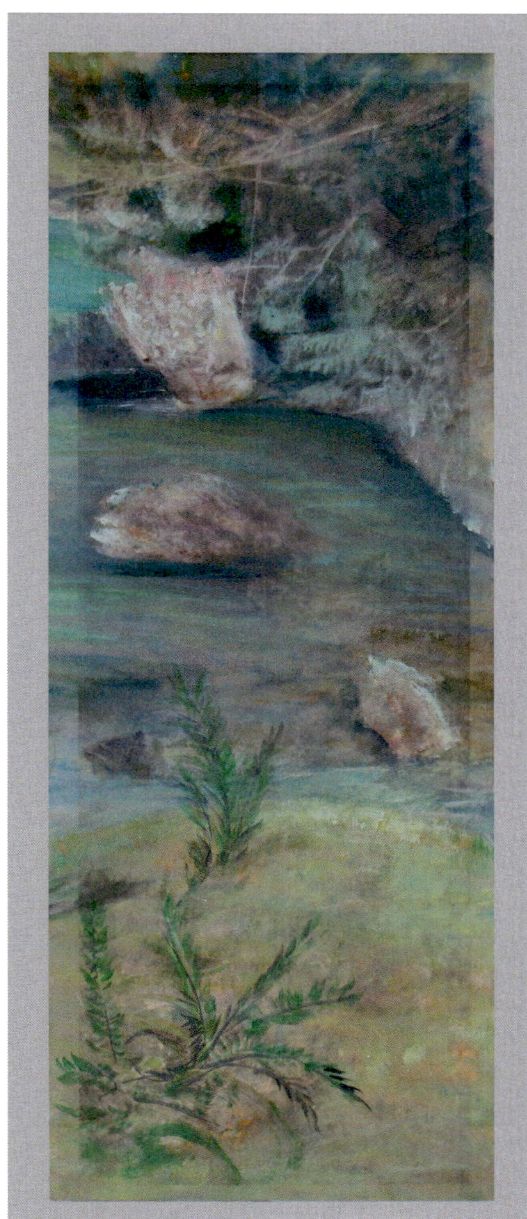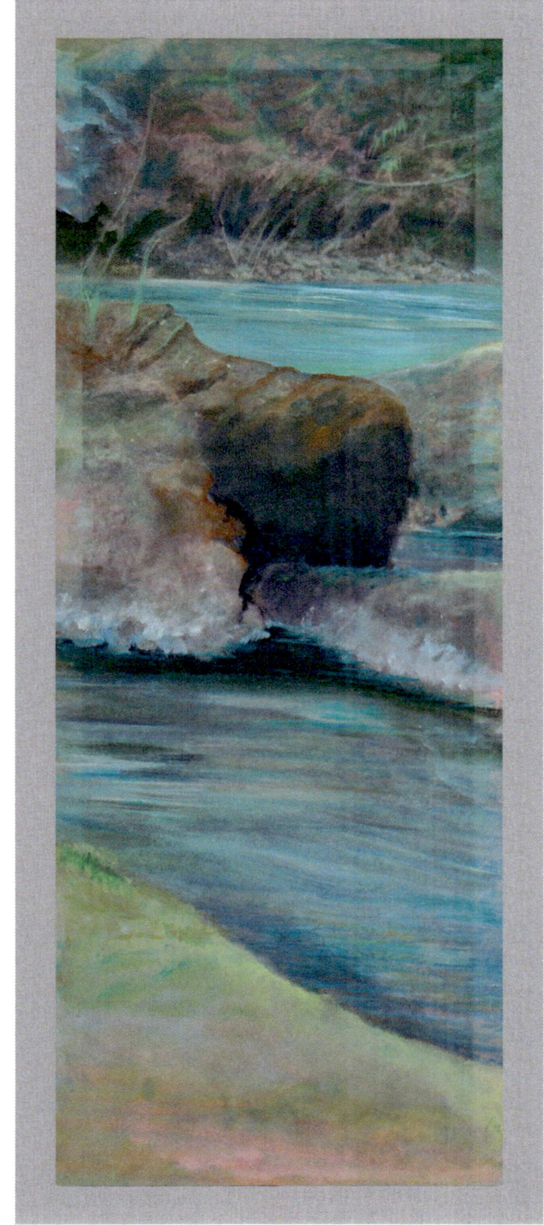

Skagit Triptych I (2007) 43 x 18 in. each panel

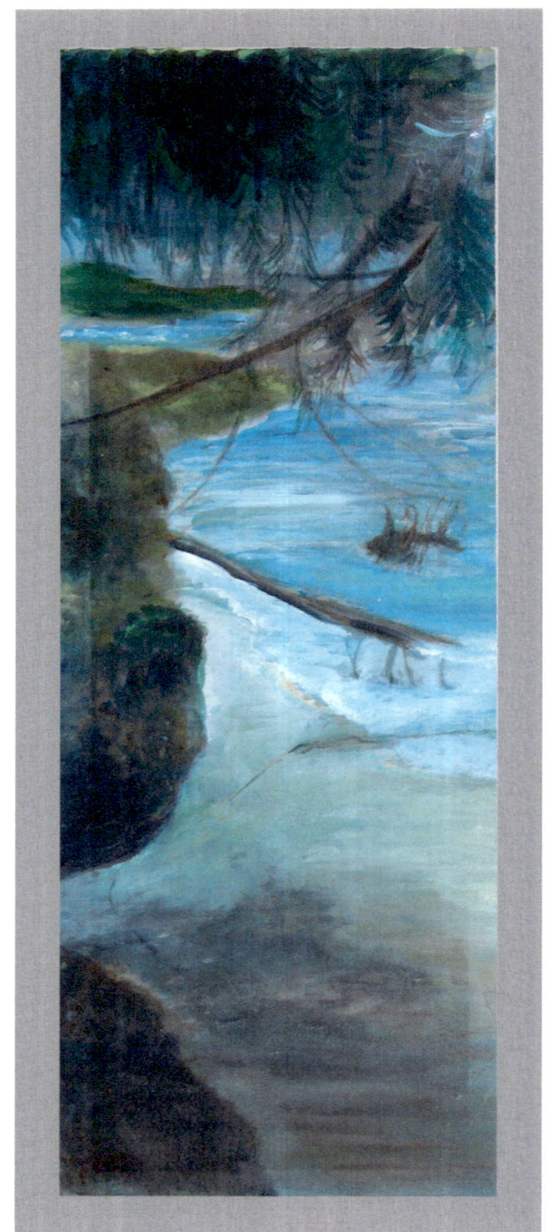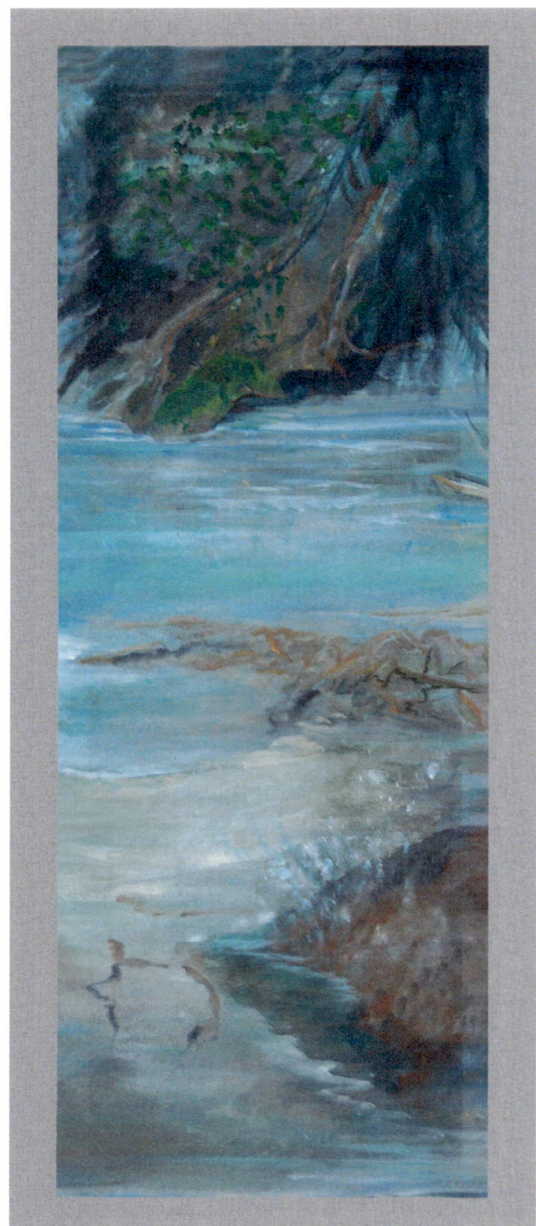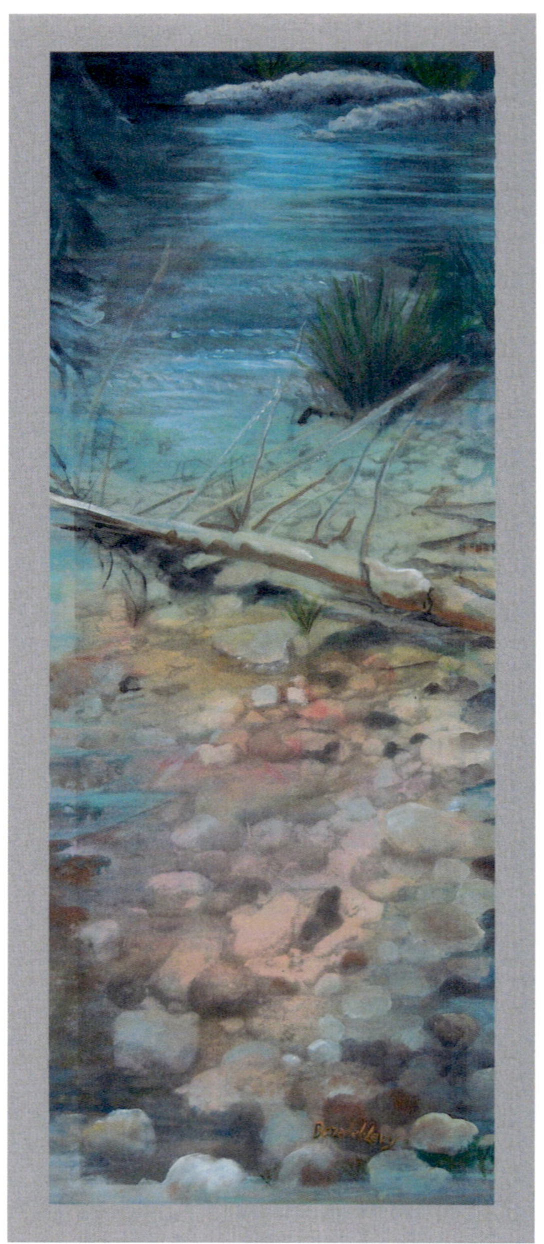

Skagit Triptych II (2007) 43 x 18 in. each panel

78

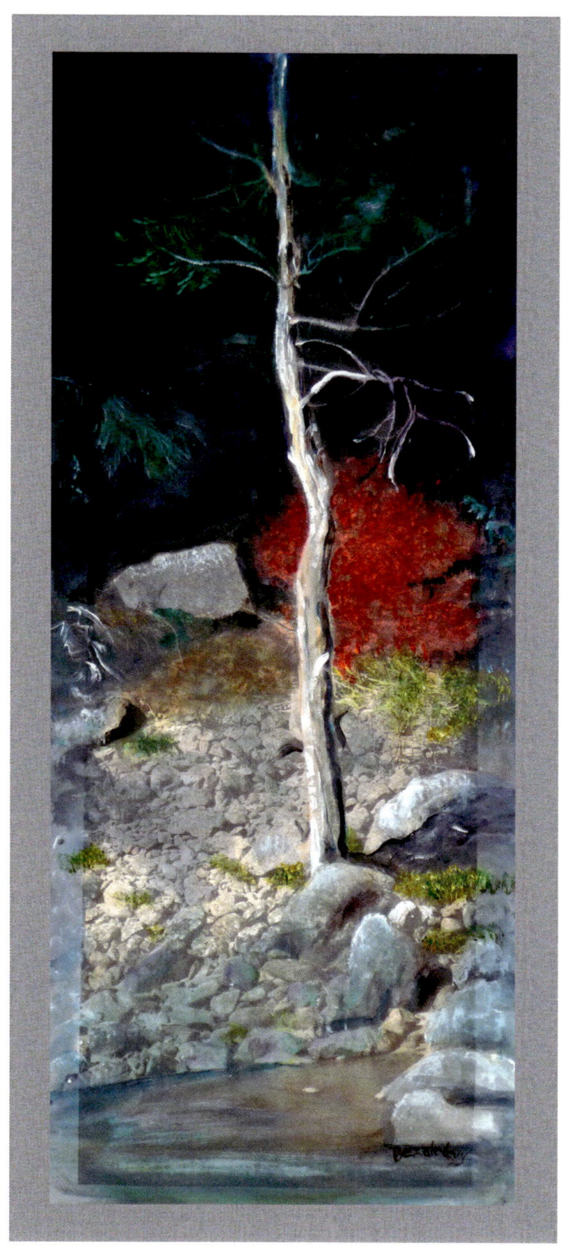

Wenatchee Riverside (2008) 36 x 16 in.

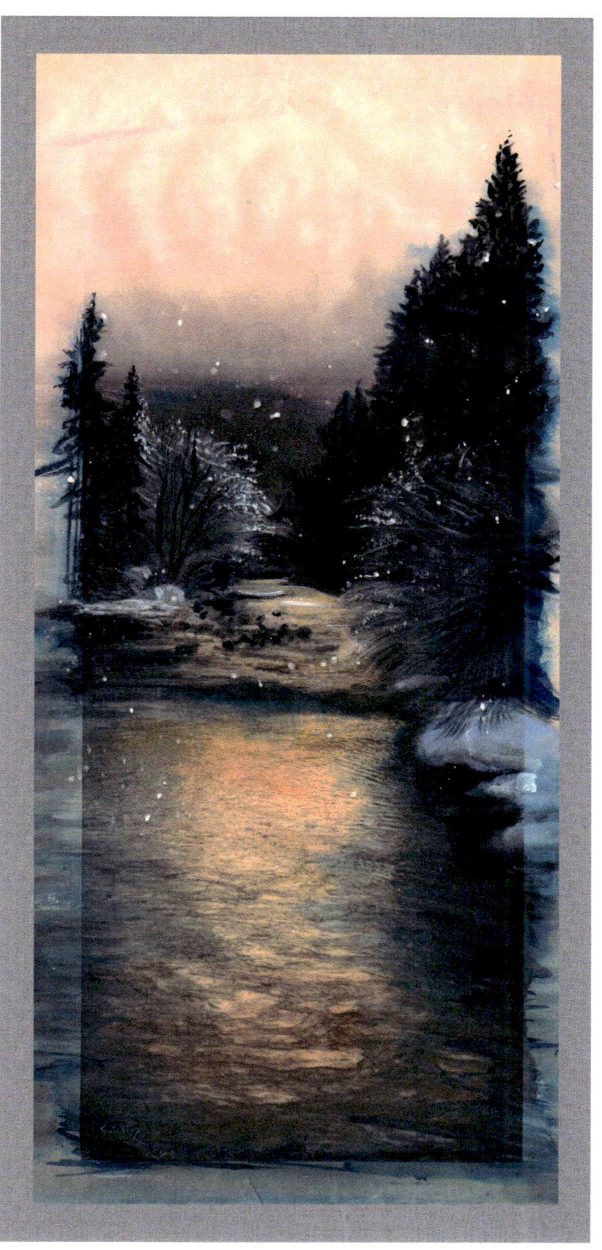

Snowfall, Skykomish River (2004) 43 x 20 in.

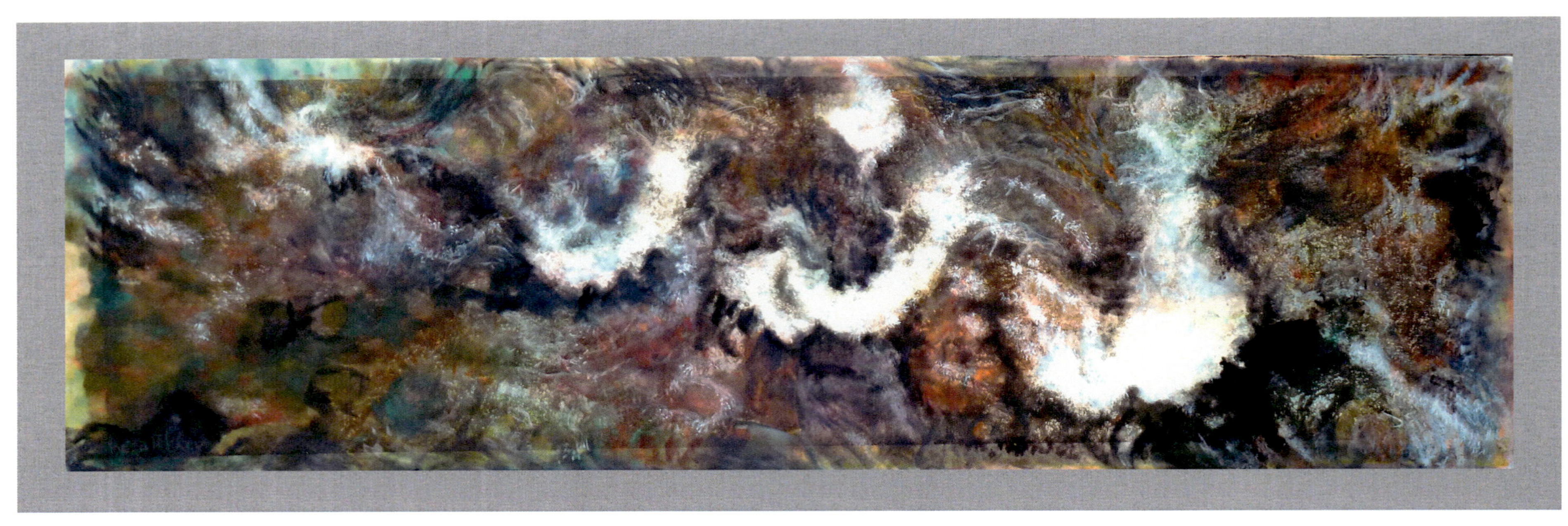

Rapids, Wenatchee River (2011) 18 x 60 in.

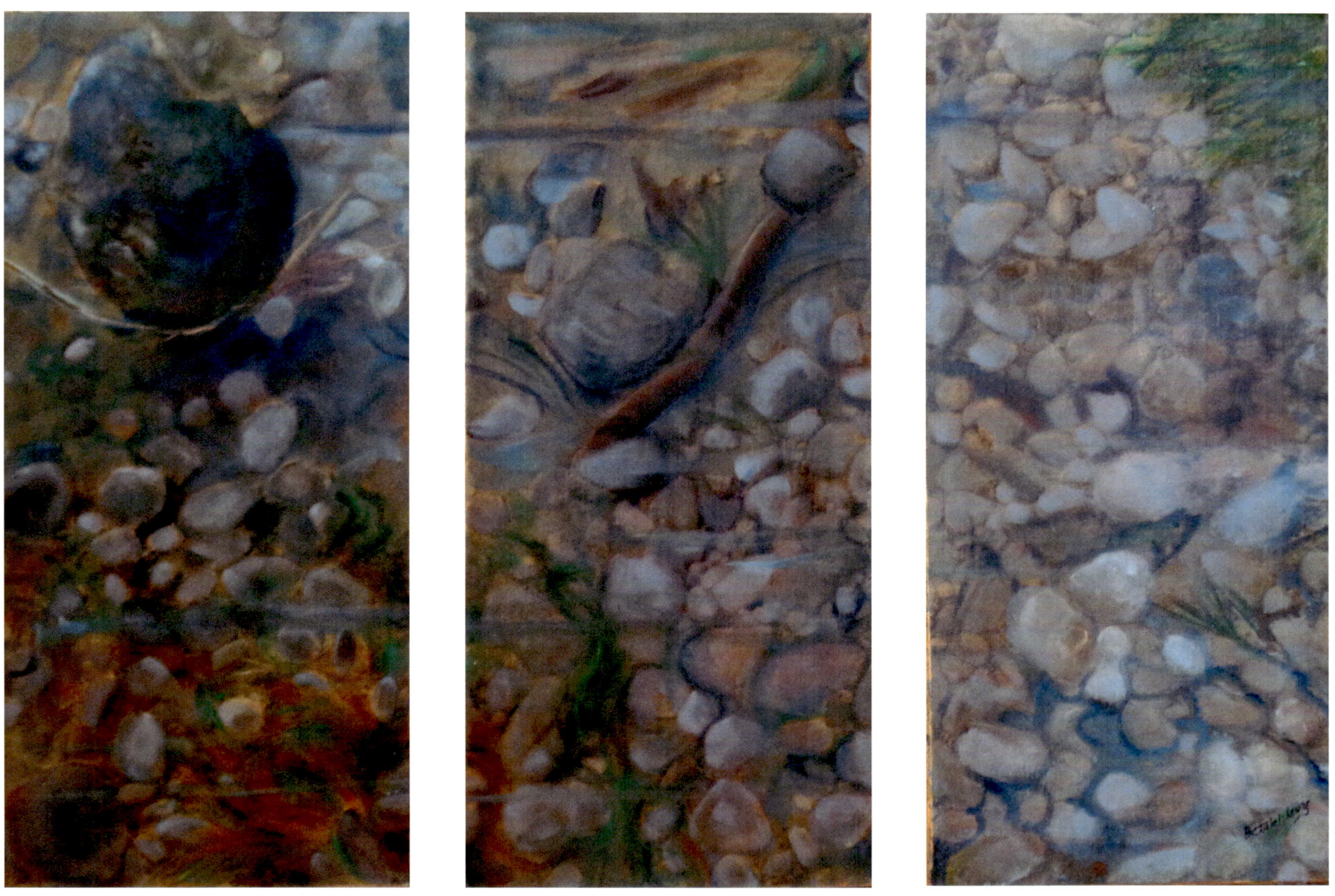

Wenatchee Riverbed (2011) mixed-media on linen mounted on birch, 29 x 13 in. each panel,

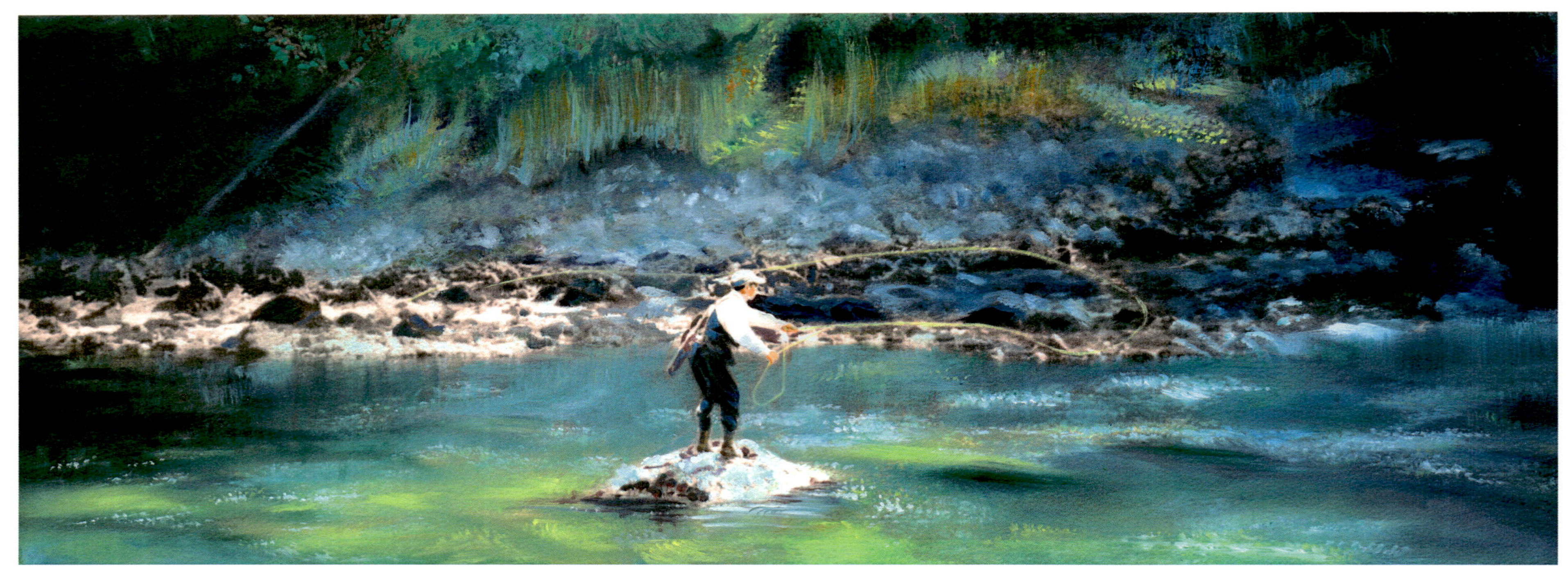

Fly Fishing on the Skykomish (2002) mixed-media with water based oils on paper, 11 x 30 in.

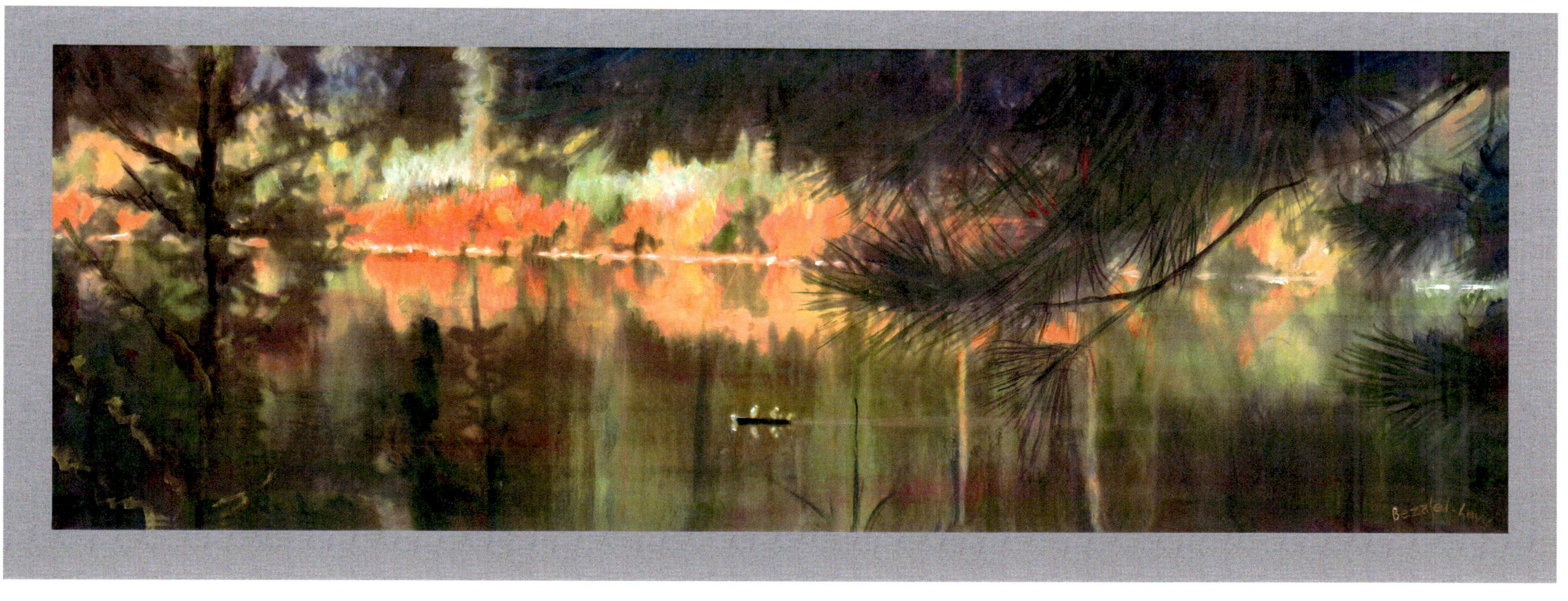

Fishing on Lake Wenatchee (2009) 24 x 60 in.

At this point, I think it is appropriate to mention our parents. Jack Ballard, Yonnah's father, was an avid fisherman and booster of the Pacific Northwest. In fact, in 1961 *Look Magazine* ran an article about him: *A very special man, Look, v. 27, no. 7 (Mar. 27, 1962), p. 34-36.* Here is the description of the photographs for that article as archived in the Library of Congress: *"Photographs show sales manager Jack Ballard, of Washington state, and his family; at home; entertaining friends at a dinner party; Ballard playing tennis; with wife and children in house; Ballard at his office. Includes the family on a camping and fishing trip; packing family station wagon; on a ferry through the San Juan Islands; at the campsite; Ballard and son Dean fishing from a boat."*

When he died we scattered his ashes, according to his wishes, from the bridge at Rockport on the Upper Skagit River, his favorite fishing spot. My own father, Saul Spilke, is buried on the property in Catskill, NY, not far from the Van Orden graves. On his headstone, coincidentally, are the very same works: "a very special man."

The Cascade Mountains and the Passes

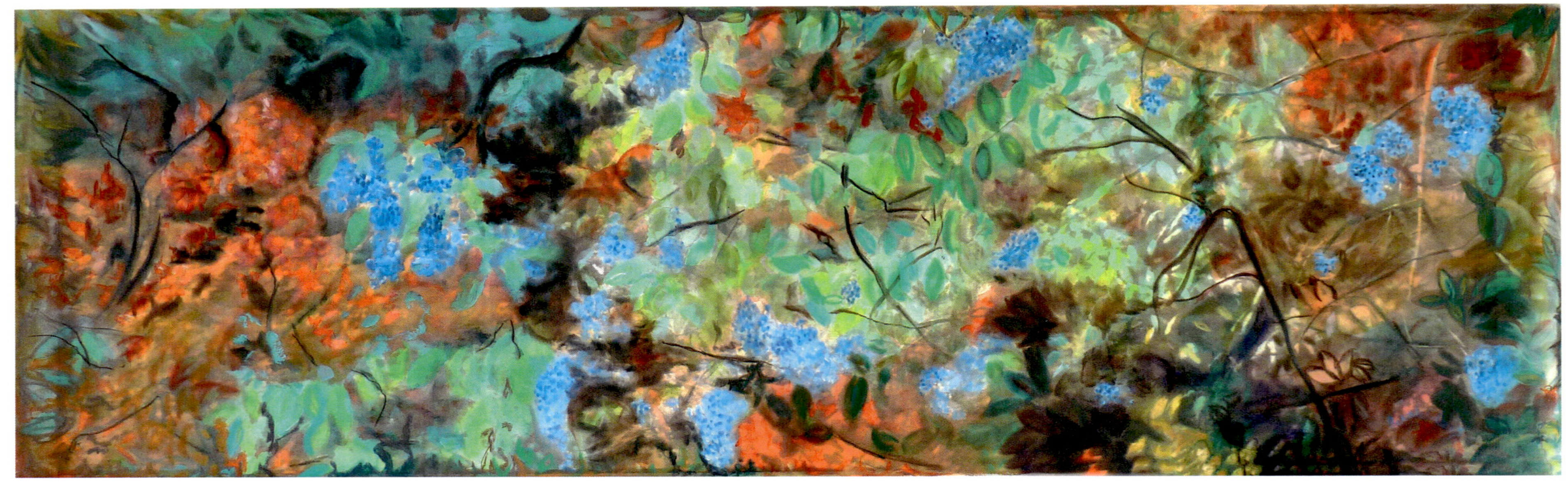

Cascade Autumn Horizontal (2011) 36 x 96 in. mixed-media with pastels on Rives paper

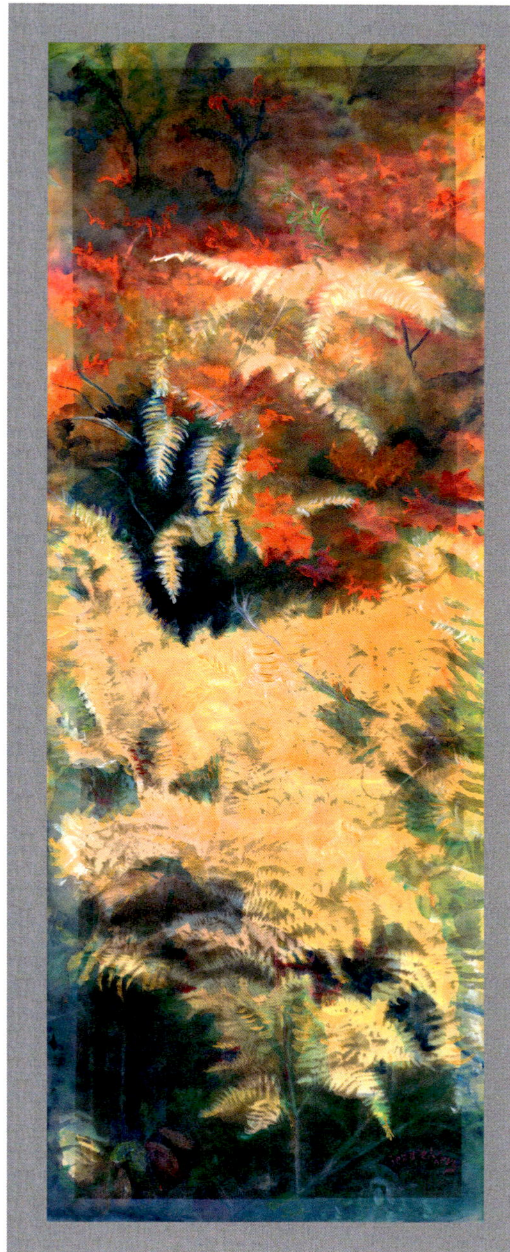

Cascade Autumn I (2007) 43 x 18 in.

My Husband, a Landscape

We often
find ourselves on field trips
of one sort or another
Walking talking ingesting the
trees   flora   fauna
and white billowy clouded
skies
I fill the scrolls of such vistas
easily with washes of
pure and mixed colors
Lovingly laid down with
cool   calm   restful strokes
or sometimes quickly
in impetuous delight
With intrigue I turn
to my husband and
climb into the hills and valleys
of his body and arms
What imprints my life
the after effects of those
landscapes
like my new digital camera chip
these images intertwine
into each other and fill my soul

- Yonnah Ben Levy

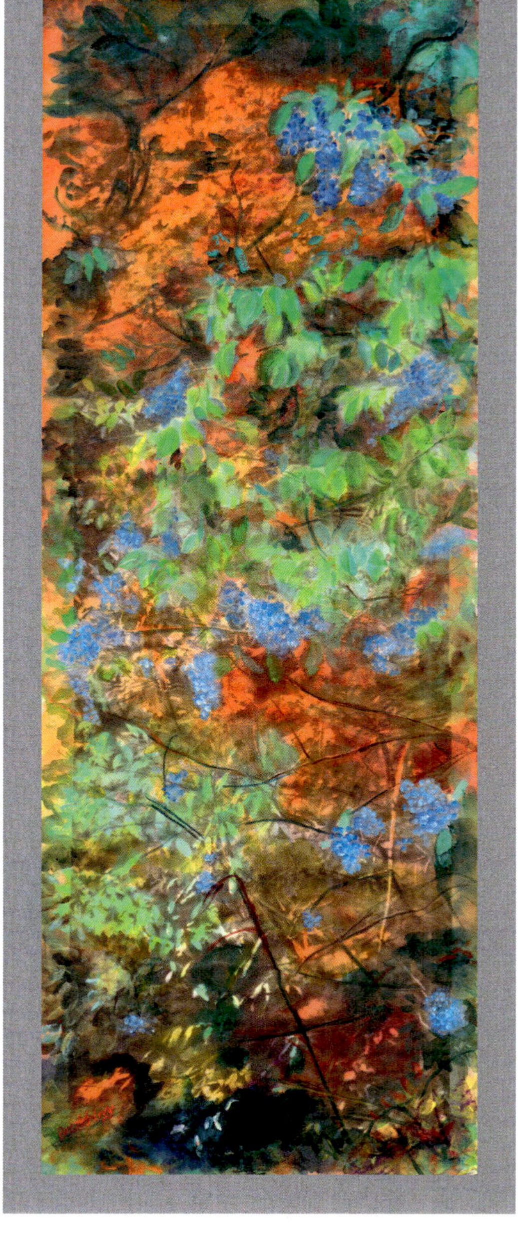

Cascade Autumn II (2007) 43 x 18 in.

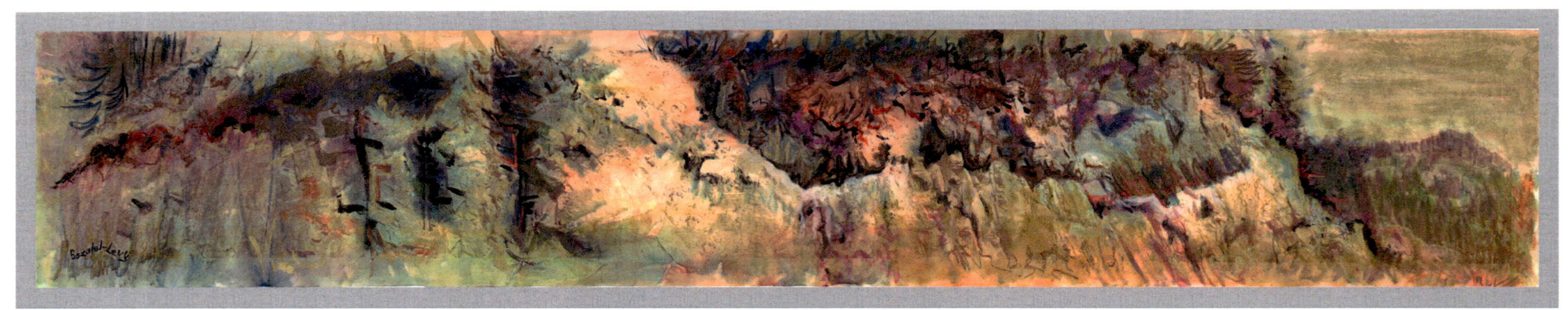

Chinook Pass (2004) 16 x 72 in.

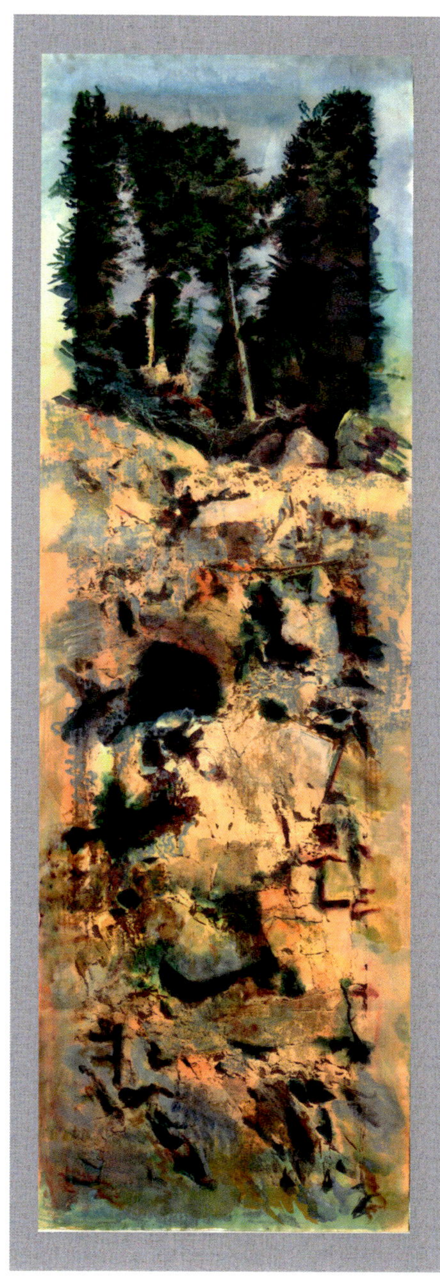

Chinook Vertical (2004) 60 x 22 in.

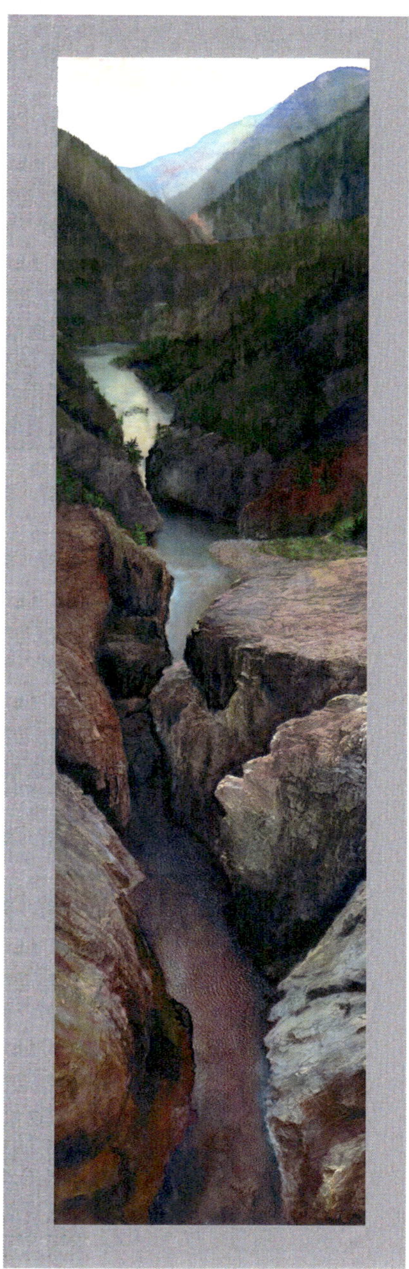

Diablo Canyon (2002) 72 x 23 in

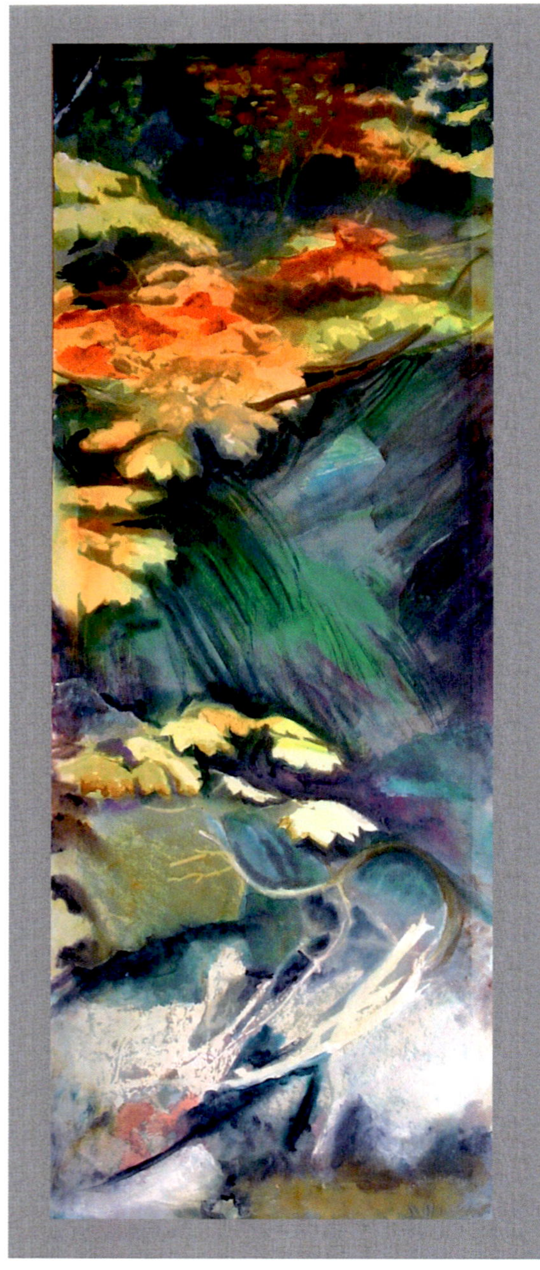

Santiem Pass I (2006) 63 x 24 in.

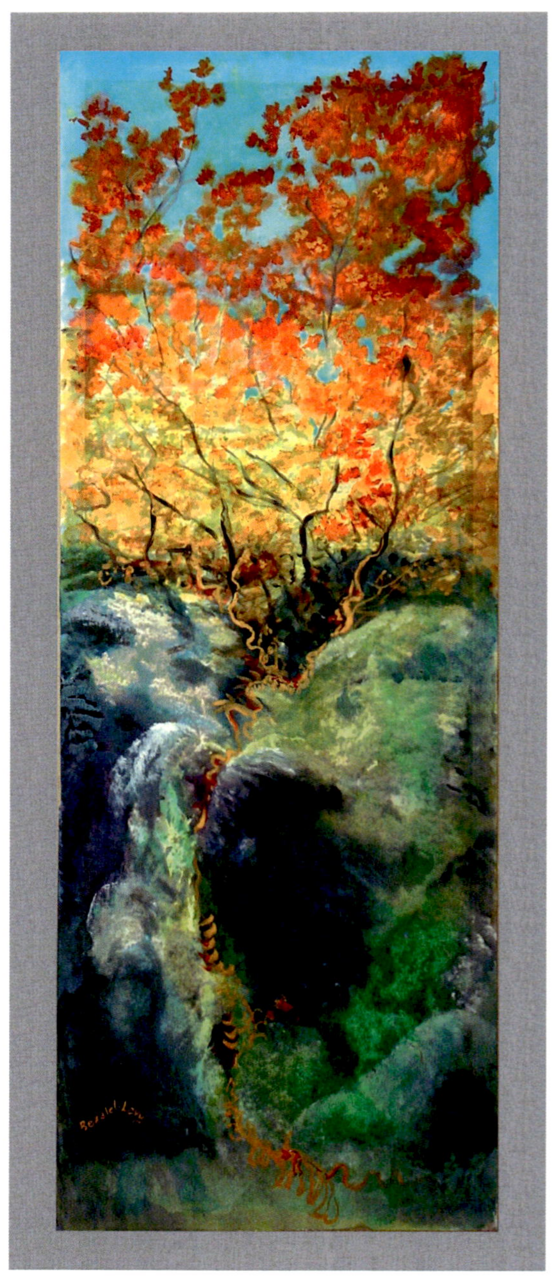

Santiem Pass II (2006) 63 x 24 in.

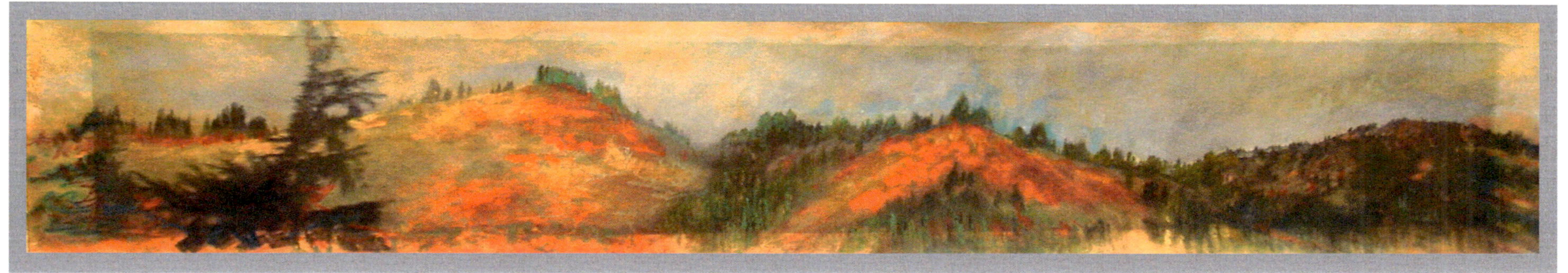

Stevens Pass (2006) 16 x 72 in.

The Fire and the Gold

Alchemy comes
  along and surprises, lifts
    and holds me in an
      altered state,
My eye shocked into
    pure delight.
We crested the mountain pass
  in waves of fog, and behold
leaves clutching their branches
    for a final fling of
      blasting glorious color
    it shines out of water
      laden clouds and sky.

With rapture we are
    transported into that
      outer yet inner space
    that reminds us of that
      special bliss of life.
  Hillsides of red and yellow
    fill the next weeks,
      tramping through the
Cascade forests and pools of
    the stuff reflected back
      like mirrors
    from the rivers and lakes.
  We wandered around

almost delirious
  as each rounding corner
    brought new
      possibilities of
    rich warm compositions,
      bending twisting
        arching trees
  the deciduous varieties
    finally having their
      place in the sun
against the blue green black
    evergreens that dominate
      these mountains and

Western terrains
Now it's back to work
 and sorting through the
  memories stored in
hundreds of photos. I'm
 kept cozy and warm with that
week in the fire and gold and
  yet challenged by the
seasonal change that peaks
  and wanes into winter. Four
more months till we
have a glimpse of lime green
  new life and new beginnings.

-Yonnah Ben Levy

89

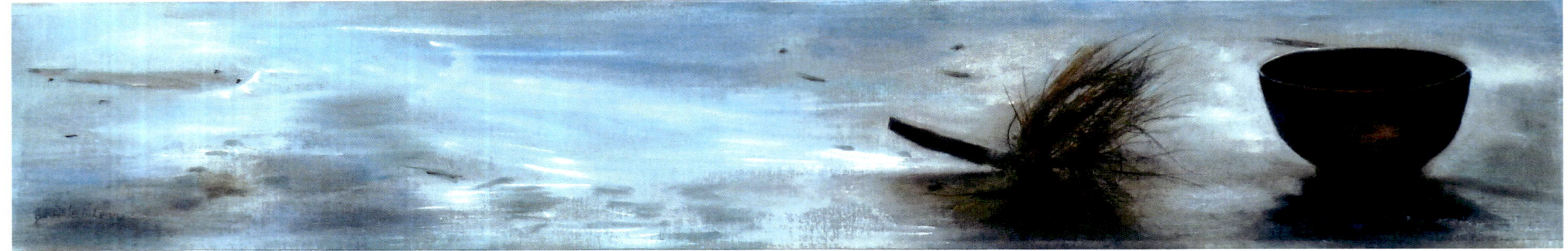

Bowl and Brush (2009) 11 x 60 in. photography and acrylics on linen mounted on birch

Though not a landscape, this composition is reminiscent of a zen scroll. The painting is of a tabletop in a studio at Grunewald Guild, where Yonnah taught painting and ceramics for ten years. As described in their website: "The Grünewald Guild is an arts education nonprofit retreat center nestled on 14 acres of Cascadian woodland, bordered by the Wenatchee River in the Plain Valley of Washington. Snowcapped peaks, rushing waters and sweet smelling ponderosa pine welcome, inspire, and create an environment in which people come to learn, to grow, and to explore the relationships between art, faith and community." The landscapes on pages 79. 80, 81, 83, 84, 85 and 86 are from photographs taken either near Plain, Washington where the center is based, or on the way, coming or going over the Stevens Pass.

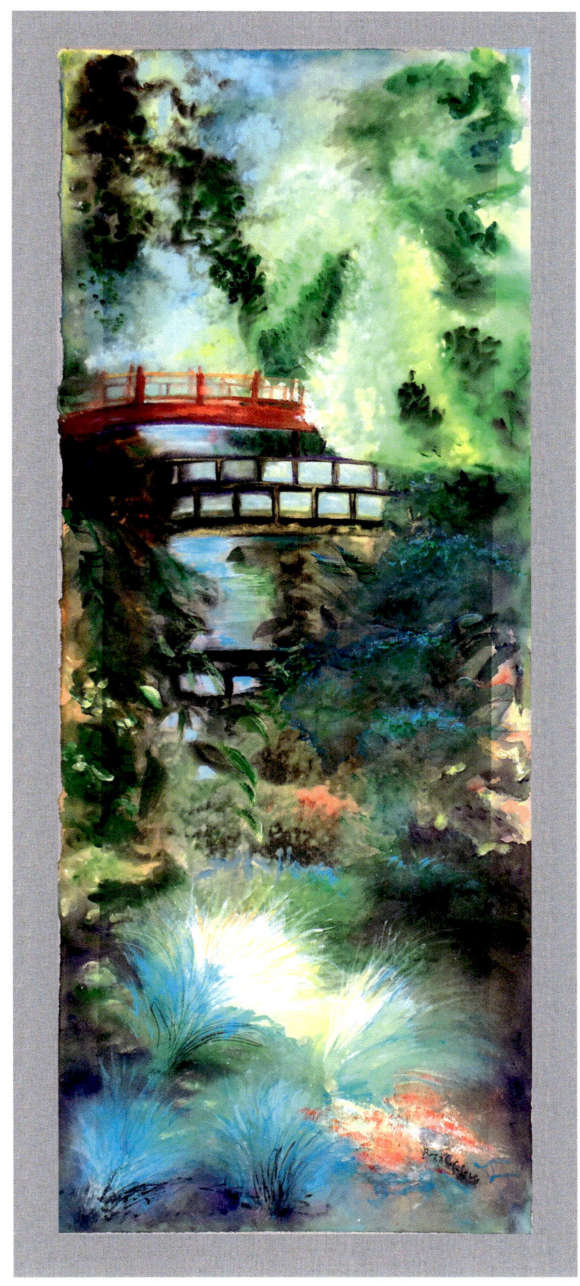

Japanese Garden, Coos Bay, OR (2005) 62 x 26 in.

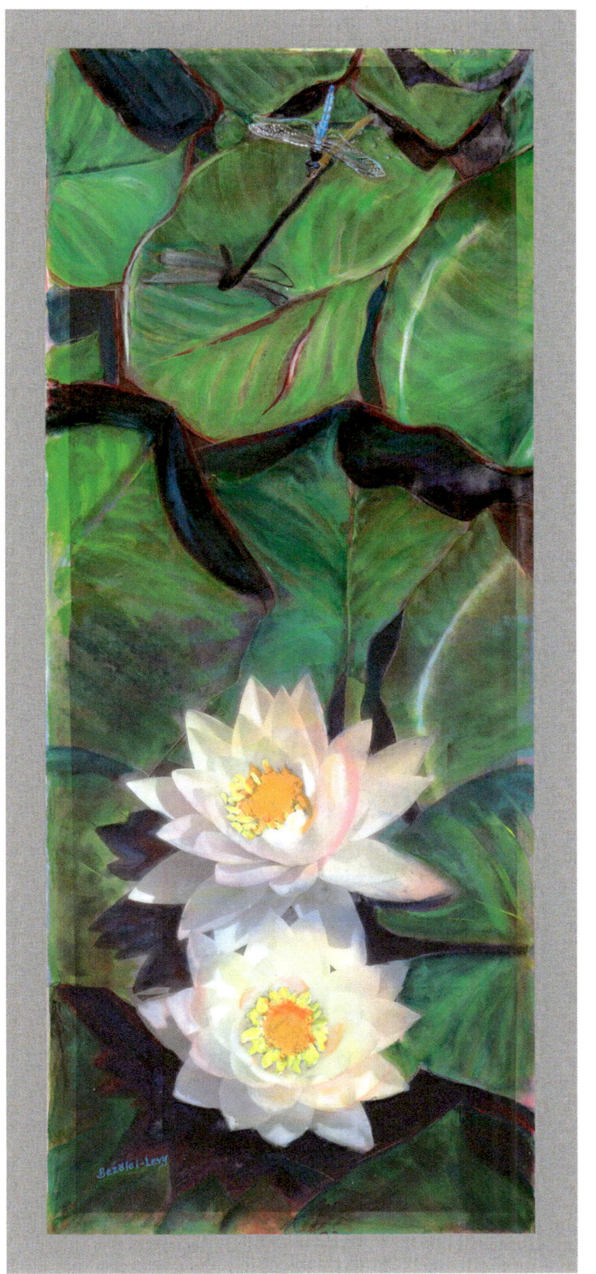

Mill Lake Park, Abbotsford, B.C. (2013) 60 x 26 in.

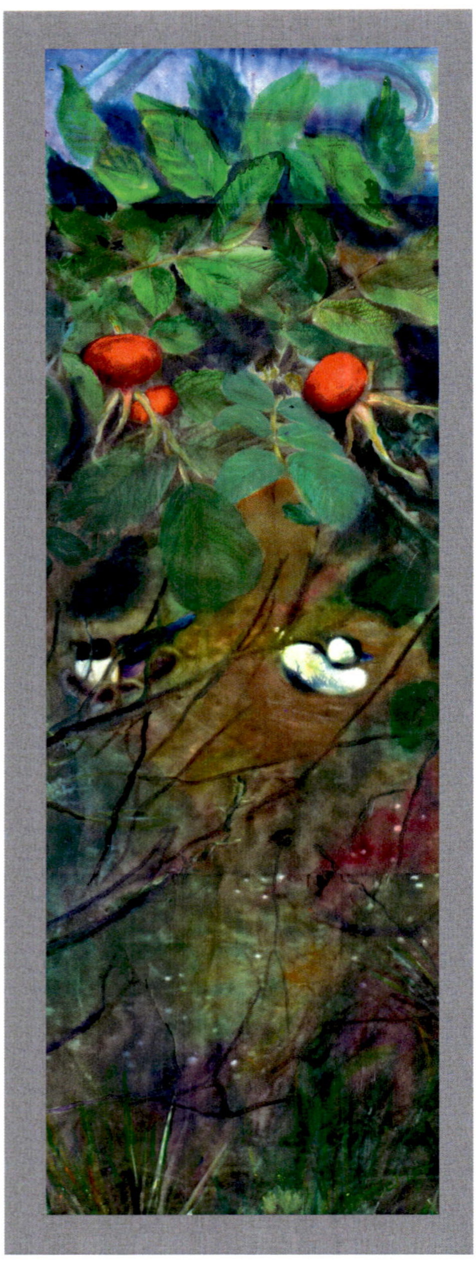

Rosehips and Goldeneyes (2008) 37 x 13 in.

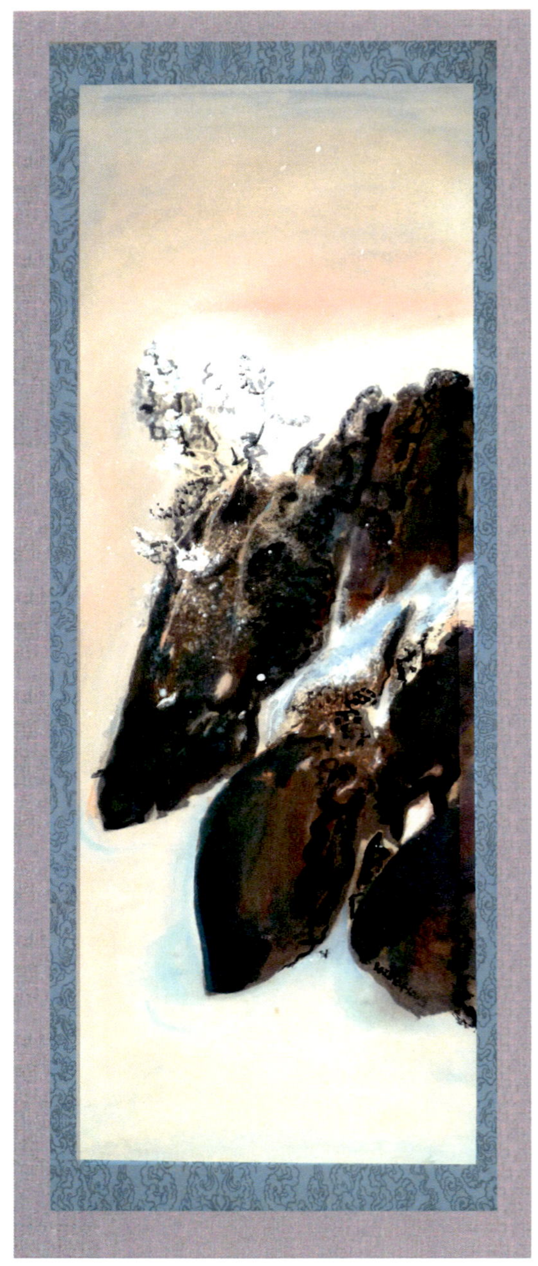

Snowfall, Mt. Rose Ski Area, Sierra Nevada (2004) 48 x 18 in.

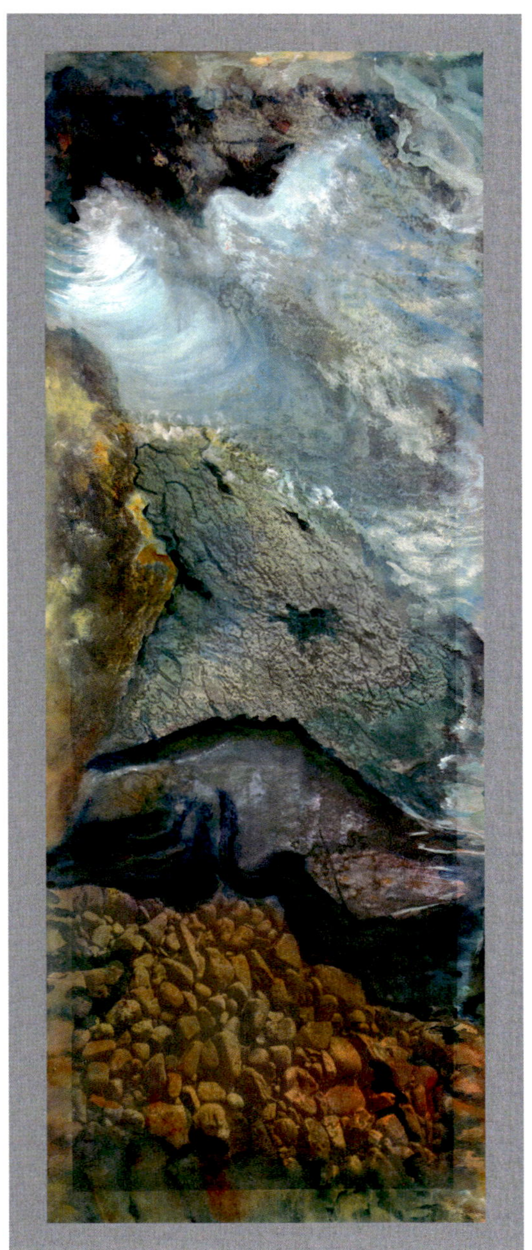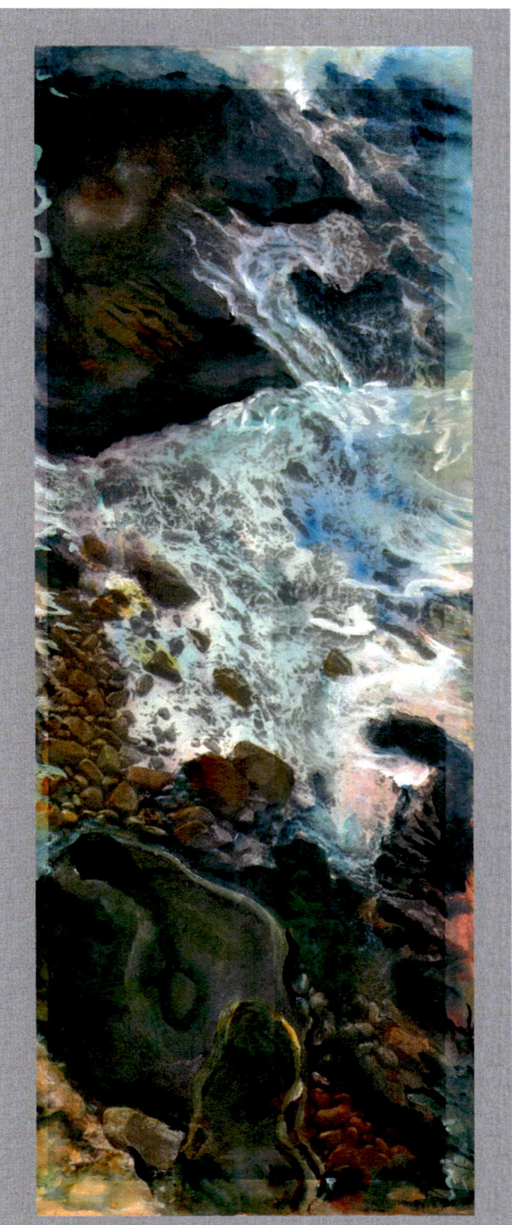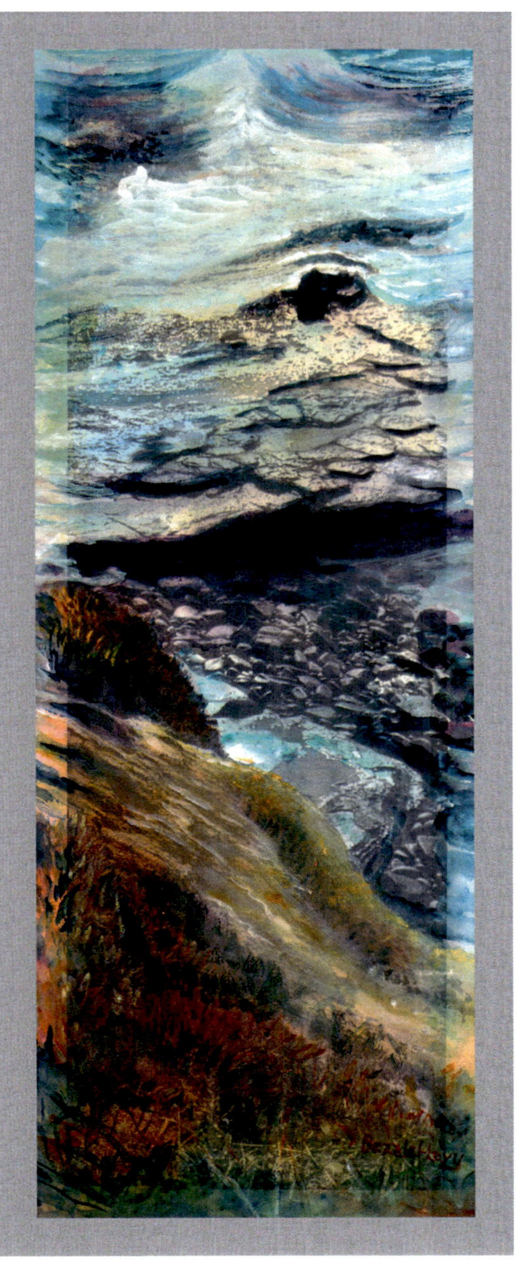

Sunset Cliffs Triptych, Pacific Beach, San Diego (2007) 45 x 14 in. each panel

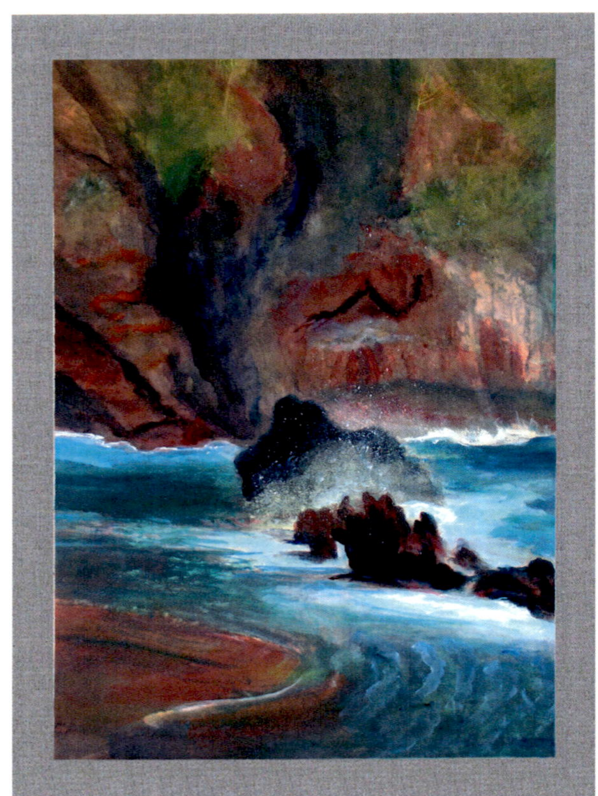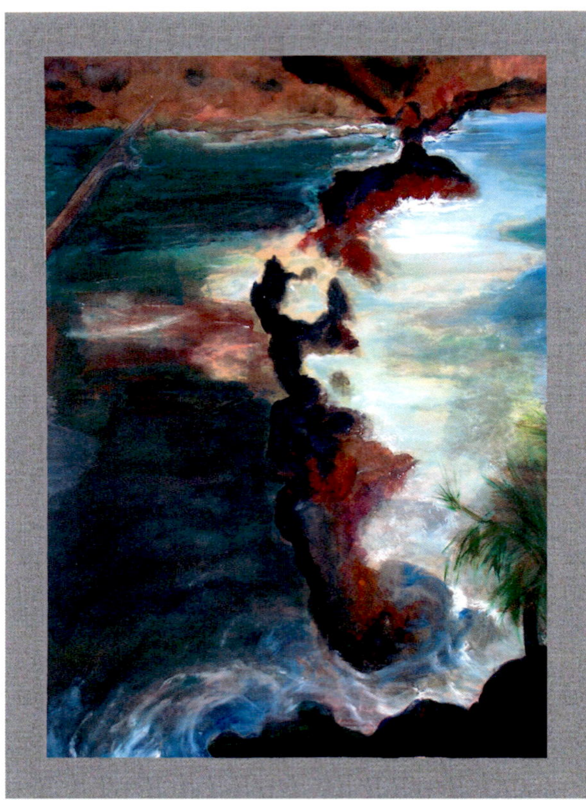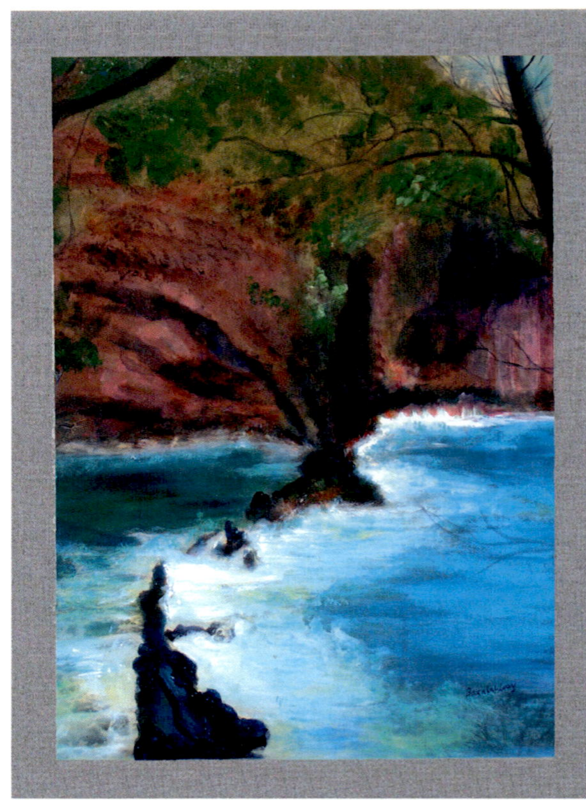

Red Sand Beach Maui (2008) 36 x 24 in. each panel

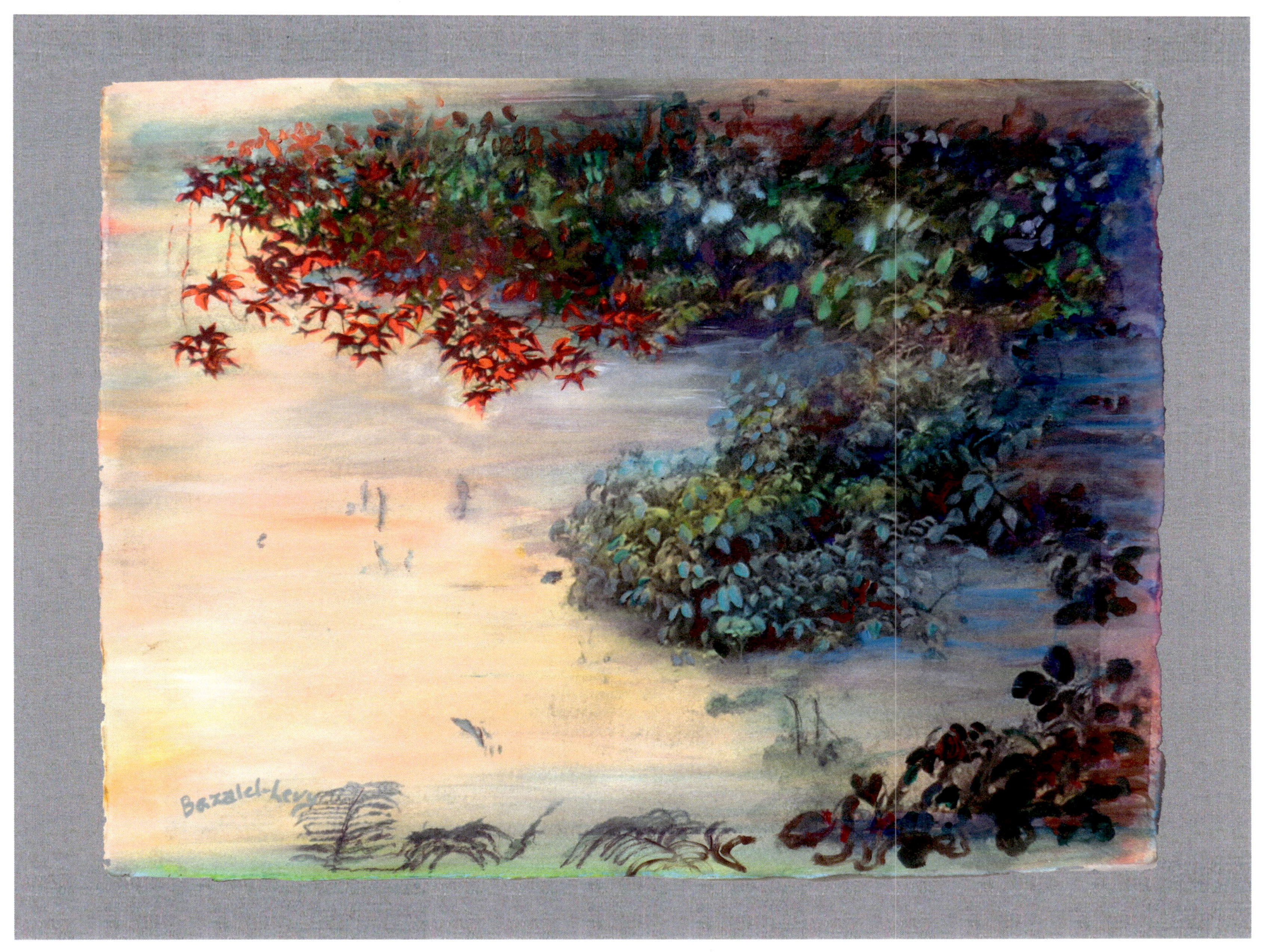

Japanese Garden I, Bellevue Botanical Garden, WA (2016) photography and acrylics on Japanese paper mounted on linen, 21 x 26 in.

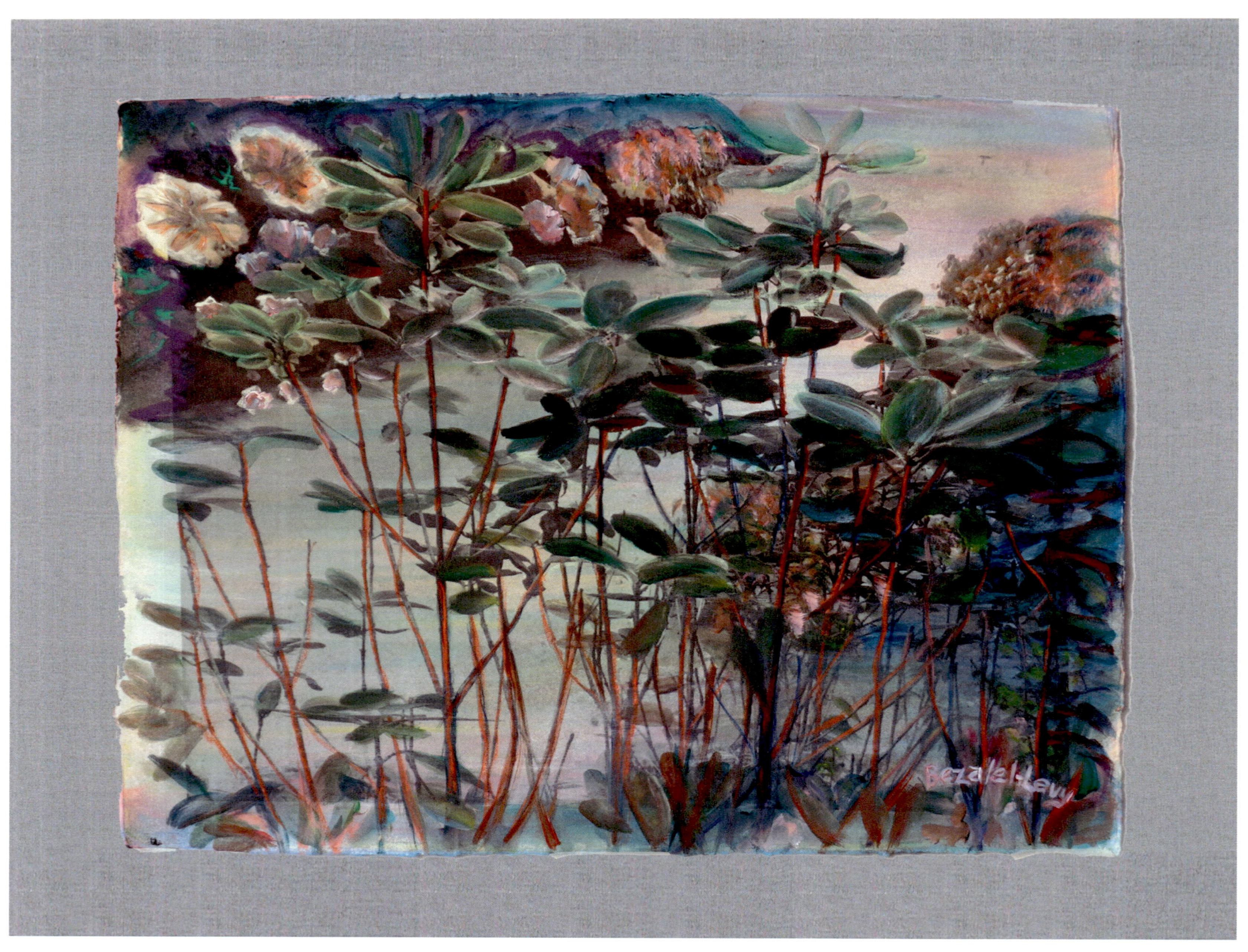

Japanese Garden II (2016) photography and acrylics on Japanese paper mounted on linen, 21 x 26 in.

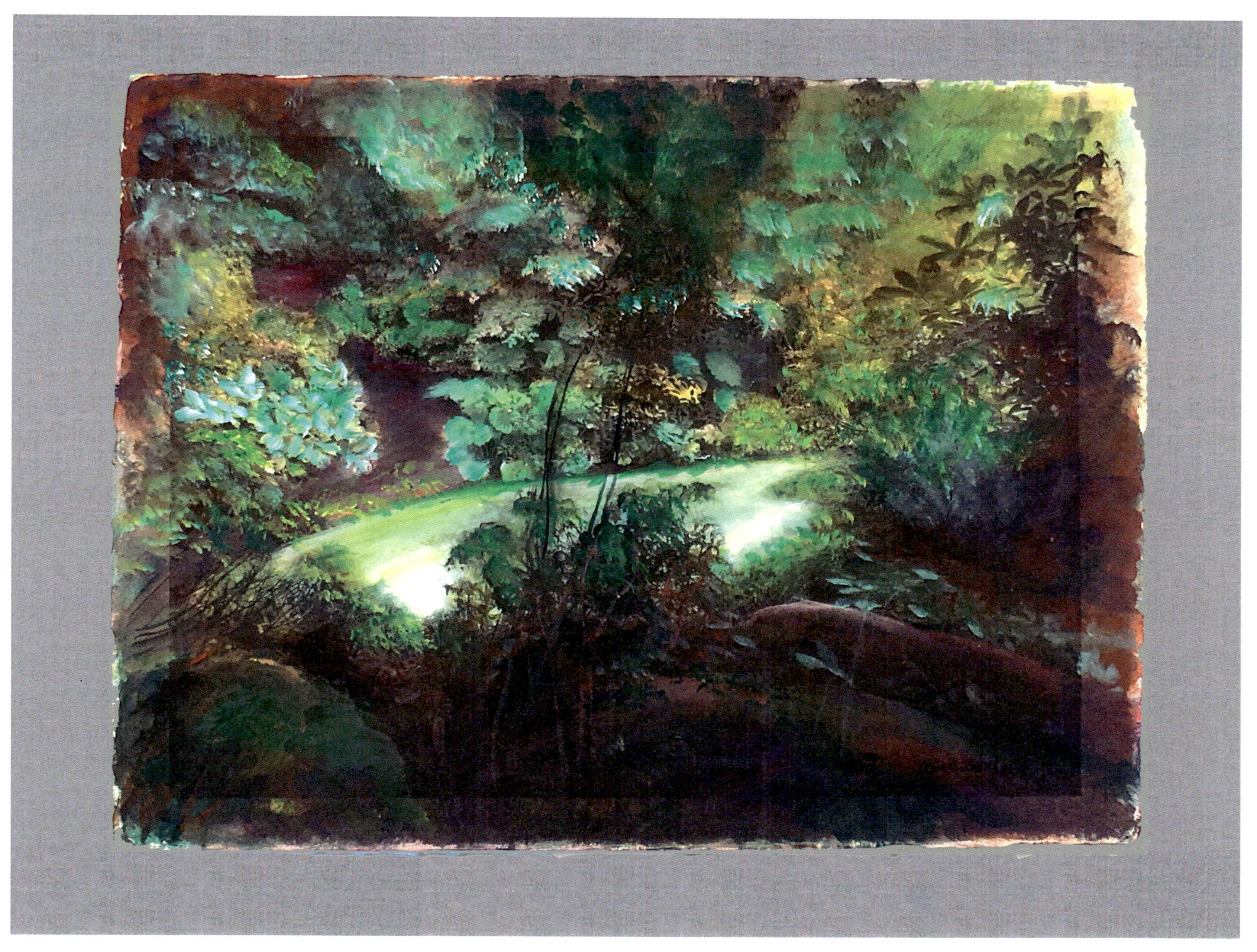

Japanese Garden III (2016) photography and acrylics on Japanese paper mounted on linen, 21 x 26 in.

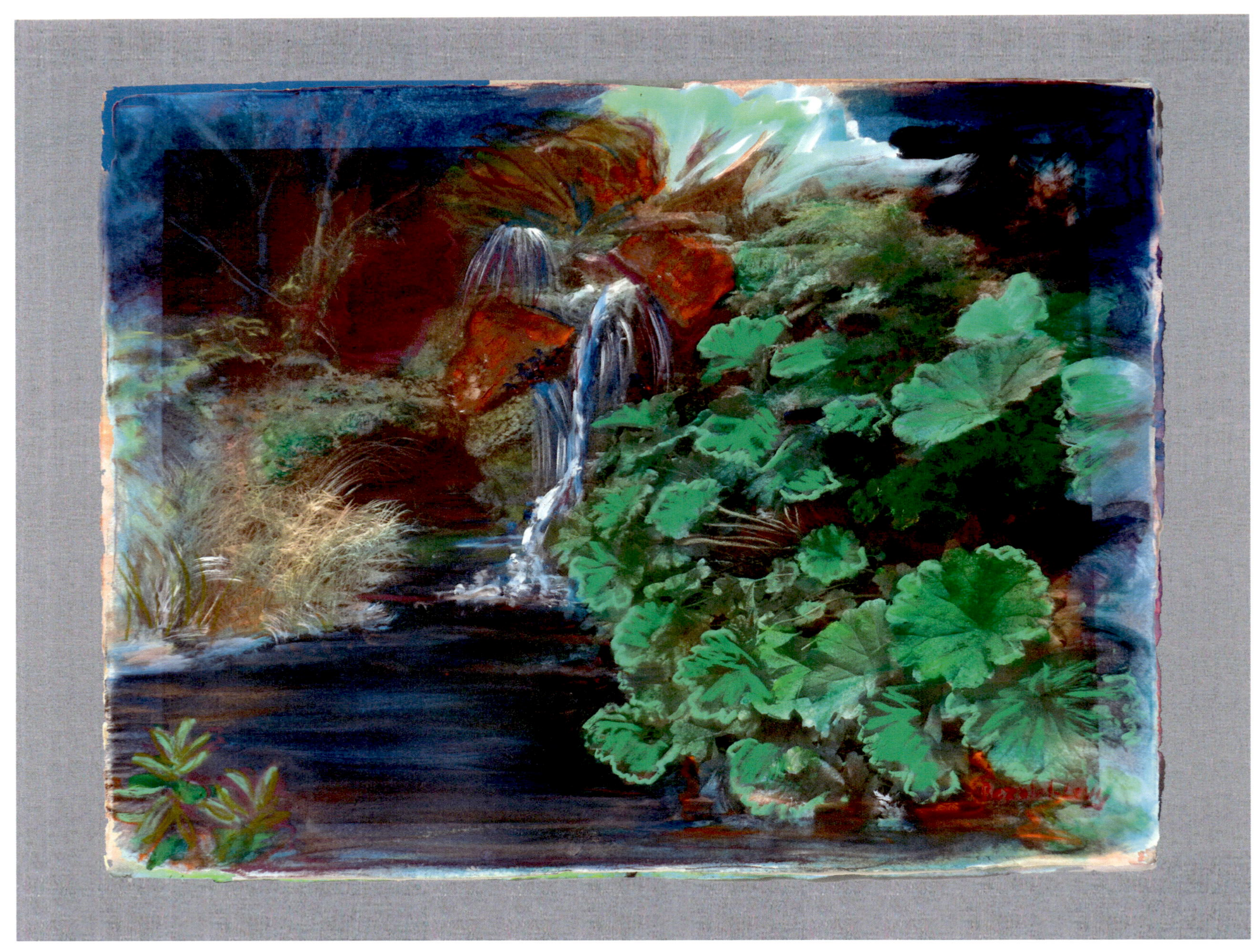

Japanese Garden IV (2016) photography and acrylics on Japanese paper mounted on linen, 21 x 26 in.

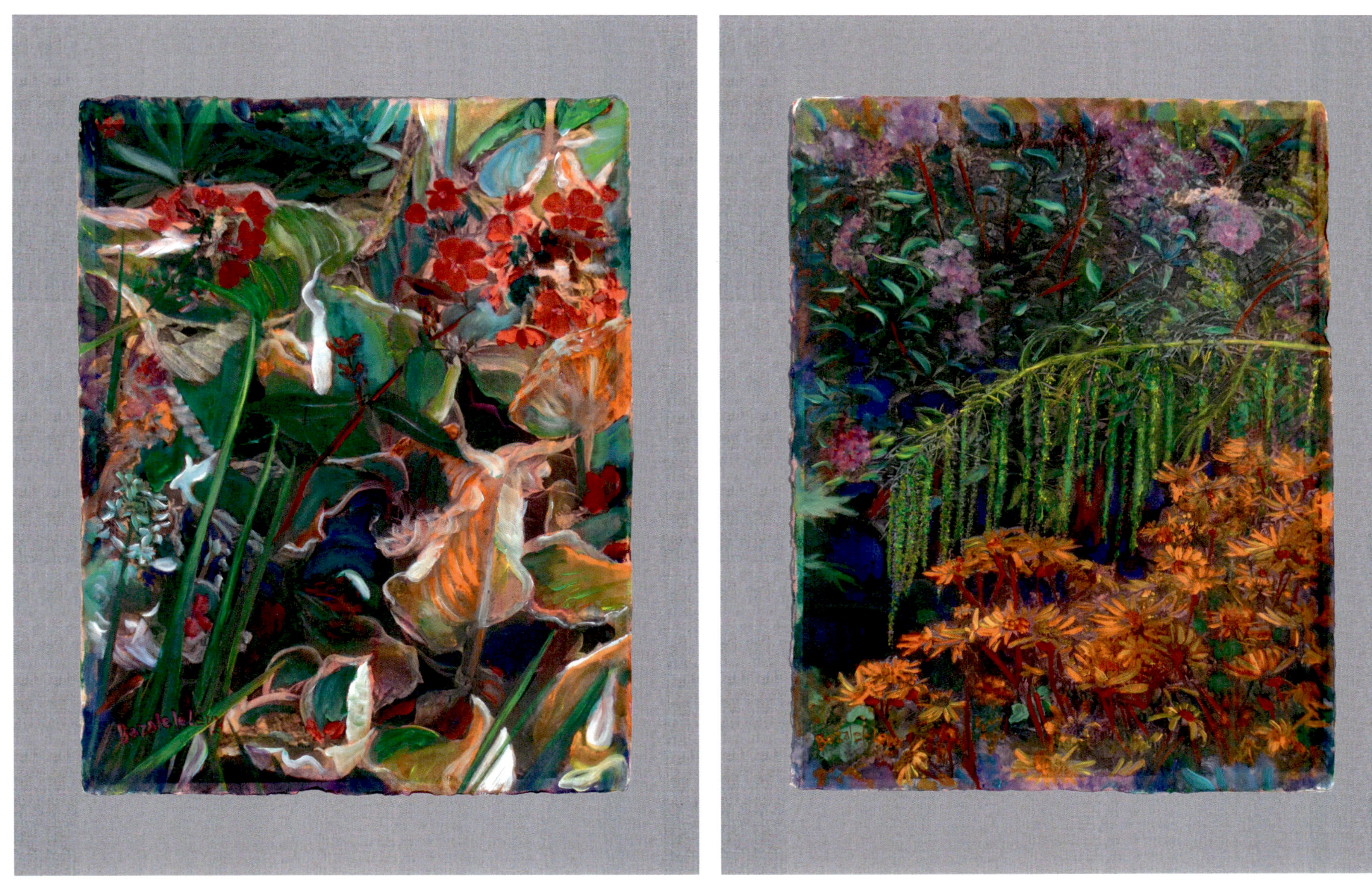

Japanese Garden V & VI (2016) photography and acrylics on Japanese paper mounted on linen, 26 x 21 in.

Desert Scrolls

In January of 2010, we mounted an exhibit in the Bay Area of California and decided to attend the opening and then spend a month as far south as possible, somewhere in Arizona. On the road at night we got lost and, to add to the tension, we had a disagreement about where to spend our first day in Arizona. Finally we compromised. We would head for Palm Springs – much closer. Making some calls from a roadside motel, we were informed that the town directly north of Palm Springs, Desert Hot Springs, was less touristy, less expensive, and actually where most of the springs were located. The next day we pulled up to the Agua Caliente (now renamed the Aqua Soleil) Hotel & Spa. When Yonnah got out to check, as her standards prevail in choice of lodging, I told her to ask them if they needed art. As it turned out, they were beginning a major remodel. As a result, we spent three Januaries in that hotel.

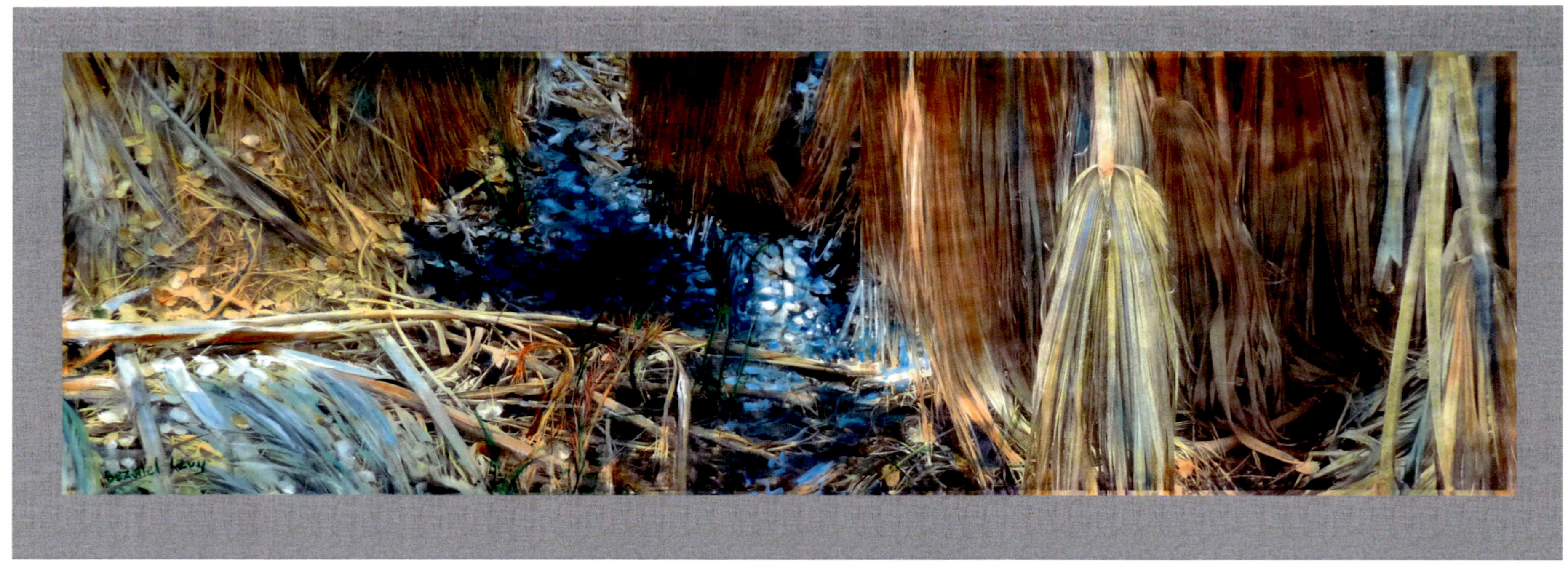

San Andreas Fault Line, Thousand Palms (2010) 27 x 72 in.

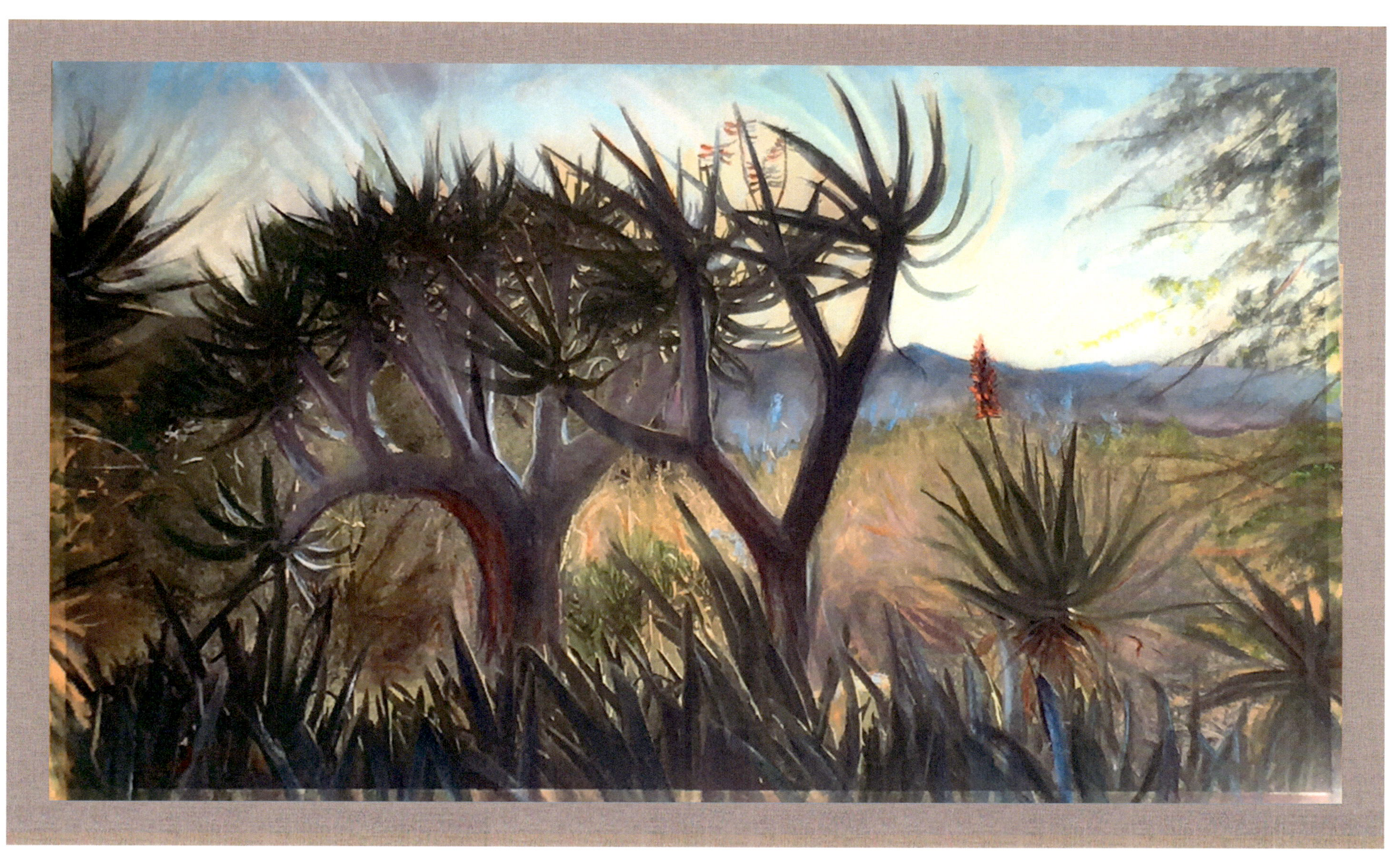

Palm Desert (2010) 24 x 46 in.

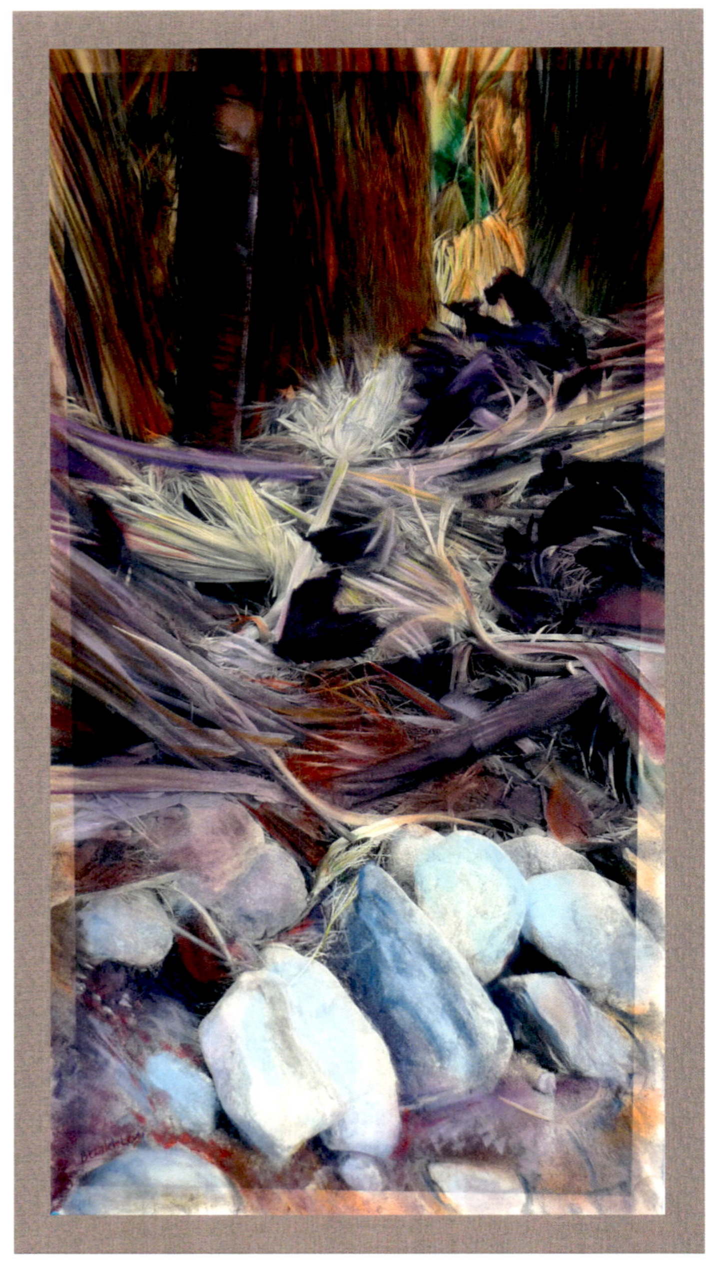

Thousand Palms (2010) 44 x 24 in.

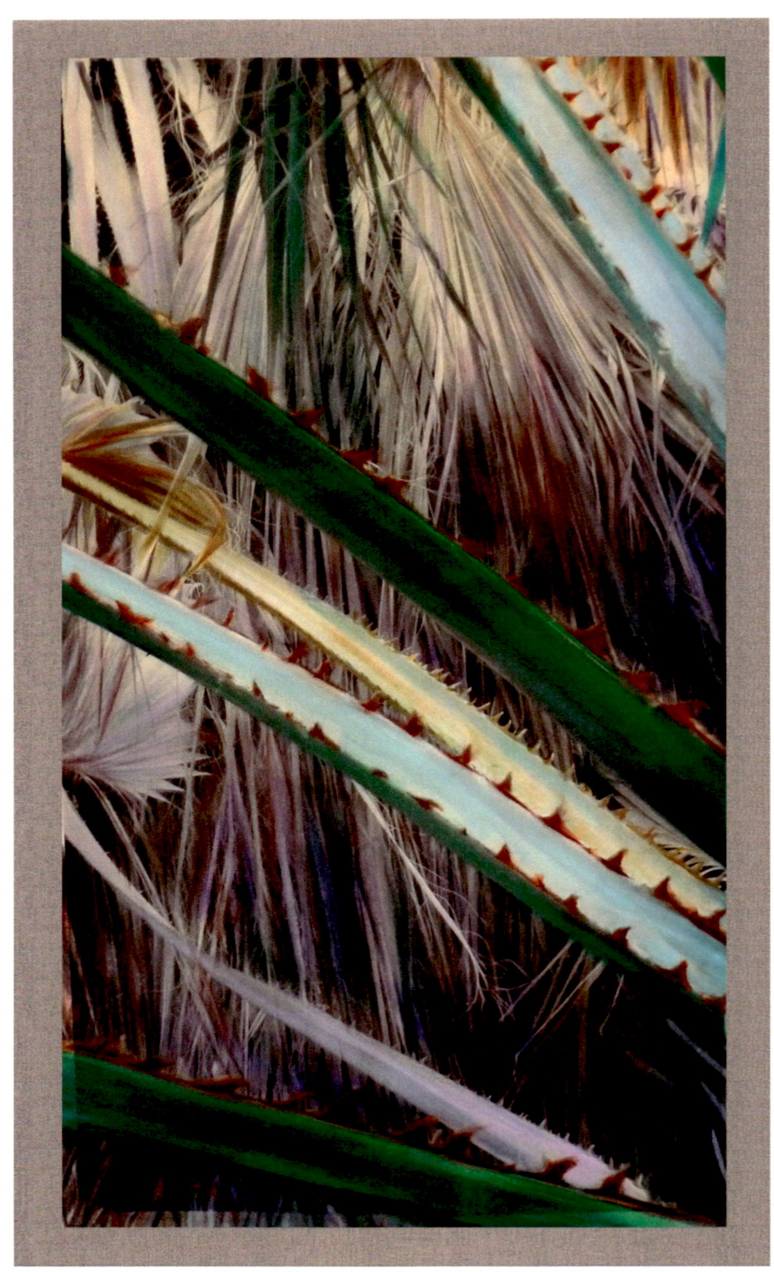

Fronds (2010) 44 x 24 in.

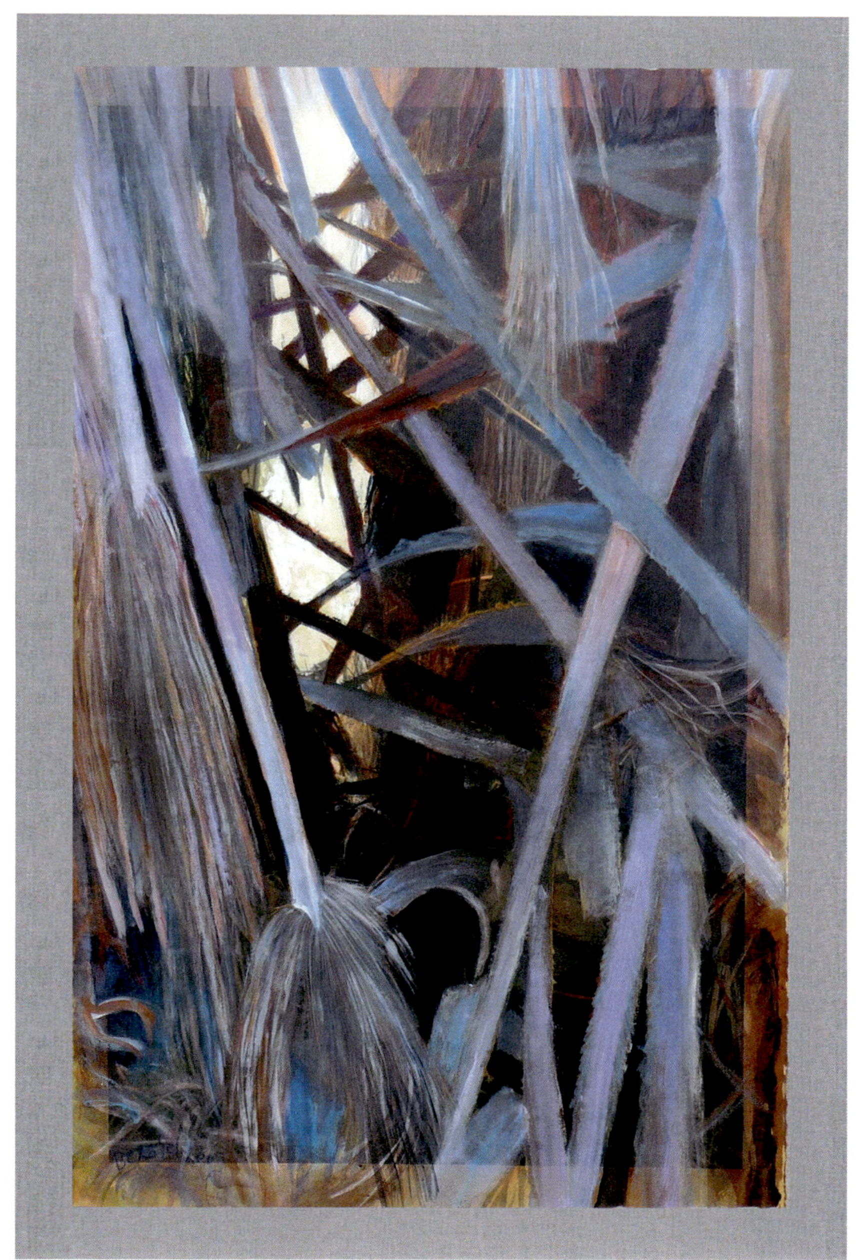 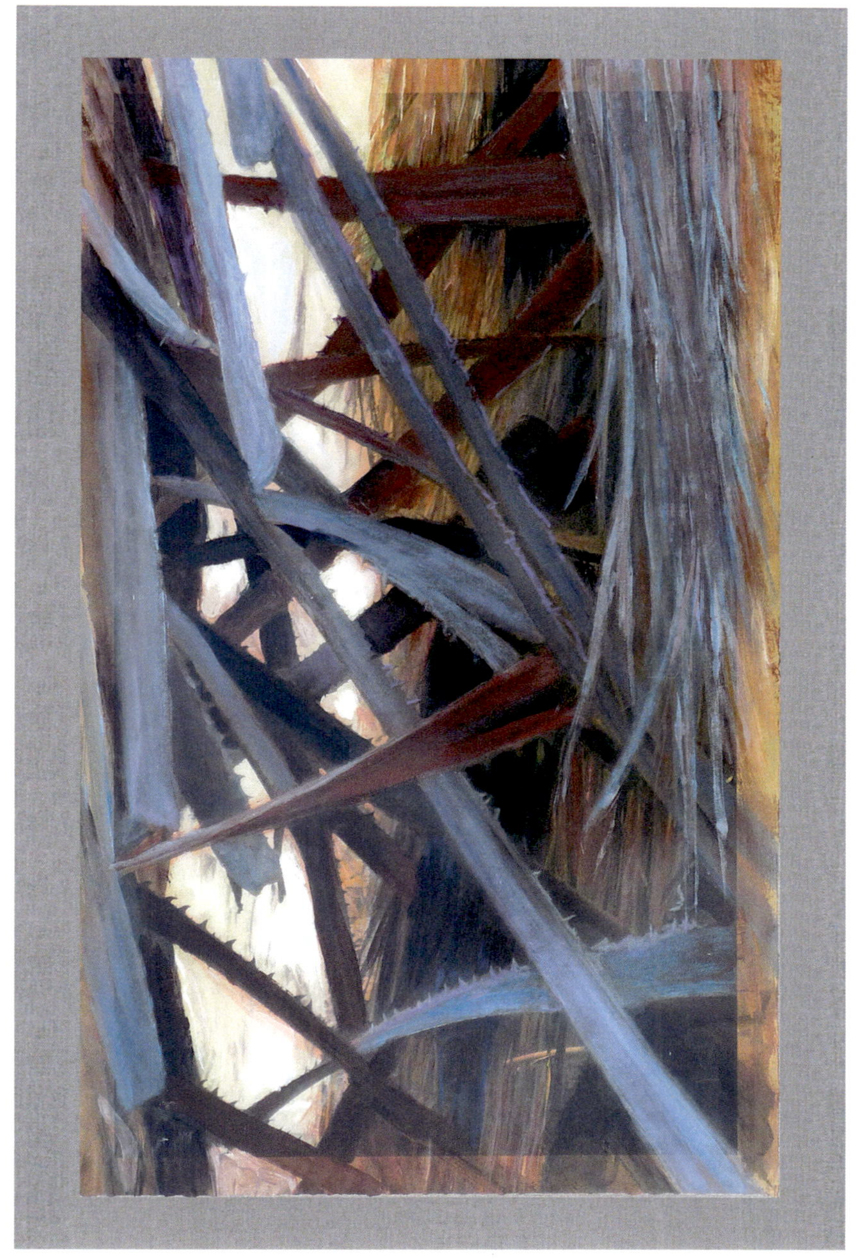

Through the Palms I & II (2010) 35 x 22 in. each

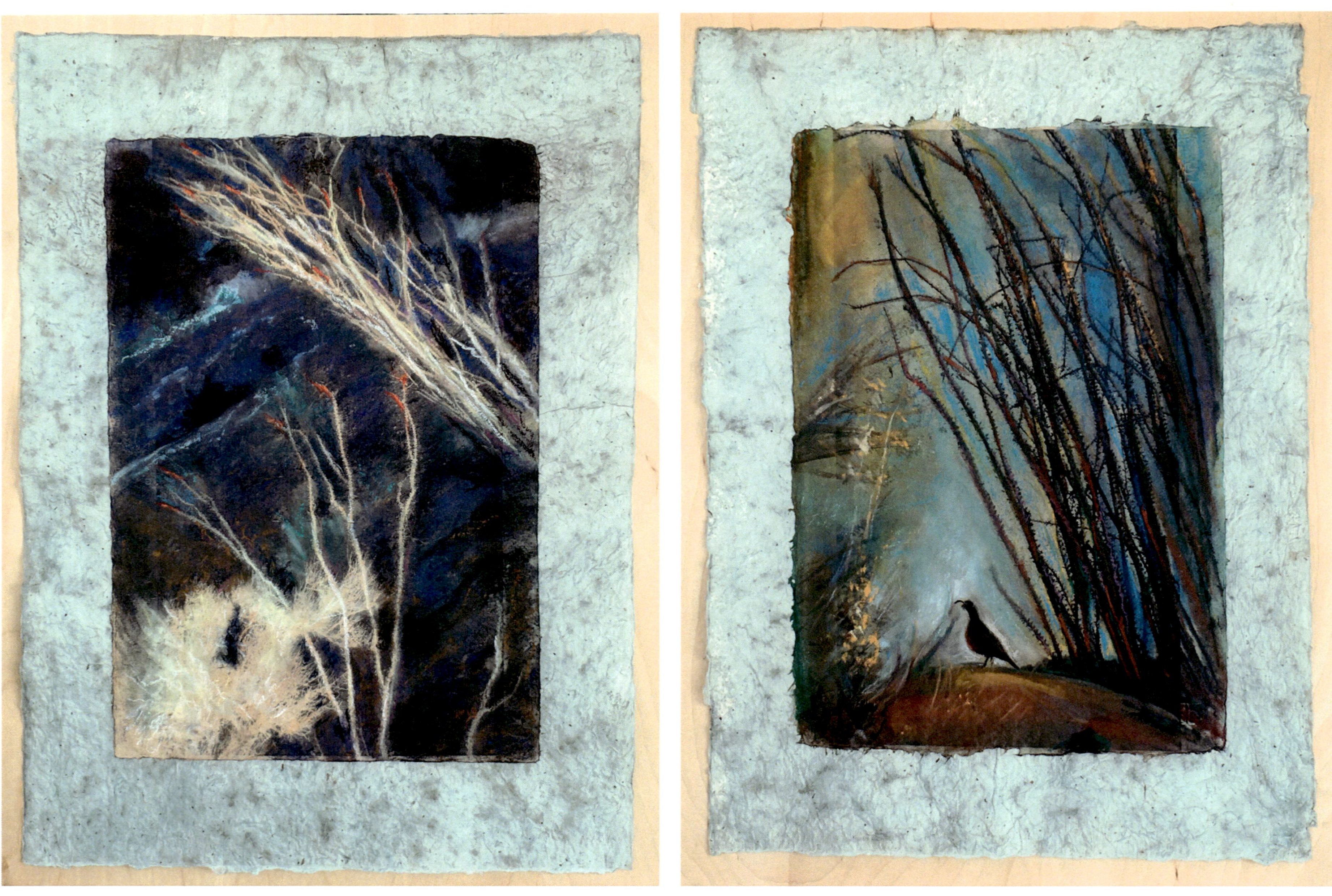

Left: **Ocotillo**   Right: **Quail**   (2010) Both are mixed-media on rice paper mounted on handmade paper, 26 x 19 in.

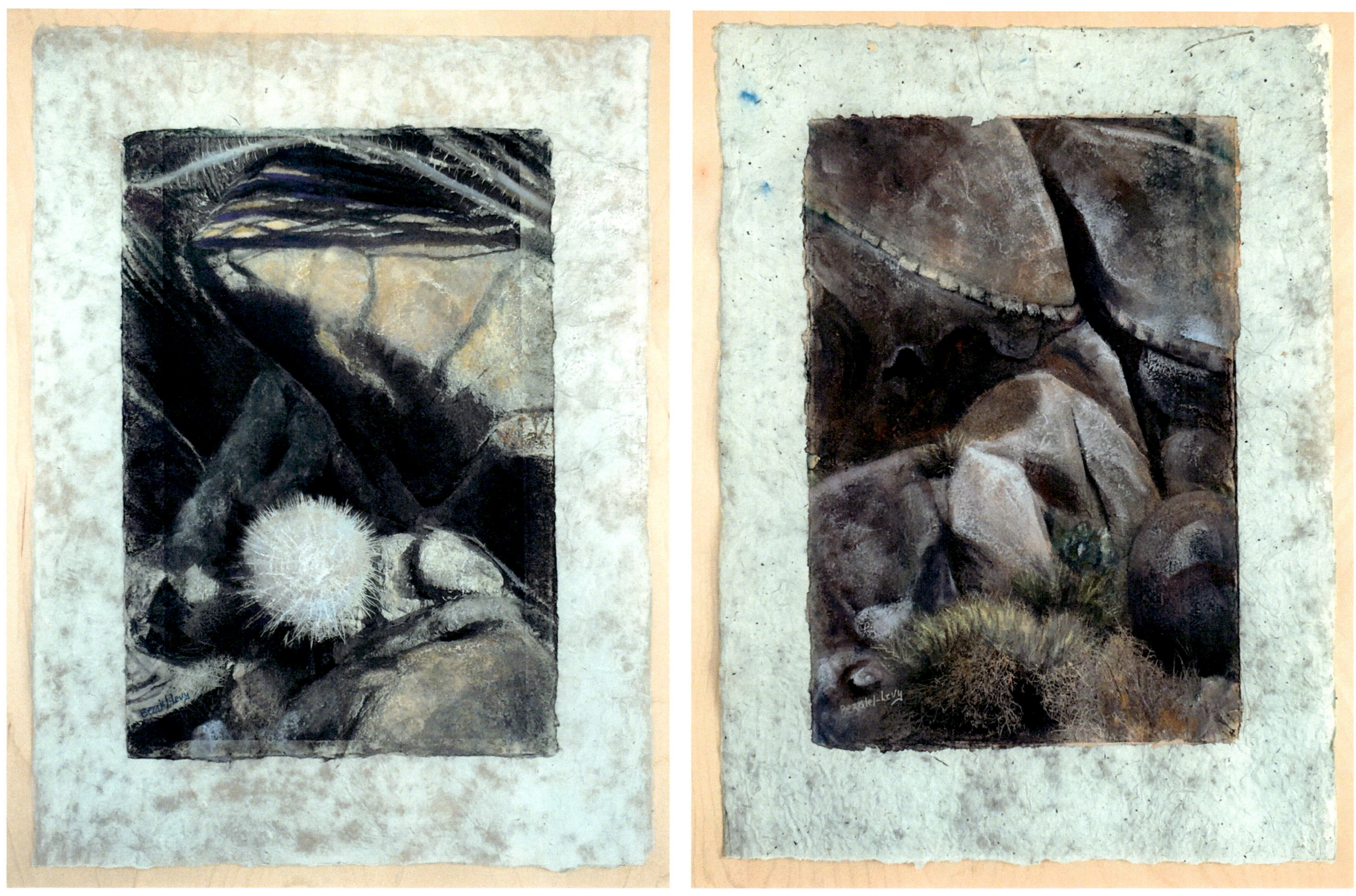

Left: **Barrel Cactus**   Right: **Rock Formation, Joshua Tree Park** (2010)   Both are mixed-media on rice paper mounted on handmade paper, 26 x 19 in.

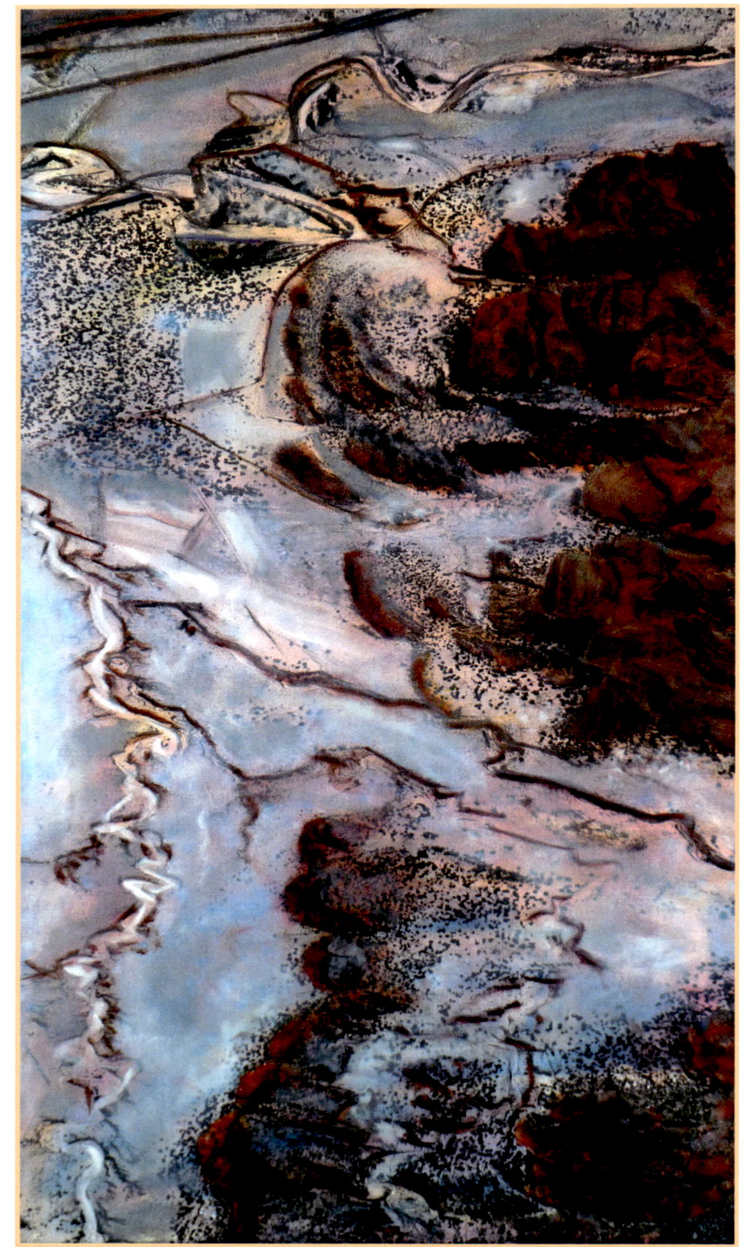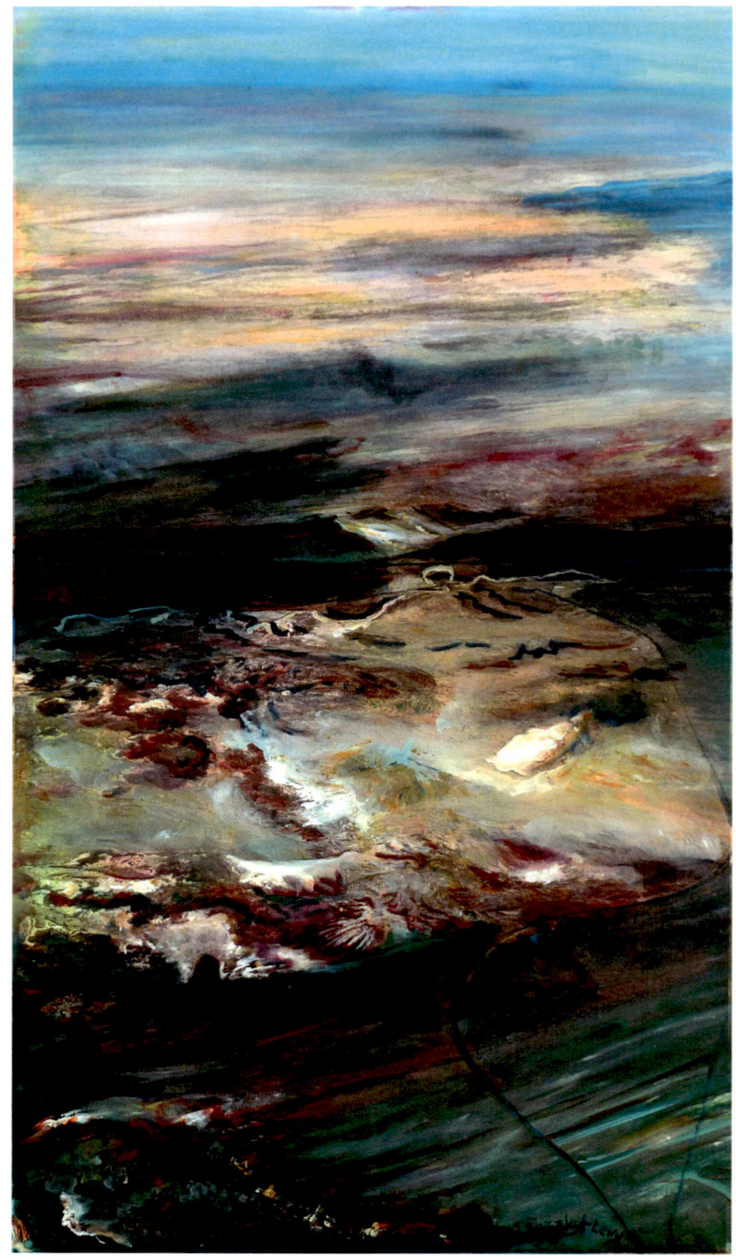

Over Arizona I & II (2011) mixed-media with acrylics on paper mounted on panel, 40 x 22

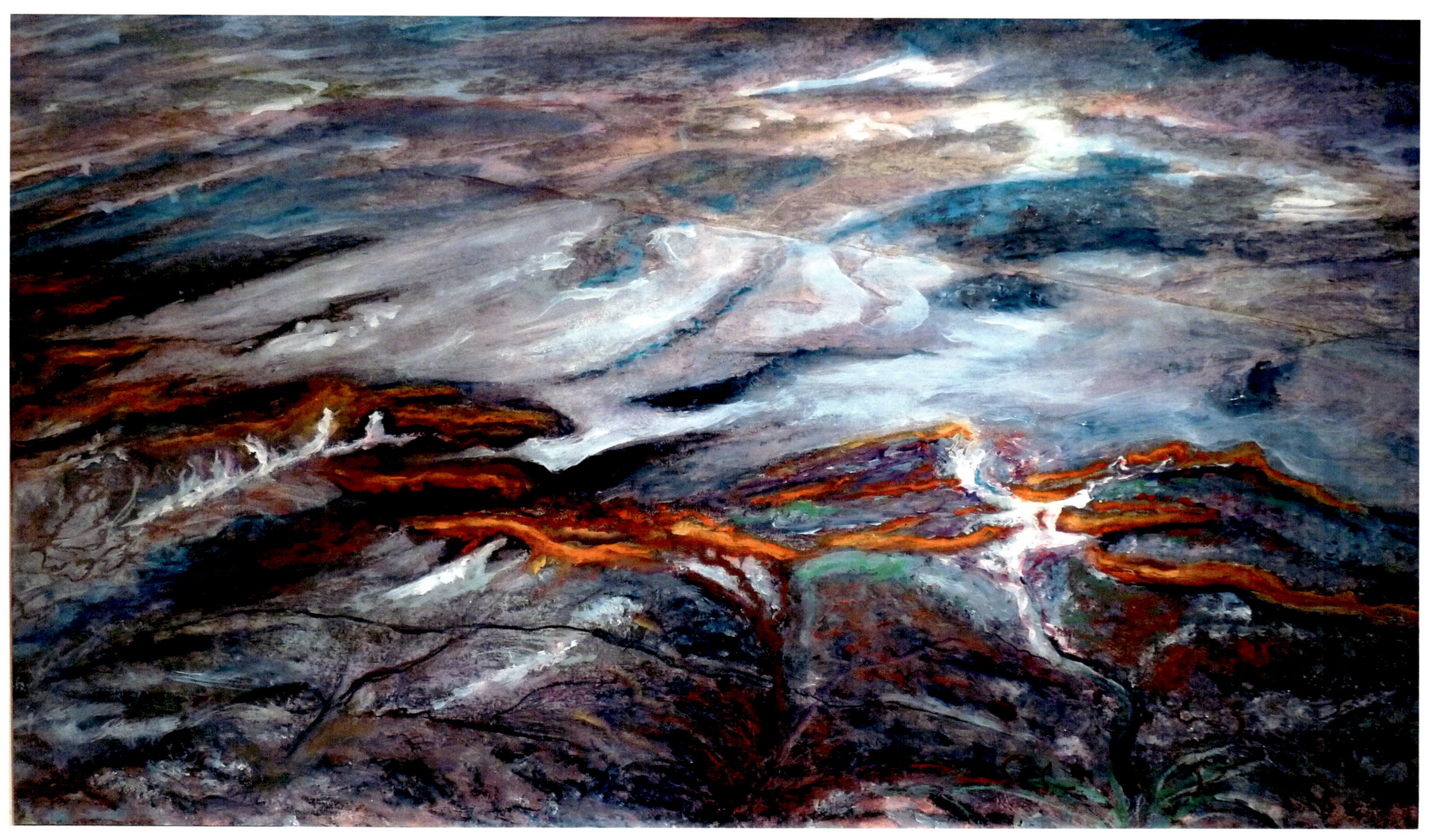

Over Arizona III (2011) mixed-media with acrylics on paper mounted on panel, 22 x 40 in.

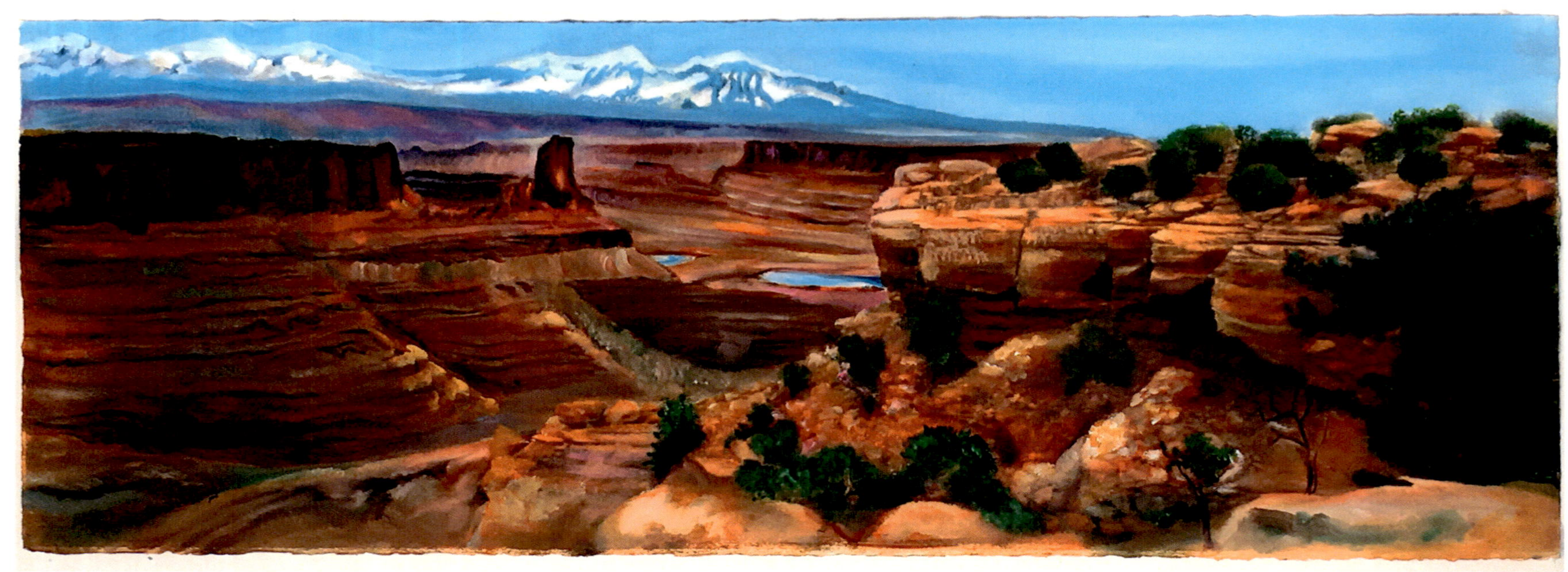

Moab, Utah (2000) mixed-media with water based oils on paper, 11 x 30 in.

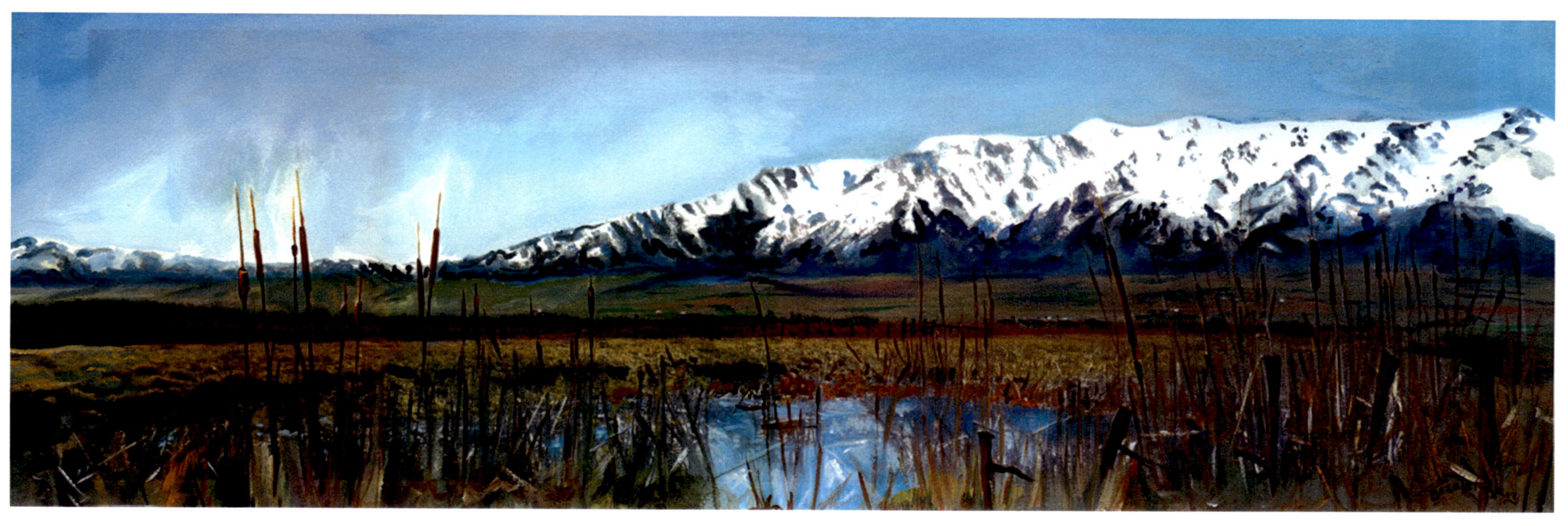

Cattails, Utah (2000) mixed-media with water based oils on paper, 11 x 30 in.

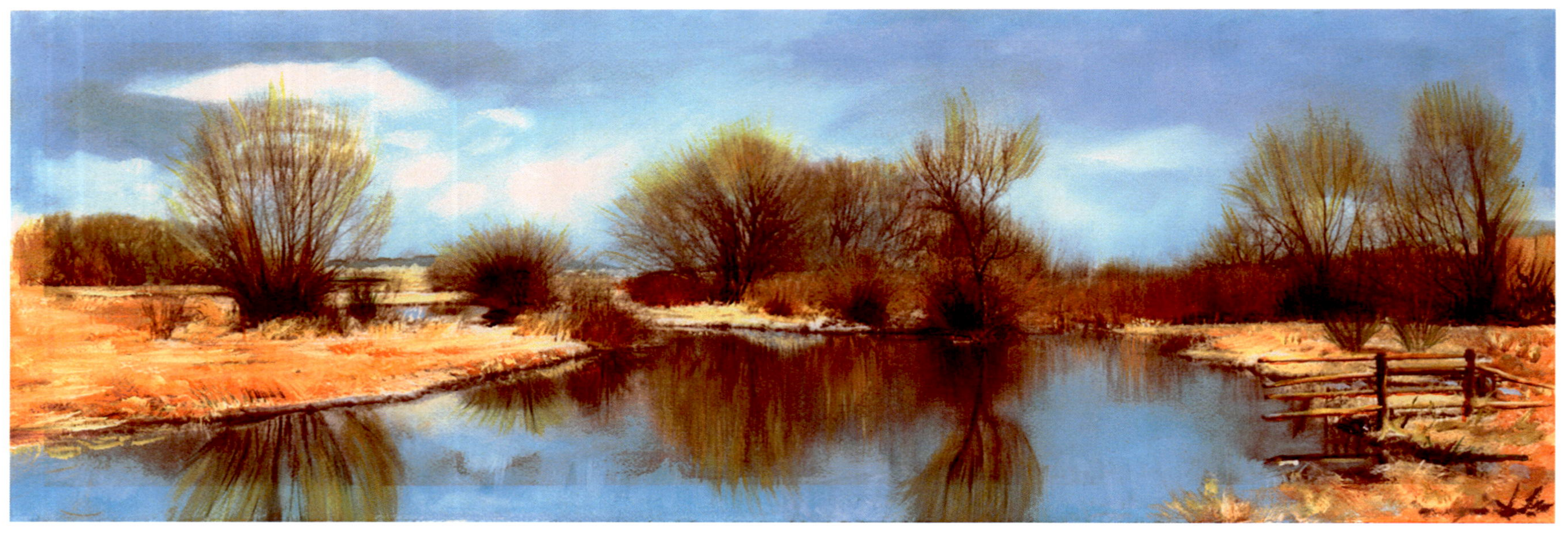

Reflections, Utah (2000) mixed-media with water based oils on paper, 11 x 30 in.

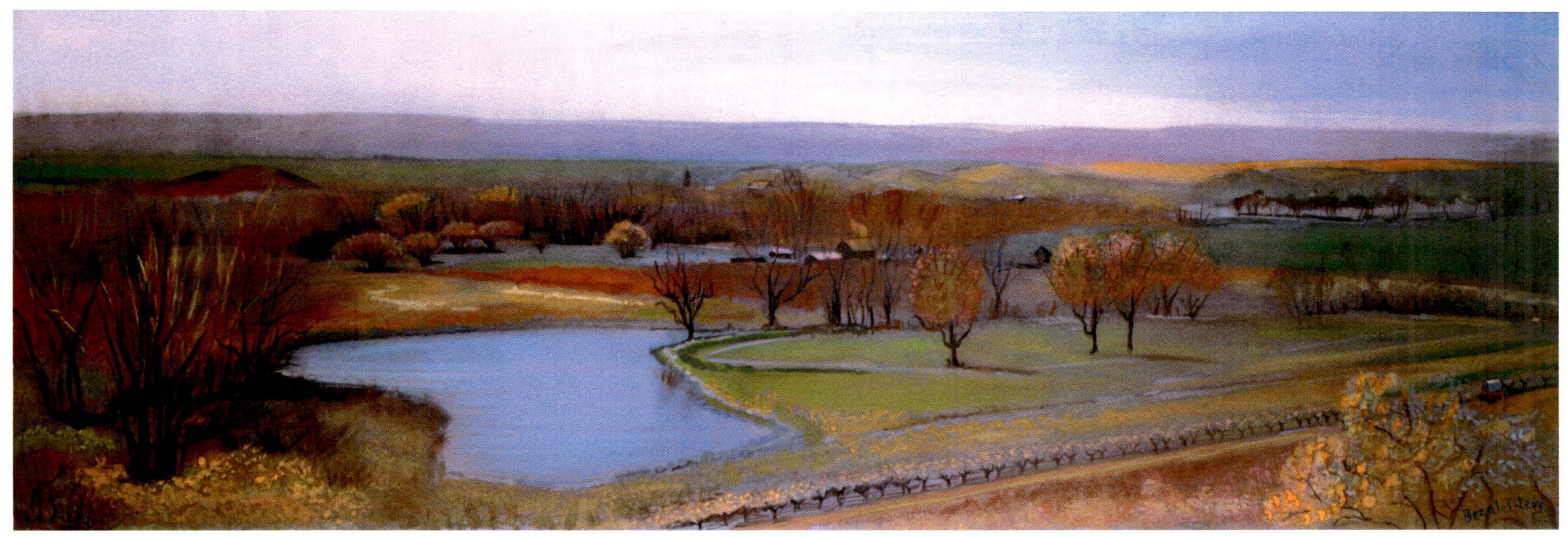

Waiilatpu, Eastern Washington (2002) mixed-media on rice paper, 18 x 48 in.

"The American Board (of Missions) have stations at Kamiah, in the country of the Nes Perces Indians, on the Kooskoos-ke, a branch of the Lewis river; at Willatpoo, on the Walla Walla, near the great bend of the Columbia, and also on the Clear Water river.

- from Hunt's Merchants' Magazine, January, 1842 (article on the Oregon Territory)

Among the first non-native settlers in the Oregon Territory were Marcus and Narcissa Whitman, a medical missionary and his teacher wife. Their mission was both religious and political, that is to convert the Indians and to open the way for settlers. After an outbreak of measles from which the whites recovered but which decimated the Indians, since they had no immunity, Whitman was accused of sorcery and along with Narcissa and twelve others massacred at their station at Waiilatpu. It is now a National Historic Site. Nearby Whitman College is named in honor of the missionaries. However, in 2016 the college changed its mascot from the "Missionaries" to the "Blues," a reference to the Blue Mountain range in Eastern Washington.

Community

If a nation has a soul, or to put it in other terms, a character, then the landscape plays a large part and should be cherished. But the other part of what constitutes a country is community. In our travels, and in our settling down we have been fortunate to find a renewed sense of community, not that it has ever really been lost.

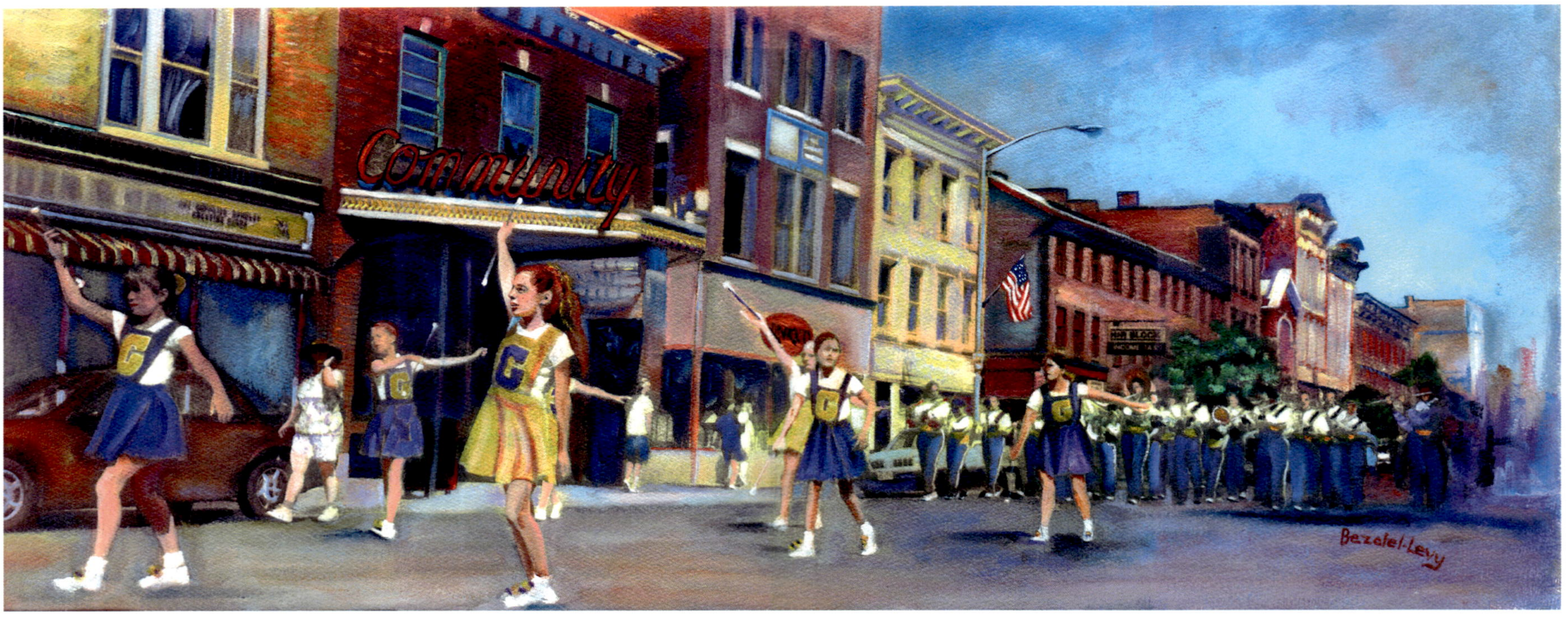

Memorial Day Parade, Catskill, NY (1998) mixed-media with water based oils on paper, 12 x 33 in.

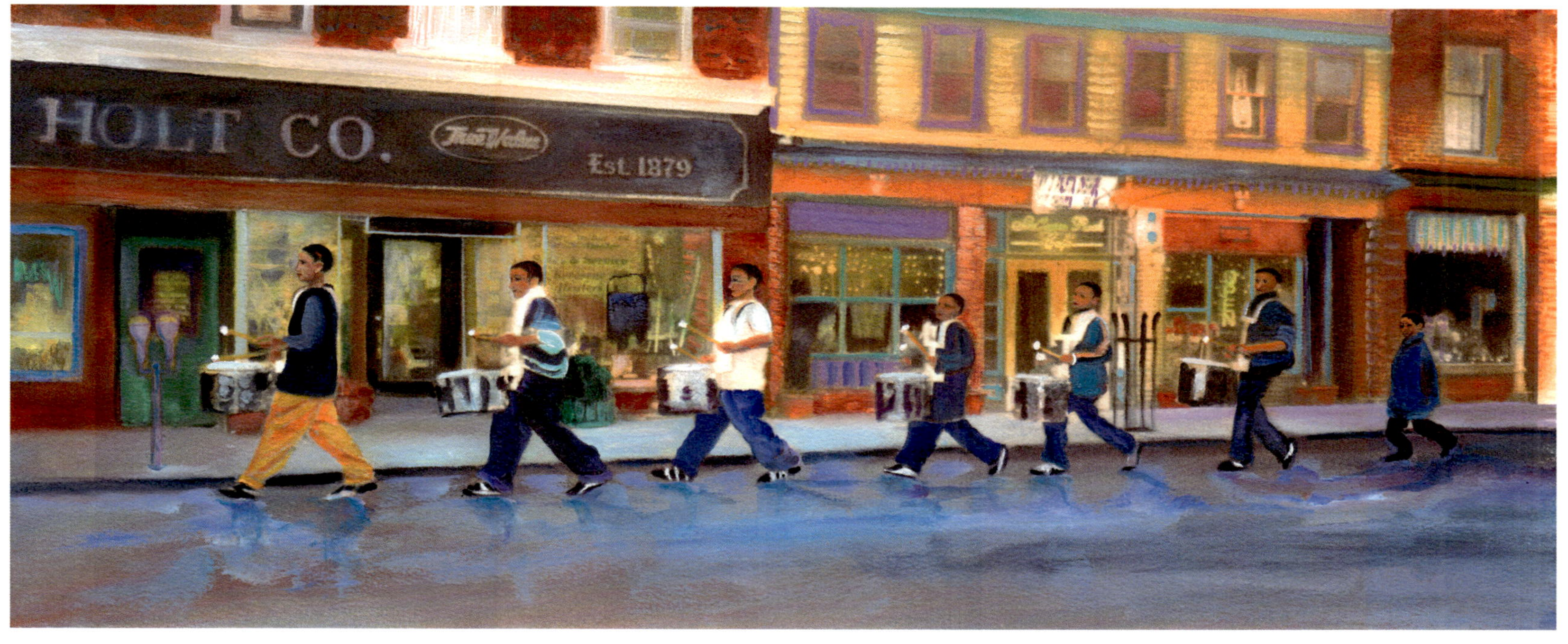

Drummers Practicing for the Parade, Catskill, NY (1998) mixed-media with water based oils on paper, 12 x 26 in.

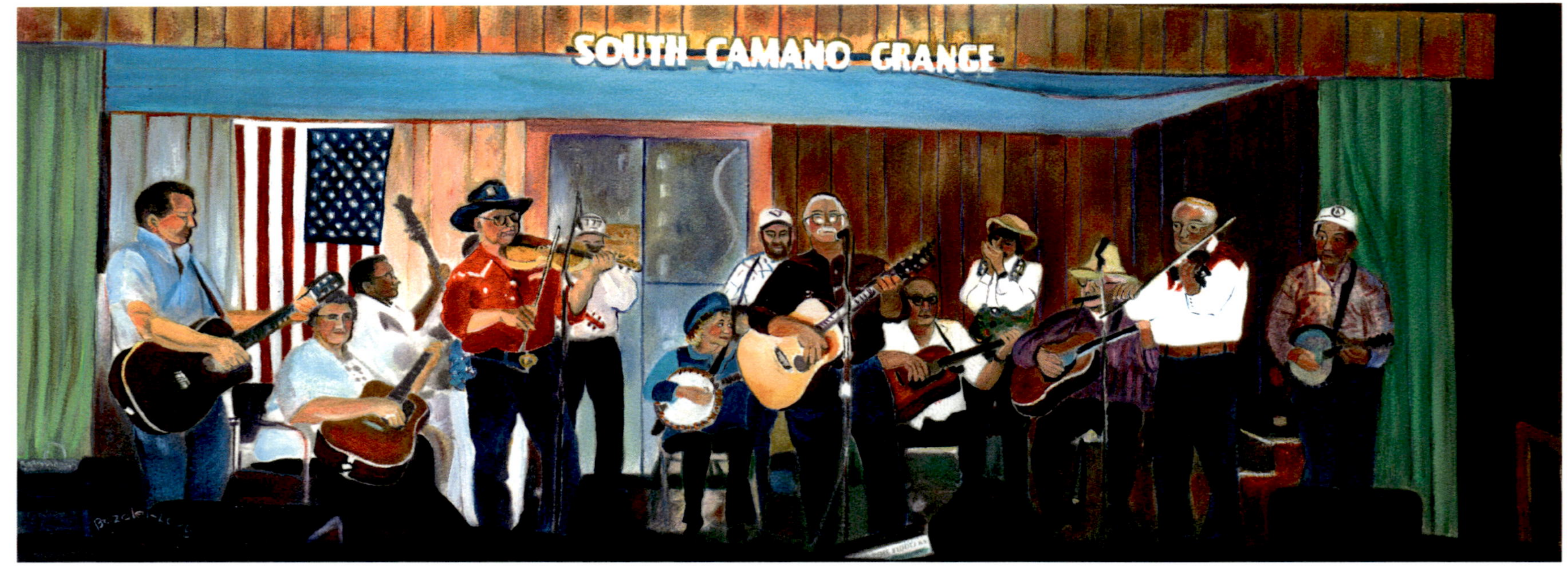

Old Time Fiddlers, Camano Island, WA (2002) mixed-media with water based oils on paper, 12 x 27 in.

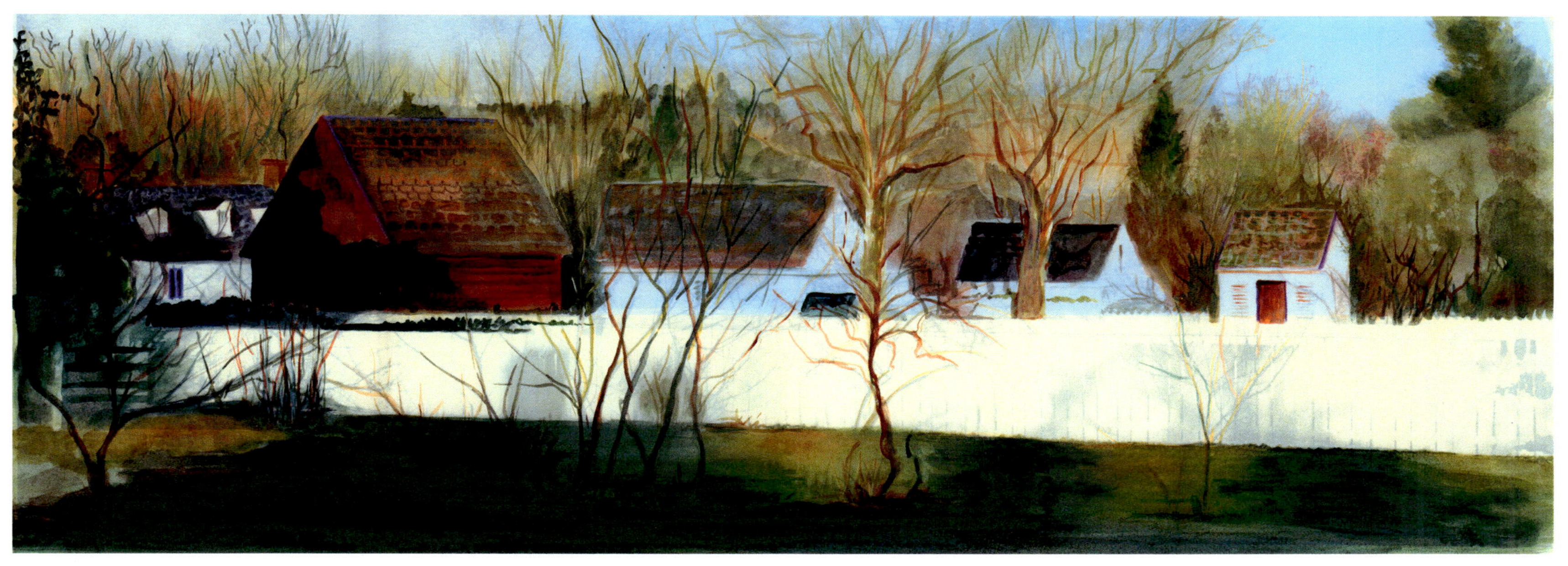

Colonial Williamsburg (2002) photography and acrylics on rice paper, 18 x 48 in.

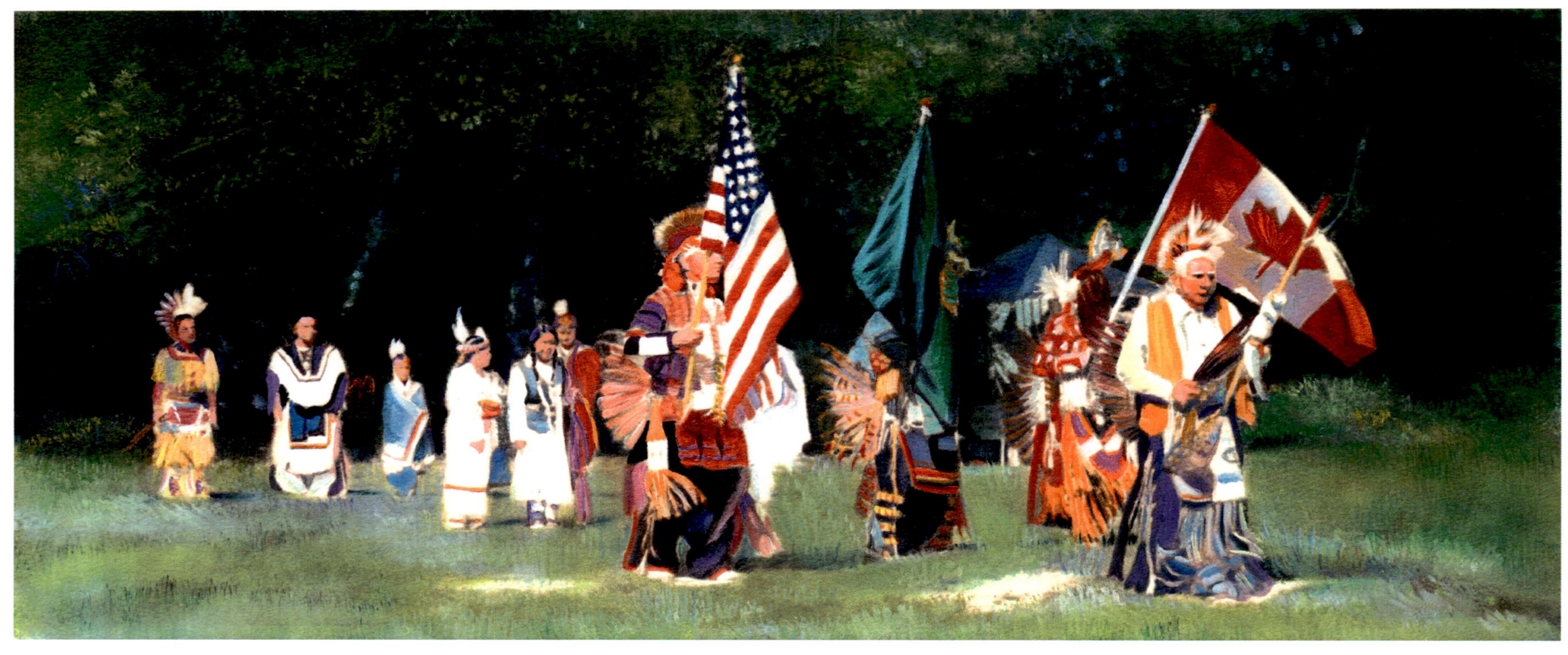

Processional, Festival of the River Powwow (2002) mixed-media with water based oils on paper, 11 x 26 in.

The Festival of the River is an annual festival and powwow hosted by the Stillaguamish tribe in Arlington, WA. The inter-tribal powwow begins with a processional bearing the flags of the United States, Canada, and Washington State. This is followed by a prayer. A traditional "fancy dance" contest is held with the accompaniment of drumming and singing.

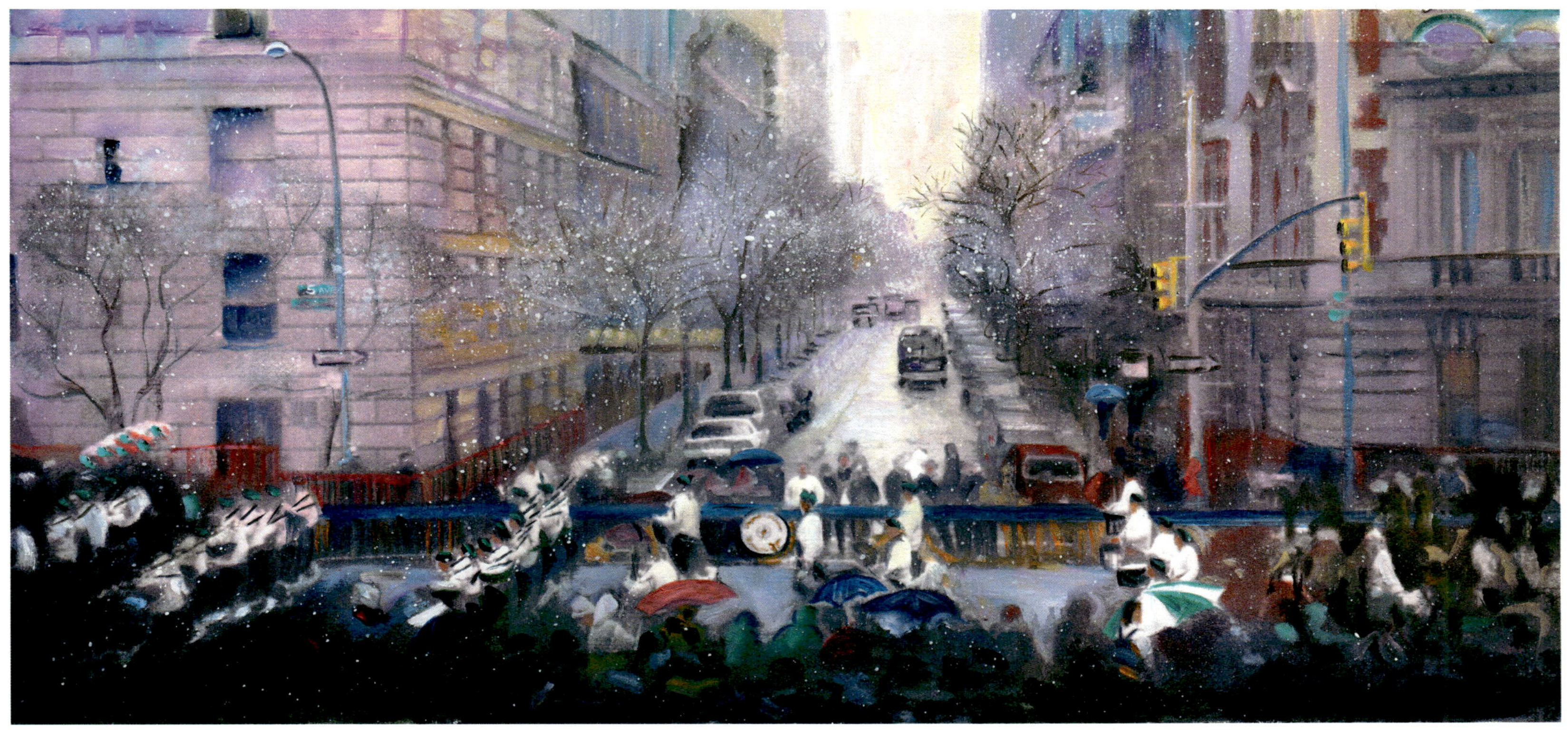

St. Patrick's Day Parade from the Steps of the Metropolitan Museum (2002) mixed-media with water based oils on paper, 11 x 25 in.

Merely six months after 9/11, the Fire Department of New York's Emerald Society Pipes and Drums marches up Fifth Avenue.

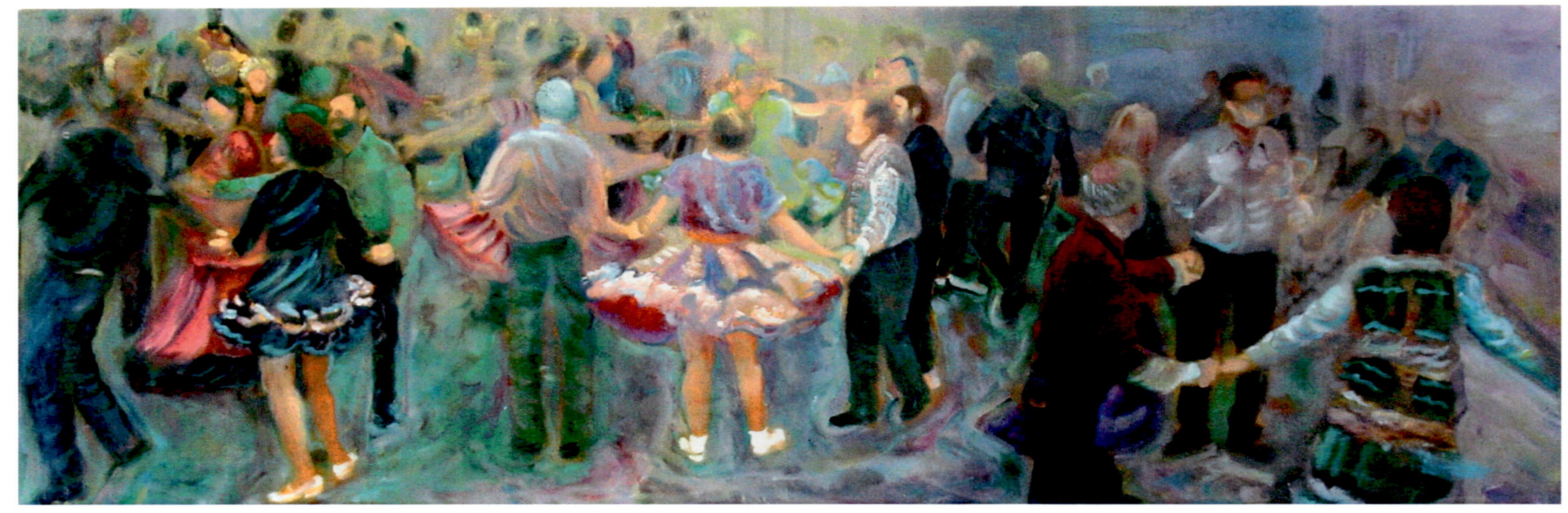

Square Dance (2007) mixed media with encaustics on paper mounted on board, 15 x44 in.

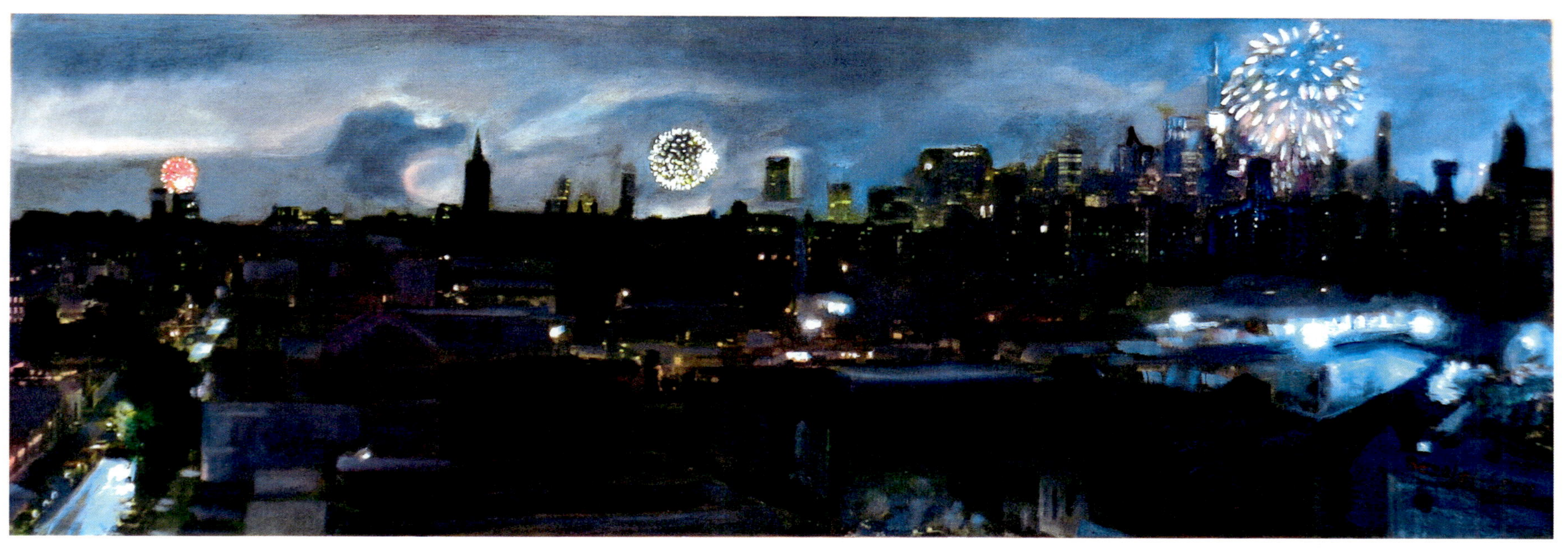

4th of July Fireworks over Manhattan (2016) mixed media with acrylics on linen, 15 x 43 in.

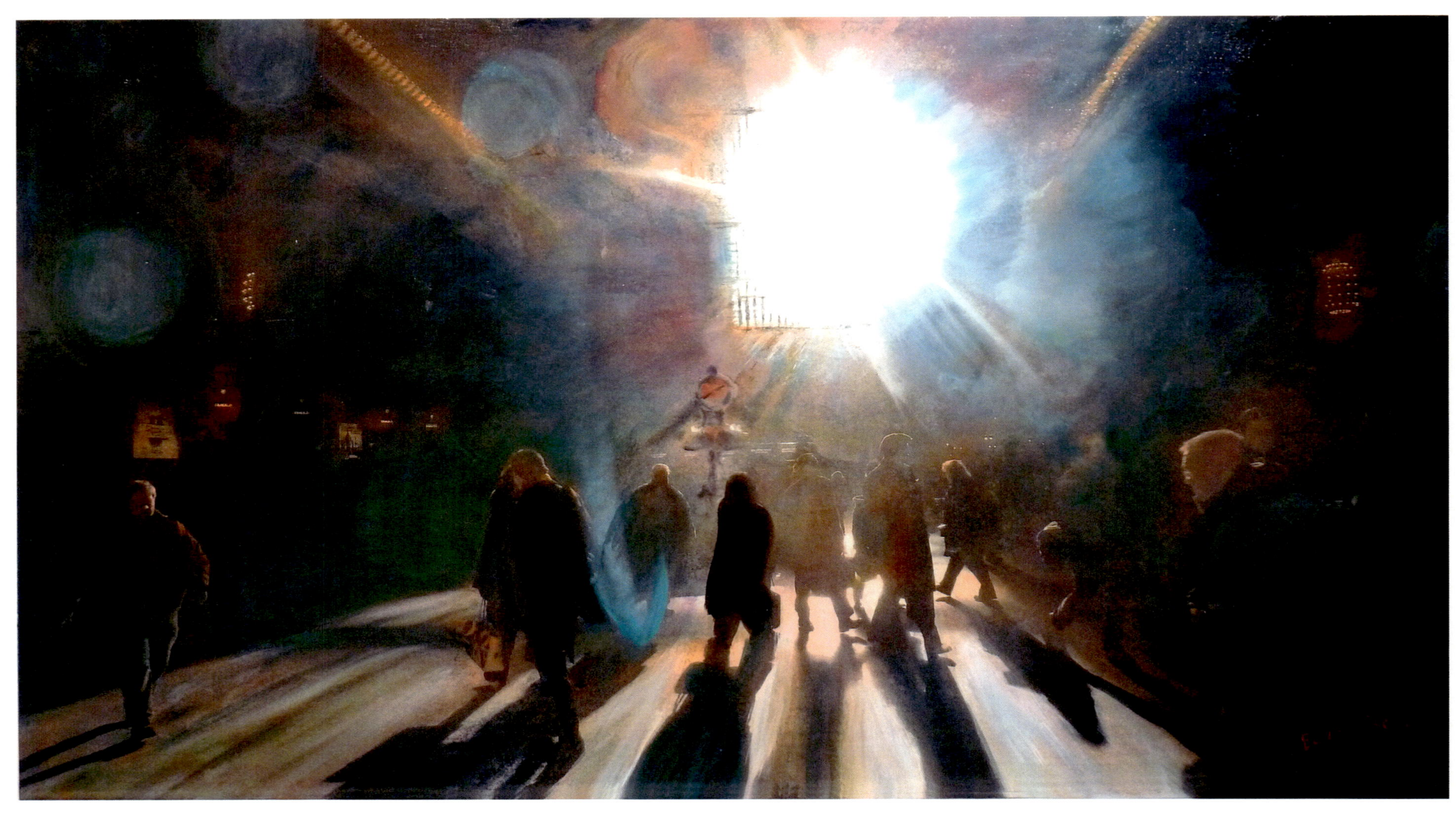

Grand Central Station, 8:11 a.m. (2011) mixed-media with acrylics on paper mounted birch, 22 x 39 in.

Gulf Scrolls

We welcomed the new millennium and the next few new years from Aripeka, Florida where Chaim's sister had bought a house with a dock at the mouth of Hammock Creek on the Gulf of Mexico. Aripeka is a tiny village with a general store and a post office, a bridge where fishermen line up every day and pelicans congregate on the other side. While in Florida we visited the Weeki Wachee River, the Homosassa River, and the Corkscrew Swamp Sanctuary, all wildlife and bird preserves.

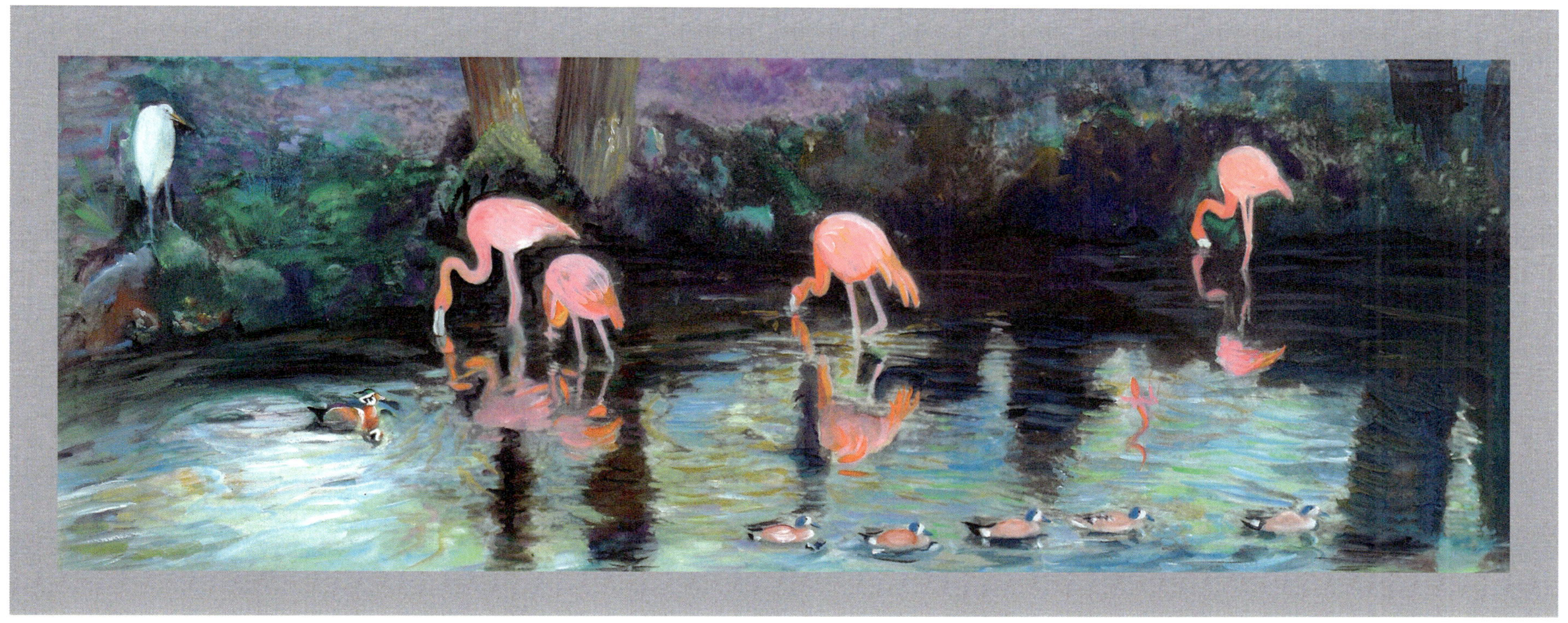

Homosassa I (2002) 24 x 56 in. photography and acrylics on rice paper mounted on linen

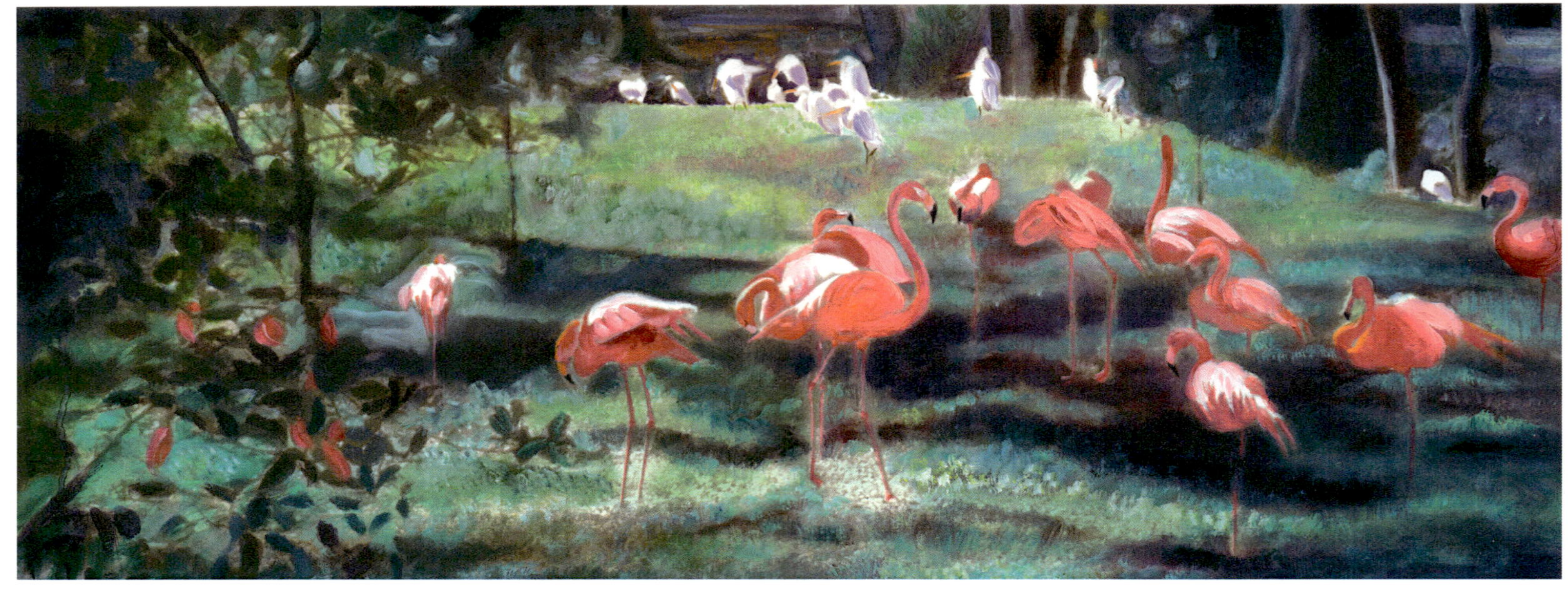

Homosassa II (2002) 11 x 28 in., photography and water based oils on Fabriano paper

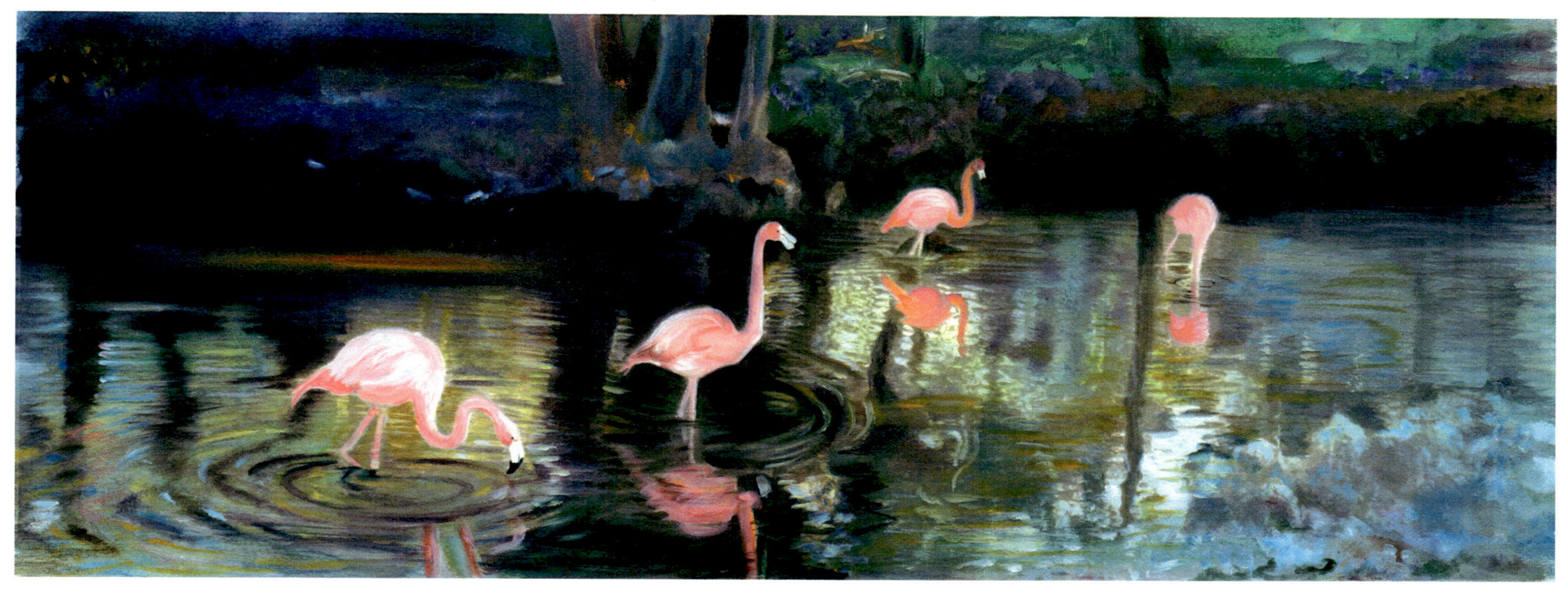

Homosassa III (2002) 11 x 28 in., photography and water based oils on Fabriano paper

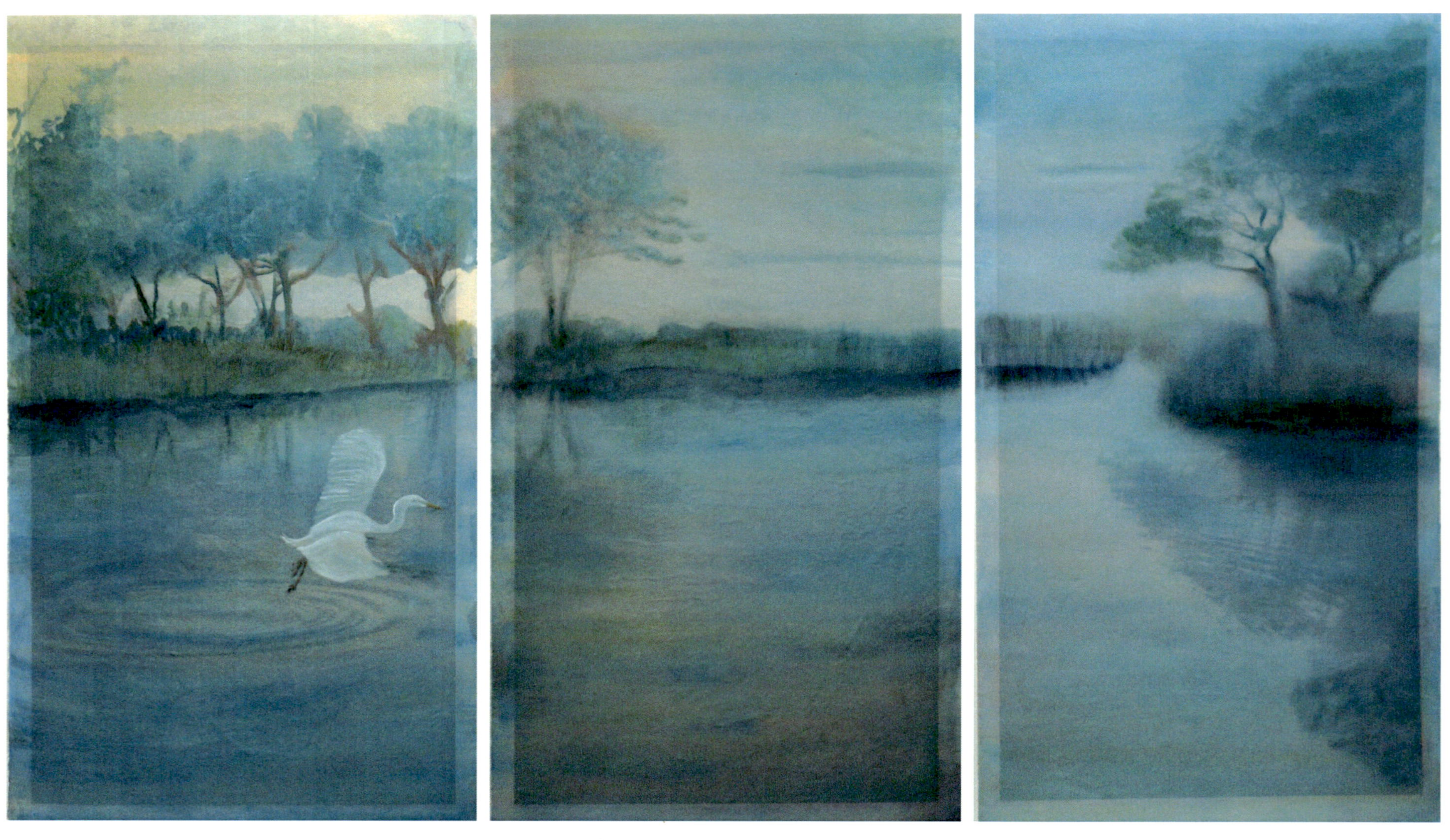

Alligator Cove Triptych (2006) 40 x 23 in. each panel, acrylics on rice paper

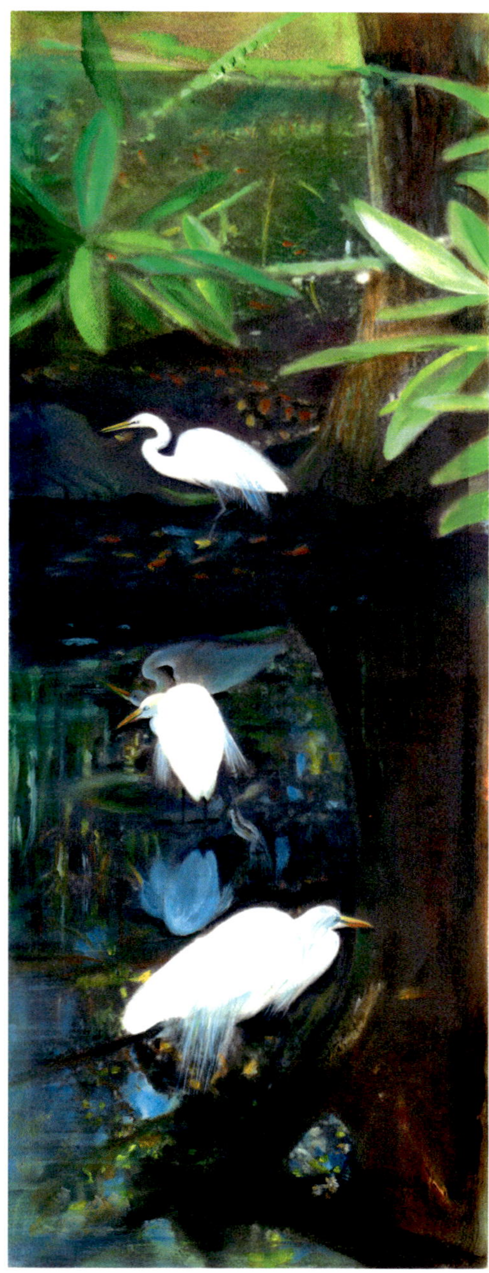

Snowy Egrets (2001) 30 x 11 in. water based oils on paper

Rivers and Springs

In a land divided by rivers we traveled,
Sometimes floating on waters named
With the Indian names in languages lost
Or nearly lost, an entire continent "tamed."

Starting in Aripeka, Seminole for bird,
Drifting down the Weeki Wachee,
Meaning little spring or winding river,
We followed the mermaid manatee.

Homosassa, "the place of many pepper plants"
In the tongue of the native Creek -
Flamingo, pelican, anahinga,
And spoonbill with a shovellike beak.

And three snowy egrets reflected in a pool
Lifted out of a Chinese scroll
White as snow and wings like lace
As delicate as a porcelain bowl.

- Chaim Bezalel

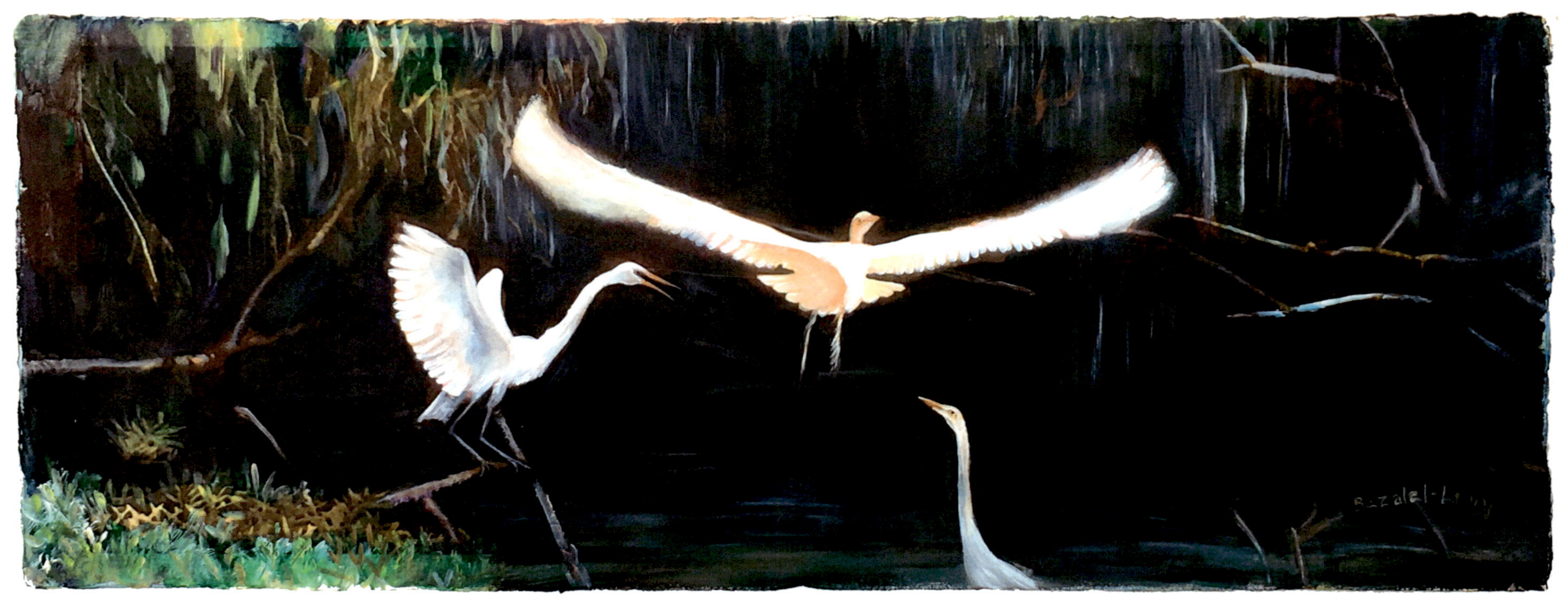

Great Egrets, Corkscrew Swamp Preserve (2017) 17 x 44 in., acrylics on handmade paper

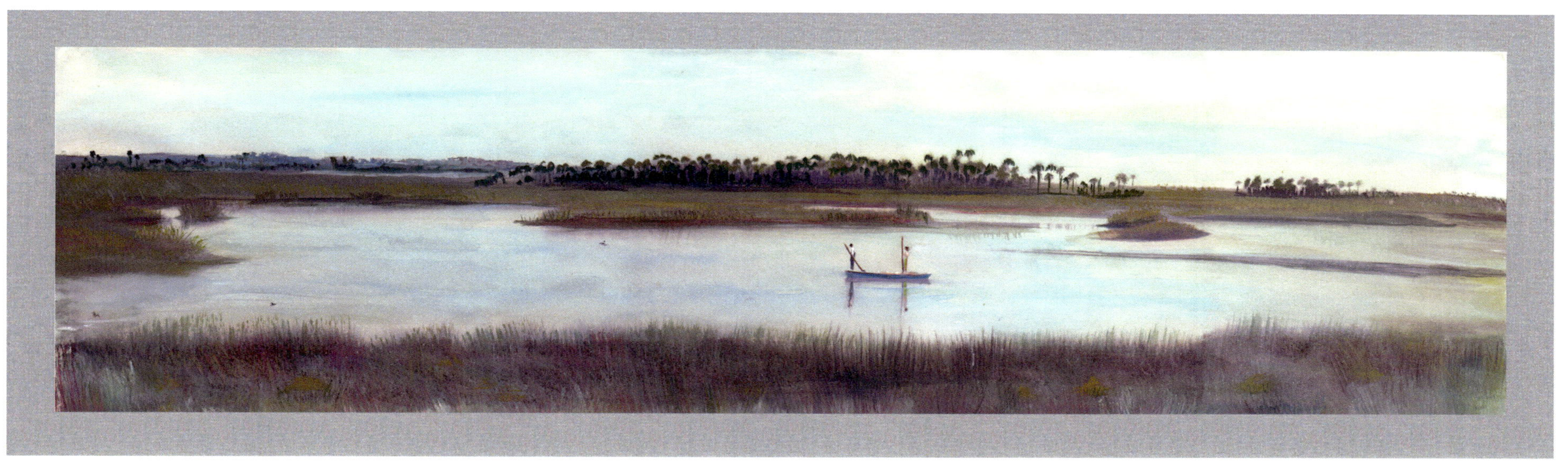

Boatmen on the Gulf, Aripeka (2003) acrylics on rice paper, 12 x 42 in.

America is an odyssey; and, like all odysseys, it's more about the journey than the destination. Even as we race to the future, there are pockets of traditional culture, full of local color. It's a journey through time as well as space. These figures drifting with the tide could be Huck and Jim. But time, like a river, flows onward, not backward. We returned to America at the turn of the millennium. We were fortunate to have the opportunity to return to familiar places of our childhood and youth and to explore new territory as well. Our journey has not been exhaustive but personal as we meet old friends and new.

Original Paintings

3. collection of the artists

4. collection of the artists (study for larger painting, Providence Regional Cancer Partnership, Everett, WA

5. collection of the artists

6. collection of the artists

7. corporate collection - Millburn Ridgefield Corporation, Greenwich, CT

8. collection of the artists

9. collection of the artists

10. collection of the artists

11. collection of the artists

12. collection of the artists

13. collection of the artists

14. collection of the artists

15. private collection

16. collection of the artists

15. collection of the artists

17. collection of the artists

18. collection of the artists

19. (left) collection Richards, Kibbe, & Orbe, LLP, NYC (right) collection of the artists

20. collection of the artists

21. collection of the artists

22. collection of the artists

23. (left) private collection (right) private collection

24. (left)collection of the artists (right) collection of the artists

26. collection of the artists

27. collection of the artists

28. (left) collection of the artists (right) private collection

29. private collection

30. collection of the artists

31 private collection

32 collection of the aritsts   collection of Malibu Camp, BC, Canada

33. (top) collection of the artists (bottom) collection of the artists

34. (top) collection of the artists (bottom) collection of the artists

35. private collection

36. private collection

37. collection of the artists

38. collection of the artists

39. (left) private collection (right) collection of the artists

40. collection of the artists

41. (left) private collection (center) private collection (right) collection of the artists

42. private collection

43. collection of the artists

44. (left) private collection (right) private collection

45. collection of Peninsula College, Port Angeles, WA

46. private collection

47. collection of Malibu Camp, BC, Canada

48. private collection

49. private collection

50. collection of the artists

51. private collection

52. (left) collection of the artists (right) private collection

53. private collection

54. (left) collection of the artists (right) collection of the artists

55. collection of the artists

56. collection of the artists

57. private collection

58. collection of Skagit Valley Regional Hospital, Arlington, WA

59. private collection

60. collection of Skagit Regional Clinics, Smokey Point, WA

61. private collection

62. (left) private collection (right) collection of the artists

63. private collection

64. collection of the artists

65. collection of Skagit Valley Hospital, Mount Vernon, WA

66. collection of the artists

67. collection of the artists

68. collection of the artists

69. (left) private collection (right) collection of the artists

70. collection of the artists

71. collection of the artists

72. collection of the artists

73. private collection
74. private collection
75. private collection
76. private collection
77. collection of the artists
78. collection of the artists
79. (left) collection of the artists (right) collection of Marysville Public Library,
   Marysville, WA
80. collection of the artists
81. private collection
82. collection of the artists
83. collection Snohomish County Courthouse, Everett, WA
84. collection Providence Everett Hospital, Tower Complex
85. (left) collection of the artists (right) collection of the artists
86. collection of the artists
87. (left) collection of Whitman College, Walla Walla, WA (right) collection of
   Skagit Valley Regional Clinics, Riverbend Complex, Mount Vernon, WA
88. (left) collection of the artists (right) collection of the artists
89. collection of the artists
90. private collection
91. (left) collection of the artists (right) collection of the artists
92. (left) private collection (right) collection of the artists
93. private collection
94. collection of the artists
95. collection of the artists
96. collection of the artits
97. collection of the artists
98. collection of the artists
99. (left) collection of the artists (right) collection of the artists
100. collection of Aqua Soleil Hotel Spa, Desert Hot Springs, CA
101. collection of the artists
102. (left) collection of the artists (right) collection of the artists
103. (left) collection of the artists (right) collection of the artists
104. (left) collection of the artists (right) collection of the artists
105. (left) collection of the artists (right) collection of the artists
106. (left) collection of the artists (right) collection of the artists
107. collection of the artists

108. collection of the artists
109. collection of the artists
110. private collection
111. collection of Whitman College, Walla Walla, WA
112. collection of the artists
113. private collection
114. private collection
115. collection of the artists
116. collection of the artists
117. collection of the artists
118. collection of Veterans Administration Hospital, Tacoma, WA
119. collection of the artists
120. collection of the artists
121. collection of the artists
122. collection of the artists
123. collection of the artists
124. private collection
125. private collection
126. collection of the artists
127. private collection

Exhibitions of the Paintings

2005 - "Pacific Scrolls" at Coos Art Musum, Coos Bay, OR
2005 - "Pacific Scrolls" Knutzen Family Theater Gallery, Federal Way, WA
2006 – selections from "Autumn Scrolls" and "Pacific Scrolls" at Solvei
   Gallery, Everett, WA
2008-2009 – "Pacific Scrolls" at Mt. Hood College, OR; Lower Columbia
   College, WA; Peninsula College, WA
2009 - "Pacific Scrolls" at Moses Lake Museum, WA
2012 - "Desert Scrolls" at Moses Lake Museum, WA

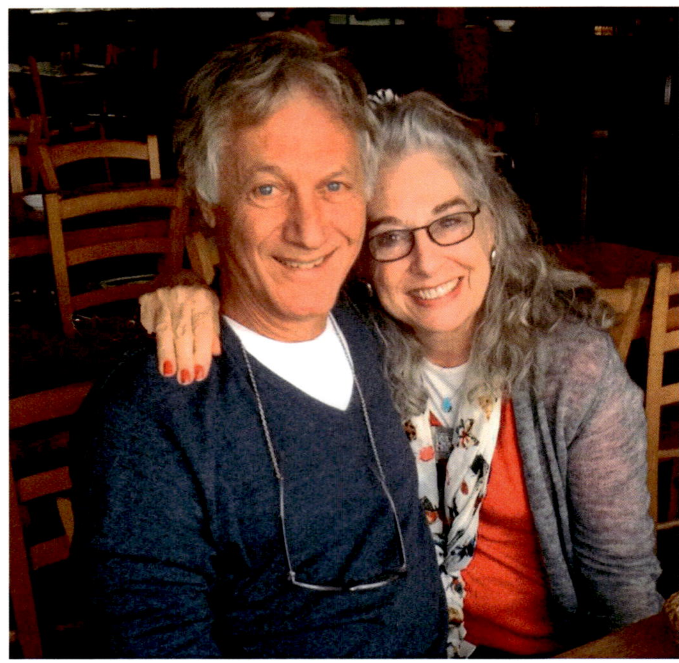

Yonnah Ben Levy and Chaim Bezalel met in Jerusalem in 1988. They are dual citizens of Israel and the United States. Yonnah was raised in Seattle, Washington. She is a lifelong versatile artist and teacher having received her Masters of Art for Teachers at University of Washington. She also studied ceramics at the Corcoran Gallery in Washington D. C. with Teruo Hara, a renowned master potter. Chaim Bezalel studied film at Northwestern University and works in mixed-media including photography, painting, ceramics, writing, and music. Chaim and Yonnah collaborate under their combined signature, Bezalel-Levy. Their homes and studios are in Stanwood, WA and Ashkelon, Israel.

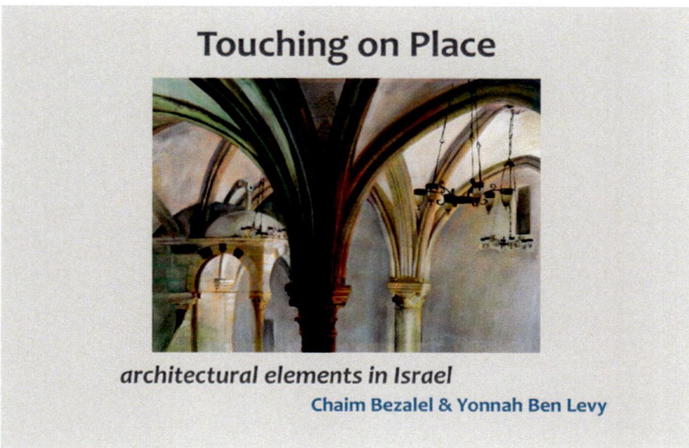

ISBN 978-0-9995958-0-0, paperback, 90 p. 6" x 9"

Seventy-seven original paintings done over twenty-five years convey the history of the past two millennia in this historic land. The book is arranged geographically with an explanation of each region and site. $20

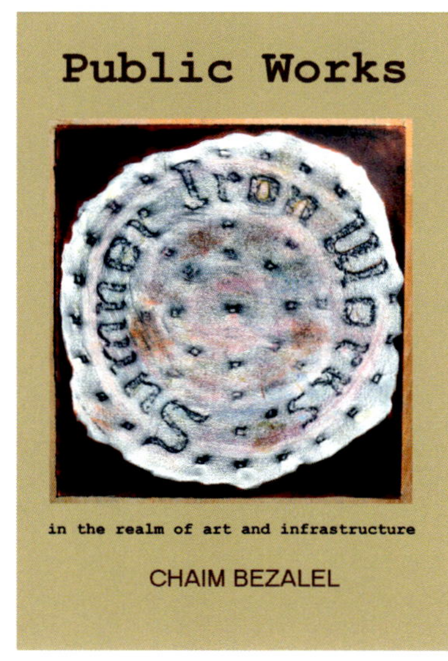

ISBN 978-0-9995958-2-4, 120 p. 9" X 6"

A cross-genre exploration of the meaning of community through art, poetry, song lyrics, and 6 essays. $20

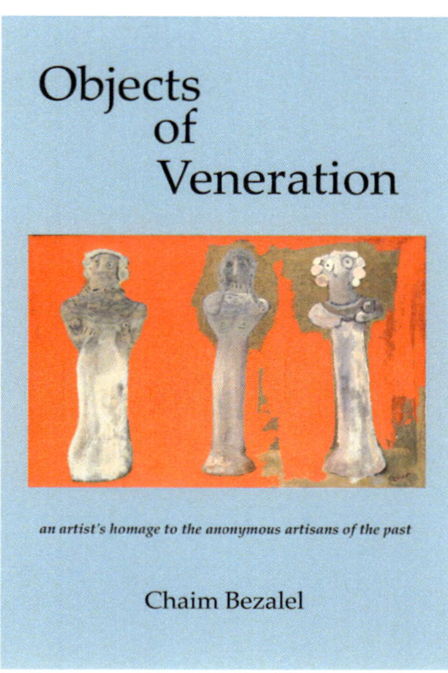

ISBN 978-0-9995958-1-7, 96 p. 9" x 6"

Paintings and sculpture inspired by devotional objects from around the world in the artist's or in other private and public collections. Includes a 33 page essay, "The Talmud, a Brief Travelogue." $20

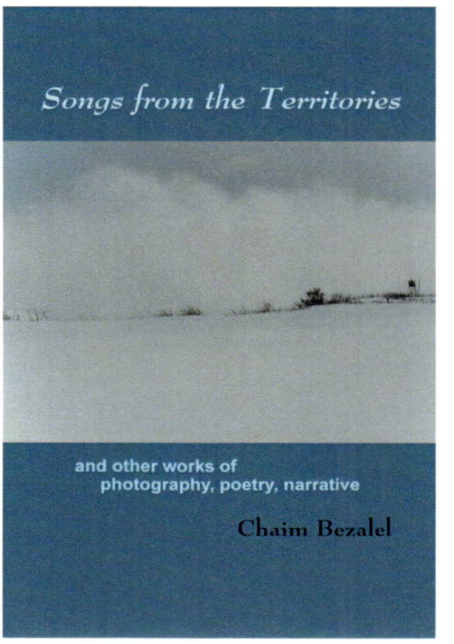

ISBN 978-0-9995958-5-5, 120 p. 9" x 6"

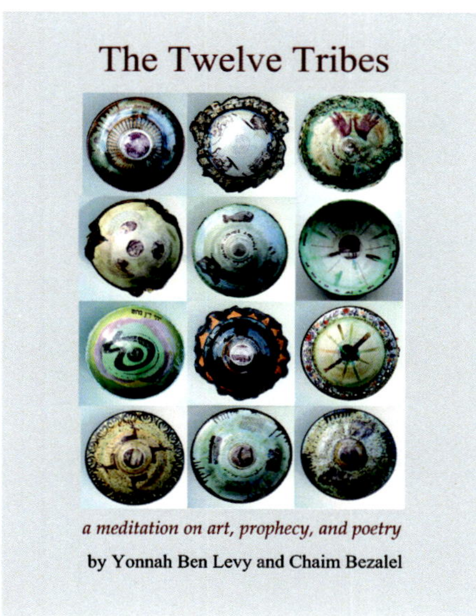

ISBN 978-0-9995958-3-1, 54 p. 8 ½' X 11"

2 art projects: "Bowls of Blessing," 12 bowls illuminate Jacob's and Moses' blessings over 12 sons who became 12 tribes. "Urim and Thummim" is 12 multi image panels exploring the meaning and role of Israel. $20

Songs from the Territories

In 1988, a 38 year old ex-hippie, ex- stockbroker on the lam boards a plane to Israel, where he has never been, with a one way ticket and two suitcases. Two years later, during the Gulf War, he is drafted into the Israeli army reserves. This is his journal. $15

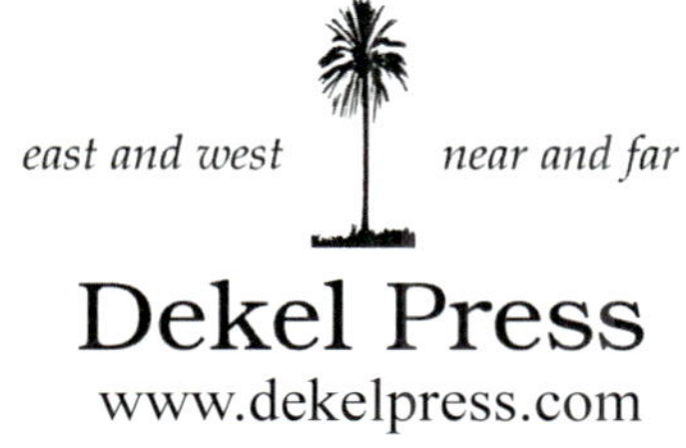

Dekel Press
www.dekelpress.com

The typeface used in this book is Palatino Linotype, an old-style serif typeface designed by Hermann Zapf, and initially released in 1949. As the designer himself describes it: "Named after 16th century Italian master of calligraphy Giambattista Palatino, Palatino is based on the humanist types of the Italian Renaissance, which mirror the letters formed by a broad nib pen." Today it is a pre-installed font on most computers.